CLARENDON LAW SERIES

CLARENDON LAW SERIES

AN INTRODUCTION TO TORT LAW

TONY WEIR

Fellow of Trinity College, Cambridge

OXFORD
UNIVERSITY PRESS

OXFORD

UNIVERSITY PRESS

Great Clarendon Street, Oxford OX2 6DP

Oxford University Press is a department of the University of Oxford.
It furthers the University's objective of excellence in research, scholarship,
and education by publishing worldwide in

Oxford New York

Auckland Cape Town Dar es Salaam Hong Kong Karachi
Kuala Lumpur Madrid Melbourne Mexico City Nairobi
New Delhi Shanghai Taipei Toronto

With offices in

Argentina Austria Brazil Chile Czech Republic France Greece
Guatemala Hungary Italy Japan Poland Portugal Singapore
South Korea Switzerland Thailand Turkey Ukraine Vietnam

Oxford is a registered trade mark of Oxford University Press
in the UK and in certain other countries

Published in the United States
by Oxford University Press Inc., New York

First published 2002
Second edition 2006

British Library Cataloguing in Publication Data

Data available

Library of Congress Cataloging in Publication Data

Data available

Typeset in Ehrhardt
by RefineCatch Limited, Bungay, Suffolk
Printed in Great Britain
on acid-free paper by
Biddles Ltd, King's Lynn

ISBN 0-19-929037-7   978-0-19-929037-6

1 3 5 7 9 10 8 6 4 2

Contents

Preface

People who claim to have suffered harm or an invasion of their rights often seek satisfaction—usually money—from the party they suppose responsible. The aim of this little book is to show how the courts react to such claims. This involves a description of the different kinds of complaint and the different ways the law deals with them.

The book is not, however, purely descriptive. Sometimes it is quite critical, both of decisions by the courts and of the statutory rules they purport to apply. If the criticisms occasionally seem severe, it should be remembered that, as Hobbes said, it is not wisdom but authority that makes a law, and the authority of our courts or Parliament, though now restricted, is not in issue. As to the authority of particular decisions, however, it should be borne in mind that many of them are, or would be, reversed on appeal; that the final decision may be overturned by legislation; and that a good few of the decisions still on the books were reached by a very slim majority in the final court, perhaps reversing a majority of judicial opinions below.

The criticisms are not based on the view that 'tort' is a single discrete product of thought or experience to which some specific purpose may be imputed. The Dean of an American Law School once asked me over lunch 'And what is your normative theory of tort?' It was rather a poor lunch and, as I thought, a very stupid question. Tort is what is in the tort books, and the only thing holding it together is their binding. In contract matters the courts may be predominantly a debt-collection agency (and creditors can now use the Internet), but in tort they function as a complaints department—with the difference that the claimant, unlike the customer, is not always right—and the complaints are of such different kinds that many various reactions may be appropriate. Naturally there are horses for courses, and the tort course sports quite a lot of horses, of very different breeds and speeds. In any event, before producing a 'normative theory' or even discussing the purpose of 'tort', it is surely desirable to become familiar with what that ragbag actually contains: otherwise we shall be like adolescents spending all night discussing the meaning of life—before, perhaps instead of, experiencing it.

It is therefore not in relation to any supposed purpose of the tort shambles, much less any single purpose, that criticisms are ventured here, but in terms of whether the results in particular situations seem sensible, whether the rule laid down is one which can be applied by country solicitors in such a way as to reduce unjustified hopes and tiresome litigation, and whether it is in line with values surfacing here and there in the system and approved by society—values which do not, as yet, embrace the view that every harm or grievance calls for official assuagement or that citizens can properly expect the State, like God after Armageddon, to wipe every tear from the eye.

There are many excellent textbooks on tort, some very large. Of their rich contents this Introduction can do no more than give a foretaste: a condensation would be highly indigestible, like a bouillon cube. Likewise, constraints of space make it impossible to attach to every statement the qualifications and modifications which would be required if it were a statutory provision; this is doubtless an advantage, for otherwise the book would be as unreadable (and unread) as statutes usually are. Greater coverage could probably have been obtained if certain cases were treated less frequently or at lesser length; but it seems sensible to get as much as possible out of single decisions, and one may have to squeeze fairly hard in order to extract all the *jus*. In consequence some decisions and observations keep reappearing. This may irritate anyone (if such there be) who reads the book straight through, but the fact is that in a common law system (if it can be called a system) decisions and rules have no fixed abode; they are not anchored as they seem to be where there is a civil code (and consequently a system).

In the four years since the first edition much has changed and much has had to be added. The result has been to turn what was intended to be whole cloth into rather a thing of shreds and patches: shreds of the old and patches of the new. The most significant change has been the incorporation of the European Convention on Human Rights through the Human Rights Act 1998. It has had some effect, of course, on the outcome of actual cases, but the more important change it has brought about is less easily documented: it has started to alter our vocabulary, our interpretation of enactments, our treatment of precedent, and, actually, our whole mode of thinking and discourse. We may have drafted the Convention, but we are not its principal interpreters, and it would be surprising if the deference due to Strasbourg (in addition to the obedience owed to Luxembourg) were to have no deep effect on our traditional mindset and practice, for those courts are dominated by jurists brought up to speak and to think very differently from ourselves.

While the facts presented are, I hope, more or less up-to-date (to February 2006), I recognise that the opinions and their expression may be thought to be a trifle old-fashioned, that is, unfashionable, not quite *à la mode*, as they used to say in the United States as they piled ice-cream on the pie.

Tony Weir
Trinity College, Cambridge
March 2006

Table of Cases

Table of Legislation

Table of Statutes and Statutory Instruments

Abbreviations

The following abbreviations are used in the footnotes.

A 2d	Atlantic Reporter (Second Series) (from 1938)
AC	Law Reports Appeal Cases (from 1891)
All ER	All England Law Reports (from 1936)
App Cas	Law Reports Appeal Cases (1875–1890)
BLR	Building Law Reports (from 1976)
BMLR	Butterworths Medico-legal Reports (from 1992)
Ch	Law Reports Chancery (from 1891)
CMLR	Common Market Law Reports (from 1962)
EHRR	European Human Rights Reports (from 1979)
EMLR	Entertainment and Media Law Reports (from 1993)
Env LR	Environmental Law Reports (from 1992)
ER	English Reports (to 1865)
FLR	Family Law Reports (from 1980)
FSR	Fleet Street Reports (from 1978)
ICR	Industrial Cases Reports (from 1973)
IRLR	Industrial Relations Law Reports (from 1972)
KB	Law Reports King's Bench (1901–1952)
LGR	Knight's Local Government Reports (1922–1998)
Lloyd's Rep	Lloyd's Law Reports (from 1970)
LR # CP	Law Reports Common Pleas (1865–1875)
LR # Exch	Law Reports Exchequer (1865–1875)
LR # HL	Law Reports House of Lords ((1866–1875)
LR # QB	Law Report Queen's Bench (1865–1875)
LTJ	Law Times (1843–1965)
NE2d	North-Eastern Reporter (Second Series) (from 1934)
NLJ	New Law Journal (from 1965)
QB	Law Reports Queen's Bench (1891–1900, 1952 to date)
QBD	Law Reports Queen's Bench (1875–1890)
RPC	Reports of Patent, Design and Trade Mark Cases (from 1981)
RTR	Road Traffic Reports (from 1970)
SC	Court of Session Cases (Scotland) (from 1821)
SJ	Solicitors' Journal (from 1857)

SLT   Scots Law Times (from 1893)
TLR   Times Law Reports (from 1990)
US   United States Supreme Court Reports
WLR   Weekly Law Reports (from 1953)

Note: The citation [year] EWCA Civ ## denotes decision no ## in [year] by the Civil Division of the Court of Appeal for England and Wales. This identifies the decision but not its earthly location: the text is in cyberspace whence it can be retrieved.

I

Introduction

Suppose a motorist knocks you off your bicycle; can you sue him for 'damages' (monetary compensation)? If a policeman stops you in the street for no good reason, is this a wrong you can sue him for? Your neighbours keep making an intolerable noise; can you get a court to stop them (injunction)? To find the answer you look in a book on tort law. If the courts would accept your claim, we say that the defendants are 'tortfeasors' and 'liable' to you. So the law of tort is about when 'liability' exists (leaving aside any other ground of liability, such as breach of contract), and 'a tort' is conduct which renders the defendant liable unless he has some defence.

All systems of law from the earliest times onwards seem to have afforded a person injured by someone else a claim to some reparation, subject to whatever conditions seemed appropriate in that society. At any rate all modern legal systems have a chapter on tort: in Scotland and Germany it is called 'delict', from the Latin, while the French, from whom we get our word, call it 'responsabilité civile', that is civil (not criminal) liability, or, more suggestively, civic responsibility. Tort is one part of the law of obligations, which tells us when others are liable to us, usually to pay us money. The other parts are contract and unjust enrichment ('restitution'). Underlying each of them is an idea about how people in society should behave towards each other, but the actual legal rules cannot simply be inferred from the idea, as the natural lawyers thought: the legal scope of each is limited. This is right. The understandable urge to bring legal standards up to those of delicate morality should be resisted, or there would be no room for generosity or for people to go beyond the call of legal duty. For example, one issue on which strong views are held is this: is there, or should there be, a legal duty to try to help a stranger in mortal danger when one could do so without risk to oneself? In our legal system, unlike many others, the answer is 'No': you may ignore an infant drowning in a pond unless it is your infant or your pond or you are the lifeguard. The point was quite well put by Lord Atkin in 1932: '. . . liability is no doubt based upon a general public sentiment of moral wrongdoing for which the offender must pay. But acts or omissions which any moral code would censure cannot in a practical world be treated so as to give a right to every person injured by them to demand relief. In this way rules of law arise which limit the range of complainants and the extent of their remedy. The rule that you are to love your neighbour becomes in law, you must not injure your neighbour . . .'.[1]

Lord Atkin was speaking of the tort of negligence, but his point can be expanded. Thus while contract is based on the notion that you should do what you said you would, you can only be *sued* for not doing what you said you would if you asked for something in return (consideration), though you may be *estopped* (prevented) from exercising your rights if you said you wouldn't, even if you asked for nothing in return. Restitution is based on the idea that you shouldn't take unfair advantage, as by keeping what you weren't supposed to have, for example, what has been given to you by mistake, but here again there is a limiting requirement: there must be an 'unjust' factor in the situation. Likewise in tort: although the underlying notion is that you shouldn't harm other people, you don't always have to pay for the harm you do: in many cases you only have to pay if you were at fault—at least careless—in causing it. Other systems, too, sometimes require fault and sometimes do not. In France, for example, the basic article in the *Code Civil* of 1804 (art 1382) makes you liable for any harm you are at fault in causing, but then comes another article (art 1384(1)) which makes you liable, even if you are not at fault, for harm done by any thing under your control, a provision whose importance can be seen when one realises that injury to the human body is generally due to the impact of a thing, especially a hard and fast thing such as a car or truck. Even this strict liability was thought to provide inadequate protection for the victim of highway accidents, and France has now introduced a much stricter system. Germany is different. It has no general principle of liability without fault for damage done by things, but it does allow victims of highway accidents to recover damages without proving fault. Britain is very unusual in holding that victims of traffic accidents get no damages at all unless they can find someone to blame, someone at fault; victims of industrial accidents, however, can quite often obtain damages without proving that their employer or the person in control of their workplace was in any way to blame. These two classes of accidents form the bulk of tort litigation, though courts are increasingly having to deal with accidents in hospitals, schools, and on holiday.

[1] *Donoghue v Stevenson* [1932] AC 580.

DEVELOPMENT

This is no place for a detailed history of the law of tort in England, but the general trend must be noted. The development has been almost uniformly in favour of claimants, doubtless because a society is thought to be progressive to the extent that it increasingly meets its citizens' complaints, that is, gives judgment for the claimant, in tort, at any rate. This is clear if we consider what has happened in the last hundred years. Until 1934 you couldn't sue if the tortfeasor died (and this was regrettable since quite often the driver who injured you killed himself in the process); till 1945 you couldn't sue the tortfeasor if you were at all to blame for your injury (and this was regrettable since most accidents can be avoided if the victim takes greater care); till 1947 you couldn't sue central (as opposed to local) government (this was not too regrettable since most harmful activities are delegated by central to local government); till 1948 you couldn't sue your employer if a fellow-employee injured you, as was often the case; till 1957 it was hard for a guest to sue the host on whose premises he was injured; till 1960 you couldn't sue the highway authority unless it had actually made the road worse than it was; till 1962 you couldn't sue your spouse even if he injured you by bad driving; till 1964 you couldn't sue the Chief Constable for the torts of lesser constables; till 1971 you couldn't sue a farmer who carelessly let his beasts escape on to the highway and cause an accident; till 1972 you couldn't sue the landlord for culpable failure to repair the premises on which you were injured; till 1977 your claim might be barred because the defendant had exempted himself from liability; till 1997 you couldn't claim for harassment, unless you were threatened with immediate violence. And now we have the Human Rights Act 1998 which allows you to sue public authorities for invading the manifold rights it contains, or even failing to protect them from invasion by others.

Thus ever since 1846, when for the first time widows and orphans were allowed to sue the person who tortiously killed their husband and father, the trend has been almost entirely in the direction of increased liability. These changes were all brought about by statute; the legislature intervened because the judges refused to modify a rule which their predecessors had laid down, even though it had become unacceptable. Sometimes, however, the courts themselves have imposed liability where none had existed before. In 1789 they held that a liar was answerable for the harm caused by his deceit although he obtained nothing by his false pretences. In 1862 they held it tortious knowingly to persuade a person to break his contract with the plaintiff. In 1866 they held the occupier of premises liable for failing to make them reasonably safe for people who came there on business. In 1891 they allowed injured workmen to sue for breaches of safety legislation. In 1897 they held it tortious to play a nasty practical joke which made the victim ill. In recent years the courts have increasingly held defendants liable for failing to protect people against third parties, or even themselves; this really started in 1940 when an occupier was held liable to his next door neighbour for not defusing a danger created on his property by a trespasser, and it has since been expanded to many other cases where the defendant could and arguably should have prevented the occurrence of the harm, though he had done nothing to contribute to the danger.

Both the legislature and the courts have been very loth to restrict liability. Very rarely has an existing liability been abolished. In 1970 a husband lost his right to sue a third party for harbouring, enticing away, or committing adultery with his wife or (perhaps prematurely) seducing his children—but then all law goes peculiar when a family is involved. In 1982 an Act abolished the claim for the mere fact that one's life had been shortened, though one can still claim damages for feeling bad about it. For their part, the courts decided in 1991 that they had gone too far thirteen years earlier when they had imposed liability on a local authority for failing to save the buyer of a jerry-built house from his unfortunate purchase,[2] and in 1964 they made the mistake, while expanding liability for intentionally causing economic harm, of restricting the use of damages in order to punish the defendant rather than compensate the claimant.[3] Nevertheless the trend has pretty uniformly been in the direction of expanding rather than restricting liability in tort.

Without question, however, the two major steps taken by the courts to increase the range of liability were taken in 1932 and 1963, in the cases of *Donoghue v Stevenson* (snail in ginger beer)[4] and *Hedley Byrne & Co v Heller and Partners* (misleading banker's reference).[5] The former decision generalized the conditions of liability for unreasonably dangerous conduct and the latter, somewhat less generally, extended this to conduct which was not dangerous at all (in the sense of being likely to damage person or property), but only damaging to the claimant's pocket. They call for extended discussion later.

---

[2] *Murphy v Brentwood DC* [1990] 2 All ER 269.
[3] *Rookes v Barnard* [1964] 1 All ER 367.
[4] [1932] AC 580.   [5] [1963] 2 All ER 575.

TORT AND CONTRACT

The increase in tort liability is matched by a decline in the potency of contract. In the nineteenth century it was axiomatic that individuals should be free to organise their lives within the limits of the practicable and acceptable, and this they did by doing deals with each other in the hope of mutual gain. Such contracts were to be upheld, almost as 'sacrosanct'. In 1875 it was famously said that 'if there is one thing more than another which public policy requires, it is that . . . contracts, when entered into freely and voluntarily, shall be held sacred. . .'.[6] Bargains, even bad bargains, were bargains. 'Vous l'avez voulu, Georges Dandin' as the man said. The courts were so reluctant to strike down agreements as being unreasonable, unfair, or 'contrary to public policy' that they allowed parties to exempt themselves from liability in tort, or at any rate liability in negligence: unless such 'exemption clauses' could be misconstrued—and the courts were quite good at misconstruing contracts, given their practice with statutes—they were upheld and the plaintiff lost his claim in tort. In 1977 the legislature intervened by enacting the Unfair Contract Terms Act, a statute rather wider than its title, which makes it impossible for any agreement or notice to insulate people from liability if they have caused personal injury or death by negligence.

This dramatises the triumph of tort law over contract. Nowadays 'the public policy consideration which has first claim on the loyalty of the law is that wrongs should be remedied. . .',[7] and the almost subsidiary role of contract was emphasised by Lord Goff in a decision which held, effectively, that every negligent breach of contract is automatically a tort: he said that 'The law of tort is the general law, out of which the parties can, if they wish, contract',[8] but failed to add that the extent to which they can contract out of the law of tort is now very limited, though very occasionally the courts will refuse to impose liability for negligence where that would perturb the sensible arrangements of the parties. Individual human beings who deal with a business can now avoid not only exemption clauses but a much wider range of 'unfair' clauses; indeed, they can often change their mind about whole contracts already formed. Such 'consumer protection', largely emanating from Brussels, can be seen as mirroring the extensive protection offered by the law of tort to victims of

---

[6] *Printing and Numerical Registering Co* (1875) LR 19 Eq 462 at 465.
[7] *X v Bedfordshire County Council* [1995] 3 All ER 353 at 380.
[8] *Henderson v Merrett Syndicates* [1994] 3 All ER 506 at 532.

personal injury, seeing that in both the dispute is almost always between an individual and a company, be it a supplier, an employer or an insurer. Although a person's consent now plays a much reduced role in the law of tort, it is not yet entirely irrelevant. If you agree to go to the police station, you cannot sue for arrest, you cannot sue a surgeon for cutting you open if you have agreed to the operation, and if you go into the boxing ring you cannot sue your opponent for fairly and squarely hitting you. Consent is thus a defence to a claim in *trespass*, but where the defendant has been *negligent*, the general principle that one cannot claim for a harm to which one has consented is increasingly being disregarded. In one astonishing case a quite sane prisoner on remand strangled himself with his shirt in the police cell; although he very clearly intended to kill himself, the House of Lords held the police liable, for though they had kept him under almost constant surveillance they had been very slightly negligent in not closing a flap in the door of the cell.[9] Whether or not one regrets it, it is undeniable that the progressive socialisation of harm diminishes the responsibility, and thereby the autonomy, of the individual.

STATUTE AND JUDGE-MADE LAW

It will be seen that the interplay between legislation and judicial decision has been very important in tort law, and since tort is commonly one of the first subjects to which law students are exposed, it may not be out of place to make some general observations about how the rules from these two sources differ.

Britons seem to find cases much easier to deal with than statutes, doubtless because in cases, referred to by the names of the parties, recognisable judges who are professionally trained to be persuasive tell a story in dramatic terms, whereas statutes deal in abstract categories and are drafted by anonymous civil servants in a cryptic, almost impenetrable manner. It is, however, *essential* to overcome one's understandable distaste for legislation, for almost all tort problems involve the application of some statute or other. These include, for example, all cases involving death, injury on another's premises, contributory fault on the part of the victim and multiple tortfeasors, as well as claims for damage done by animals, airplanes, or radiation. Statutes may not play a great part in civil liability for highway accidents, unless the highway authority itself is being sued, but in industrial injury cases statutes (or worse still, statutory

---

[9] *Reeves v Commissioner of Police* [1999] 3 All ER 897.

instruments) are very important indeed. That is not to suggest that they are invariably well-conceived.

STATUTES

Statutes are very diverse. Some impose liability quite openly. For example, the Animals Act 1971 provides that 'When a dog causes damage by killing or injuring livestock, any person who is a keeper of the dog is liable for the damage . . .'. Other statutes which do not speak openly of civil liability require or prohibit specified conduct, sometimes providing that there is a duty to do it, sometimes making it an offence to do it and laying down a penalty for contravention. Whether the infringement of such a statute generates a liability in tort is a very vexed question which will be attended to later. Yet other statutes, rather than imposing a duty, confer a power on a body to do something it would otherwise not be able to do. Most public bodies owe their powers, indeed their very existence, to statute, and it is an even more vexed question whether such a body (typically a local authority which has extensive powers as regards planning, education, social services, especially child-care, and highways) is liable for the harm resulting from failure to exercise its powers properly or at all.

Just as a visitor to an art gallery should not rush past a picture which the painter took years to perfect, or a reader scurry through a sonnet over which the poet laboured long and hard, one must read statutes with something approaching the meticulous care taken by the draftsman. For example, the Defective Premises Act of 1972 imposes liability (though it speaks in terms of 'duty') on 'A person taking on work for or in connection with the provision of a dwelling'. This does *not* mean 'a person taking on work in connection with a building', for by its terms, which cannot be extended by interpretation, it applies only where the work is in connection with the *provision* of a dwelling, and the building must be a *dwelling*, that is, a building for human beings to live in: the statute is simply inapplicable to kennels or office blocks, or to mere repairs to an existing home. One must therefore scrutinise the precise wording of the statute in order to see whether the facts of one's case fall within its purview: interpretation is not so much a matter of eliciting meaning as of ascertaining coverage.

It is not, however, the original wording of the statute which is critical, but rather what the courts have made of it in the process of application, so that it is essential to discover and read the cases in which the enactment has been construed. Until recently our judges did not ask what the legislator meant to say but what was meant by what he did say; as one judge pungently observed, 'the courts are not so much concerned with what the legislature aims at as with what it fairly and squarely hits'.[10] Since 1972, however, when that remark was made, our courts have been very much influenced by the methods of statutory interpretation prevalent on the Continent, where legislation is regarded as primary (and rational) and the courts interpret it in a manner less logical than teleological (purposive). Indeed, our judges are now instructed by the Human Rights Act 1998 to interpret statutes compatibly with the European Convention on Human Rights 'so far as it is possible to do so', a provision which shows that several different interpretations are possible, that their number is not unlimited and that a particular one is to be adopted.[11]

JUDGE–MADE LAW

As to *cases* the technique of eliciting the rule is quite different. Whereas in a statute every word is law, the precise words of judges are not law at all, but merely an indication of it. After all, one can hardly imagine a statute enacted in five different wordings, but it is quite normal in the House of Lords for there to be five concurring opinions, all very differently expressed, as happened, for example, in *Hedley Byrne & Co v Heller and Partners*.[12] In order to discover what a decision is an authority for, one must first understand the relevant facts, and analyse the decision in the light of those facts, ignoring asides (*obiter dicta*). The aim is to ascertain the rule (the *ratio decidendi*) that the judge must have had in mind in order to reach his decision. Then one must decide whether that rule is applicable to the case in hand, which depends on whether its facts are different enough to enable the prior decision to be 'distinguished'; if so, the judge may disregard the prior decision or, if he thinks it right, extend it to the case in hand. As an example of distinction, we can take cases relating to the question of whether a local authority could be sued for the unreasonable exercise of its child-care powers. In 1995, the House of Lords held that that it would not be 'fair, just and reasonable' to impose liability in this delicate area where Parliament had conferred discretion on the authority. In that case the local authority knew that a child was being abused at home,[13] but failed to take any action. Four years later that decision was 'distinguished': in the later case the authority had actually

---

[10] *Charter v Race Relations Board* [1972] 1 All ER 556 at 566.
[11] *R v A* [2001] 3 All ER 1.   [12] [1963] 2 All ER 575.
[13] *X v Bedfordshire County Council* [1995] 3 All ER 353.

taken the child into care, and it was held that there might be liability[14] (perhaps because the original decision had been discountenanced by the European Court of Human Rights in Strasbourg).

A decision can only be an authority if it can be cited to a court: an attempt was made in 2001 to deter counsel from overcitation[15] but it seems to be proving as little efficacious as the injunction to submit arguments in 'skeleton' form. Nor, if citable, are all decisions of equal authority.

Apart from the status of the court in question and perhaps the age of the decision, one must take note of the litigational context. If the decision was made on facts established at trial it is of considerable value, but it can be distinguished if a particular and critical argument was not addressed to the court. Quite often, however, the decision is rendered on facts which have been merely alleged, not established by proof. In some ways this makes it easier to ascertain the scope of the decision, since the precise allegations are taken as being true; indeed, many leading cases (including *Donoghue v Stevenson* itself) were decided in this way, prior to any trial. Often, however, such a case is remitted for trial on the basis that the claimant's case is 'arguable' and that therefore the pleadings should not be 'struck out' or summary judgment given. Since many argued cases are lost, 'arguable' clearly does not mean 'bound to succeed', so such a decision must be treated with caution. Thus in a case where a woman returning from shopping saw her house afire and allegedly suffered a disabling shock, the Court of Appeal held it arguable that the men who were installing a gas fire in her home would, if shown to be negligent, be liable to her for the shock.[16] This case is no authority for the wide proposition that one can recover for shock occasioned by seeing one's property damaged, but even if it were, it might be inapplicable to a case where you saw your dog run over by a careless motorist, for in the case of the burning house the parties were not total strangers but were in a special relationship, namely occupier and visitors, and this might well be treated as a distinguishing feature.

Courts are increasingly ready to disregard a precedent on the ground that, though the case in front of them is not really distinguishable from it on the facts, they have been persuaded by an argument not raised in the earlier case. This indicates the important role of counsel in English litigation. Not only are counsel commonly specialists in the area, addressing a

---

[14] *Barrett v Enfield LBC* [1999] 3 All ER 193.
[15] Practice Direction (Citation of Authorities) [2001] 1 WLR 1002.
[16] *Attia v British Gas* [1987] 3 All ER 455.

judge who, prior to elevation, was perhaps a specialist in some quite different area, but the judges are to a great extent forced to deal with the case in terms of the arguments addressed to them, and those arguments may well be constrained by the original pleadings, drafted possibly by a young barrister still wet behind the ears or a solicitor with nothing between them. Even so a decision may be right although the reasons given, following those of counsel on the winning side, are not quite appropriate. It is always safer to follow what the courts do than what they say, for they may well bend the arguments addressed to them in order to justify the decision which, thanks to a kind of trained professional intuition operating on a sense of justice, they know to be right. Of course decisions are not always right: although those of the Court of Appeal are authoritative until reversed or overruled, it is worth considering that in the year 2004 the House of Lords disagreed with the Court of Appeal in 23 out of 45 cases.

INTERACTION

It follows from the fact that statutes cover only what falls within their precise terms and that all litigated cases are inevitably different to some degree that judge-made rules are always applied *by analogy* and that statutory rules never are. An example may indicate the difference. Suppose Farmer Giles hears barking in his field at night, and on going out sees a dog harassing his sheep. He takes his gun and shoots the dog, which belonged to Hamish. Now here Farmer Giles has deliberately destroyed a piece of Hamish's property, by direct invasion, that is, a trespass to goods. He is presumptively liable. Does he have a defence? Well, there used to be a judge-made rule that one was entitled to protect one's cattle by killing a dog if it was really threatening them and there was no other way of deterring it, but in 1971 the Animals Act was passed, at the behest of the Law Commission. This enactment expressly replaces the common law in the area to which it applies, and lays down the circumstances in which a person has a defence in proceedings for 'killing or causing injury to a dog'. But what is the law if my neighbour's cat is threatening my canary and I heave a brick at it? The *statutory* defence cannot possibly be invoked, because a cat is not even arguably a dog and a canary is not 'livestock', helpfully defined by the Act as including 'asses, mules, hinnies [!] . . . and poultry', 'poultry' being further defined as 'the domestic varieties of . . . fowls, turkeys, geese, ducks, guinea-fowls, pigeons, peacocks and quails'. So what law does apply? Answer: the old common law about damaging other people's creatures which are threatening to damage your creatures. The oddity is that the cases in which that rule was laid down were cases of dogs threatening cattle, the very cases in which the common law rule, having been ousted by the legislation, no longer applies.

WHEN IS CONDUCT TORTIOUS?

There is no *general* principle in English law to tell us when conduct is tortious (not 'tortuous') and when it is not. Contract law is different in this respect, for although transactions such as employment, sale, tenancy, insurance, and so on are quite different one from another and are in many respects subject to particular rules, often embodied in a statute, there is an underlying general principle: almost any promise or undertaking which is part of a deal generates an obligation to perform or pay. Tort is more like criminal law, for just as there are different crimes, such as burglary or blackmail or driving without due care and attention, so there are several different torts; and just as one cannot say that a person is a criminal without specifying what particular offence he committed, so a person is not a tortfeasor unless he has committed a specific tort, that is, unless all the requirements for liability in that particular tort are met, all its ingredients, so to speak, present. So to get to know the law of tort one must get to know the different requirements of the various torts, and there are quite a lot of them. Some torts have relatively familiar names, such as negligence, trespass, nuisance, harassment, conversion, defamation (= libel and slander), malicious prosecution, misfeasance in public office, breach of statutory duty, inducing breach of contract, and so on. Sometimes a tort is named after the parties to the case which established it, such as *Rylands v Fletcher*.

In the old days there used to be different forms for the different torts, 'forms of action' being best thought of as the sort of forms you get from a post office, as it might be a green one for negligence or a blue one for trespass. In order to bring the action you had to have the right form, the form appropriate to the facts you hoped to prove. Nowadays, however, we are less formal: the claimant merely alleges the facts which in his view give him a 'cause of action', that is, a ground for a successful suit. The judge then scrolls through all the torts in the book, and if the requirements of any of them are met by the facts proved, the claimant wins. Of course his counsel will cite authorities and these authorities will inevitably be located in one or other of the chapters of a tort book, perhaps the 'Negligence' chapter or the 'Nuisance' chapter, but that is the only sense in which the claimant can be said to be suing 'in negligence' or 'in nuisance'. Such phrases are commonly used, but it is just a sloppy shorthand.

THE FORUM

A claim in tort is normally brought in the county court, and claims for personal injury, for example, must go there unless the sum in issue is £50,000 or more, an exception being made for medical (clinical) negligence claims. Claims of up to £5,000 go to the small claims court, unless the damages claimed for pain and suffering exceed £1,000; claims of up to £15,000 take the fast track. There will be no jury, except in cases of false imprisonment, malicious prosecution or defamation, and even in defamation cases the judge may now, and quite often does, refuse to empanel a jury and give summary judgment himself. Public money is not generally available for parties to a tort suit, unless there is a plausible human rights issue, so the claimant may have to find a lawyer who will take the case on a conditional fee basis—that is, make no charge if the claim is lost (with insurance to pay the costs of the successful defendant), but up to double the normal fee if it succeeds, when the costs, including the insurance premium and the success fee, will be paid (up to a point) by the defendant who lost. This can be very costly for media defendants sued by dodgy claimants backed by chancy solicitors.[17]

In order to persuade parties to settle rather than bother the court with a full-scale trial, the rules as to costs are modified if either party offers to settle for a sum which is refused and proves at trial to have been adequate. Of such offers made by defendants about two in five are accepted. Indeed, in 2004 no less than 60% of claims instituted in the Queen's Bench were settled, struck out or withdrawn, leaving only 991 to be tried, of which 65% were personal injury cases.

FOCAL POINTS

Although the requirements of the various torts are different, the differences between them turn on just a few focal points. Since the basic complaint in a tort case is 'You hurt me', the three crucial focal points are, quite evidently, first, what the alleged tortfeasor did, secondly, what the claimant suffered in consequence, and thirdly, how the suffering resulted from the conduct. It is very important to keep these matters distinct, and it is not at all difficult. How the defendant behaved (the cause) is clearly distinguishable from what the claimant suffered (its effect): both of these

---

[17] See *Campbell v MGN* [2005] UKHL 61, especially Lord Hoffmann at 29 ff.

D's behaviour

Cause – effect – how behaviour caused it

are provable facts. How the conduct resulted in the harm is not quite a fact, it is a relation between the two other facts, and we call it 'causation'. Thus our focal points are conduct, harm, and causation.

THE DEFENDANT'S CONDUCT

The defendant's conduct may take different forms. He may have done something or merely spoken. Acts and speech operate differently in the world we know—even Beatrice's saying to Benedick 'Kill Claudio!' didn't kill Claudio—so the law tends to distinguish them. Thus some torts, such as trespass, require an act, while others, such as misrepresentation, fraudulent or negligent, require a communication of some sort. But the distinction is not clear-cut. Gestures can be rude, and actions can speak—louder than words, it is said—and people have been known to talk of body language and fashion statements. Although *Hedley Byrne v Heller* was a case of misrepresentation, a misleading letter, and liability was in principle imposed on that basis, this liability was quite quickly extended to the careless misperformance of services of all kinds. And as Lord Steyn has said: 'A thing said is also a thing done'.[18]

Speech and action have one thing in common, however: they are both positive—the speaker or agent adds something to the previous situation. What if the defendant neither spoke nor acted, but remained passive and silent? Here again the law draws a distinction. It is much readier to impose liability on a person who does or says something than the person who does and says nothing. Where the defendant is charged not with positively endangering or damaging the claimant but of failing to protect him from a danger or damage we speak of 'liability for omissions'. Again, the distinction between acts and omissions is not watertight—liability under *Hedley Byrne* was extended to cover an indolent solicitor who did nothing[19]—but an excellent justification for it may be found in Lord Hoffmann's speech in *Stovin v Wise*,[20] where an embankment beside the highway obstructed the sight lines at an intersection and the highway authority failed to exercise its power to have it removed.

The distinctions between act and speech and between act and omission are at the level of perceptible fact and are quite easy to draw, even for a layperson who doesn't see why they should be drawn at all. The matter is more complicated when the conduct falls to be evaluated rather than simply described. Did the defendant's conduct fall short of the standard

Stovin v Wise

Liability for omission

---

[18] *R v Ireland* [1997] 4 All ER 225 at 236.   [19] *White v Jones* [1995] 1 All ER 691.
[20] [1996] 3 All ER 801 at 806.

which the court or the legislator holds appropriate? Is the defendant to be blamed? Was he driving too fast (the word 'too' always indicating that some criterion, commonly unstated, has been applied)? Did the surgeon pull too long on the emergent baby? Was the driver's conduct unreasonably dangerous? Should the writer have realised that what he said was inaccurate or misleading? These judgments are commonly semi-objective, independent of the defendant's internal attitude or even abilities: the learner driver may be held liable for the way he drives, though we know he is doing as well as he can. Sometimes, however, there must be an inquiry into the defendant's mind. Was he conscious of what he was doing or simply inattentive? Did he know that what he was saying was false, did he realise that he was acting outside his powers? These distinctions matter, because in some torts there is no liability unless the defendant's conduct was objectively unreasonable, in others he must be shown to have behaved disreputably, and in yet others he is liable just for having caused the harm, even though his conduct was neither unreasonable nor disreputable; in this last case we say that his liability is 'strict'.

EFFECT ON THE CLAIMANT

The harm suffered by the claimant may also take different forms. His leg may be broken or his car wrecked. This is physical damage, damage to his tangible person or property. Such damage usually entails economic harm as well, such as the loss of wages or the cost of cure or repair. In other cases, however, the harm may be what we call 'purely economic', not consequent on any physical damage, as where the defendant misleads the claimant into making a bad bargain or deprives him of a prospective advantage. The claimant's complaint then is not that the tortfeasor has disabled him personally or damaged his property but only that he has been made poorer, not as rich as he was or would have been. The law of tort makes a clear distinction between these two cases. As Lord Oliver once said, 'The infliction of physical injury to the person or property of another universally requires to be justified. The causing of economic loss does not'.[21] Thus while the careless manufacturer of a defective chattel is responsible at common law for the personal injury or property damage it foreseeably causes, he cannot be sued (except in contract) for the equally foreseeable economic loss which the purchaser or consumer may suffer from the mere fact of its being defective or unproductive.[22] Likewise the

---

[21] *Murphy v Brentwood DC* [1990] 2 All ER 908 at 934.
[22] *Muirhead v Industrial Tank Specialities* [1985] 3 All ER 705.

House of Lords has held that a doctor who carelessly allows a woman to conceive or remain pregnant must pay her for the pain of bearing the unwanted child but not, if it is healthy, the cost of maintaining it.[23] The distinction between purely economic loss and physical harm, even if it is only to property, is not just a bugbear of conservative tort lawyers: for example, in the foot-and-mouth disease fiasco of 2001, the government was prompt to pay those whose physical property in the form of sheep, cows, and pigs had been destroyed but offered hardly anything in comparison to those, hotel keepers, auction houses and the like, whose harm was purely economic, though equally foreseeable. And one might reflect on the fact that while taxation—the extraction of money—is perfectly, if reluctantly, acceptable, expropriation, the taking of physical property, is not.

New kinds of harm are occasionally admitted. If so, liability is naturally expanded. In the year 2000 the House of Lords held that a reduction in a child's level of achievement could constitute actionable harm, the conduct in that case being failure to diagnose and alleviate the congenital condition of dyslexia.[24] By contrast, the occurrence of pleural plaques in a person negligently exposed to asbestos fibres does not, the Court of Appeal has held, constitute actionable damage even if they indicate an increased risk that an actual disease might develop and also cause anxiety about that possible outcome, since neither of these separately or in conjunction amount to actionable harm.[25]

The law is often criticised for making needless distinctions, but an example may show that the distinctions just mentioned are necessary, or at any rate useful. Take the daily occurrence of a traffic pile-up on the motorway resulting from crass driving by someone up front. A passenger in the following car has his head cracked open and dies; his widow suffers shock at hearing of the accident, and the firm which employs him loses his valuable services; the driver of another car suffers a broken nose but survives, while a third drives into the mess and his car is damaged, but he himself is uninjured. Meanwhile there is a whole slew of traffic backed up, at a standstill for hours, and in consequence many of the drivers and passengers lose time and money as well as their tempers. These are all perfectly foreseeable and harmful consequences of a single act of negligence, but given the different types of harm, it could not be right to treat all these victims the same.

---

[23] *McFarlane v Tayside Health Authority* [1999] 4 All ER 961.
[24] *Phelps v Hillingdon LBC* [2000] 4 All ER 504.
[25] *Rothwell v Chemical and Insulating Co* [2006] EWCA Civ 27.

HARM AND RIGHTS

Common to all these cases is that the claimant has suffered actual harm or damage, and he doesn't need a lawyer to tell him so. Sometimes, however, the claimant has suffered no actual harm but is aggrieved because he thinks his rights have been invaded. The law of tort is ready to assist him, if he is correct, because one of its roles, apart from determining whether compensation is payable for harm caused, is to vindicate essential rights when they have been invaded. English law has traditionally been reluctant to speak openly in terms of rights (as opposed to duties). As one judge put it 'In the pragmatic way in which English law has developed, a man's legal rights are in fact those which are protected by a cause of action. It is not in accordance . . . with the principles of English law to analyse rights as being something separate from the remedy given to the individual'.[26] To see that this has changed one need look no further than the Human Rights Act 1998 which lists the rights of the citizen and makes it unlawful for a public authority, including the courts, to act incompatibly with them. But in reality the change falls short of being entirely revolutionary. Since very early times a person's rights in his person and in property in his possession have been protected by the English law of tort in the form of trespass: anyone, even an official, who deliberately restricted a person's freedom of movement or touched his person or any of his possessions could be sued, even if no actual harm resulted, and it was up to him to establish, if he could, some legal justification for his act. This may apply only to rights protected by trespass law, for when the Court of Appeal held that no damage need be proved if a person's 'constitutional' rights had been maliciously thwarted,[27] the House of Lords reversed and sidelined a decision 300 years earlier that a person who was prevented from exercising his right to vote had a claim in tort although, as his candidate was actually elected, he had suffered no actual loss, only a grievance.[28]

It is quite easy to tell when the law of tort is performing its vindicatory rather than its compensatory role: first, there need be no proof of damage; secondly, the claimant need prove only that the right was invaded, not that the defendant was wrong to act as he did. The defendant must then show, if he can, that he was entitled to do what he did. Thus it is presumptively wrong to thump anyone, but you are entitled to do it in

[26] *Kingdom of Spain v Christie's* [1986] 3 All ER 28 at 35.
[27] *Watkins v Home Office* [2006] UKHL 17.
[28] *Ashby v White* (1703) 92 ER 126.

self-defence. This is structurally very like the European Convention on Human Rights, which first states the right and then lists the purposes for which alone invasion is permissible, the right being very generously construed, the defences subjected to careful scrutiny. The Convention confers many more rights than are protected by our common law of trespass, which covers only the right to freedom of movement, corporeal integrity, and undisturbed possession of property, landed or moveable: for example, Article 8 provides that 'Everyone has the right to respect for his private and family life, his home and his correspondence'. But whereas a claim in trespass lies against persons of all kinds and invariably carries a right to damages, the Human Rights Act 1998 explicitly binds only public authorities and offers damages for infringement only as a last resort.[29] On the other hand, and very importantly, liability in trespass attaches only to positive acts, whereas under the statute 'an act includes a failure to act' and the authority may be liable for failing to protect citizens from invasions of their rights by others, who are not themselves bound by the Act.

The rights protected by the law of trespass and defamation are rights which the judges have recognised; like the more relative rights which arise from contracts, they exist at common law. Many rights, however, have their source in a statute. Alongside common law rights in tangible property we have statutory rights in intangible property, such as copyrights, patent rights, and design rights; these are called 'intellectual property' since they are perceptible only to the mind or intellect, not the senses. These, too, are protected, in the ways specified in the legislation, by the law of tort or something quite analogous.

CAUSATION

In the tort of trespass the invasion of the right must result *directly* from the defendant's act. Contrary to what many students seem to think, 'direct' is not a word apt to describe either the conduct or the result; it refers only to the link or relationship between them, indicating immediacy, the absence of anything intervening between the conduct, which is the cause, and the harm or invasion, which is its result. Thus in one case where the claimant's foreshore was polluted by oil from the defendants' tanker, the defendants were not liable in trespass because they had pumped the oil on to the sea and not directly on to the claimant's property, though it was bound to end up there, and soon, through the intervention of wind and

---

[29] *R (Greenfield) v Secretary of State* [2005] UKHL 14.

tide.[30] The defendants would have been liable in negligence, however, had they been at fault (in fact they had to lighten the vessel to save the crew in an emergency for which they were not shown to be at fault), for in negligence the requirement is not that the result be directly caused by the defendant but that the harm be the *foreseeable* result, whether or not it is directly caused. Indeed, in another pollution case in which the claimant's wharf was burnt down as a clear result of the defendant's careless spillage of oil in Sydney Harbour the defendant was held not liable because all the experts said that the oil on the water could never be ignited.[31]

Foreseeability seems to be the link predominantly required in the law of tort today. Thus in yet another pollution case, this time on land, small quantities of a industrial chemical which the defendants had allowed to leak into their land gathered in the water table and polluted the claimant's water supply; this was not a claim 'in negligence', since there may be liability for such an escape even in the absence of any negligence, but the defendants nevertheless avoided liability because the pollution of the water supply was a quite unforeseeable result of the escape.[32] The 'propensity to percolate through underground channels and contaminate hidden springs' was said in another case to be a characteristic of defamatory statements.[33] Here the rule used to be that the originator of a defamatory statement was not liable for its being repeated unless he had authorised the repetition, but when newspapers reviewed the previous evening's television programme the Court of Appeal held that the BBC might well be liable for this further dissemination of its contents. 'There cannot' it was said 'be a difference in principle between negligence and other tortious conduct' and the test of foreseeability (or 'natural and probable consequence') was adopted as against the earlier rule. Here the change of test expanded the range of consequences for which liability was imposed, whereas in the pollution case it restricted it. The wrong way round, one might think.

In some torts, however, a stricter criterion is used: the result may have to be the 'calculated' effect of the conduct, meaning that it was very likely to result. Sometimes, indeed, it must be shown that the result was actually intended by the defendant or that it was one whose likelihood he recklessly ignored. But though different torts have different requirements for the link between the defendant's conduct and the harm or invasion

---

[30] *Esso Petroleum v Southport Corp* [1953] 3 All ER 864.
[31] *The Wagon Mound (No 1)* [1961] 1 All ER 404.
[32] *Cambridge Water Co v Eastern Counties Leather* [1994] 1 All ER 53.
[33] *Slipper v BBC* [1991] 1 All ER 165 at 179.

complained of, it must always be shown that the latter was indeed the result of the former, that the defendant can properly be said to have caused it or contributed to its occurrence. Unfortunately causation is a very elusive concept, about which much more will be said in Chapter 4.

RELATIONSHIP OF PARTIES

The nature of the tortfeasor's conduct, the harm suffered by the claimant and the link between them are crucial in any tort claim, but other factors may also play an important part. One such factor is the previous relationship, if any, between the parties. Sometimes the parties are total strangers, like ships that collide in the night, but very often they are not. Relationships in life vary a great deal. The parties may be cheek-by-jowl, in the same family or as neighbours, living much closer to one another than they would like. Special considerations are bound to apply. The relationship may be that of consumer and producer, where the consumer, targeted by the producer, selects the product because of its provenance. The parties may be in a voluntary relationship, as when you enter a shop, visit a tenant, or hitch a lift. The relationship may be fully contractual, as between employer and employee, or one of bailment, where one person is in lawful possession of goods belonging to another, as when you take your car to the garage or let a friend borrow it. The application of the rules of tort may be greatly affected by the relationship between the parties. This is quite right, for the law is there to answer people's reasonable expectations (a product is defective if it is not as safe 'as persons generally are entitled to expect'), and people's expectations of others depend on their relationship to them, especially when they are justifiably relying on them for advice or protection (as one relies on one's doctor or other apparent expert). In short, whether you get damages depends on whom you are suing as well as what you are suing him for. How could it be otherwise?

WHERE TORTS HAPPEN

Most accidents occur in the home, on the highway or on other people's property, often a factory or building site. Accidents at home are usually the result of the victim's own negligence, but they may be attributable to a defect in an appliance—the toaster which blows up, the unstable ladder in the shed—so that one can sue the producer, or due to some structural defect in the premises, so that one can try suing the landlord, or to some temporary hazard—the carpet-layer failed to nail down the carpet or the workman left his hammer lying about for someone to trip over. Most domestic accidents, however, tend to be the fault of the victim or another member of the household, and lawsuits are relatively rare.

By contrast, suits arising from accidents on the highway, which includes the high seas, are extremely common; this is not surprising, given that so many hard and heavy metal objects are moving about at high speed. Although there are some pure accidents, when no one is to blame, injuries on the highway are most often due to some fault of the person in control of the vehicle's movement or condition. Sometimes, however, the highway itself (including the pavement) has been badly maintained or inadequately signposted. Sometimes a builder leaves an unlit skip or debris on the highway, sometimes a branch of a tree or part of a building falls on to it from neighbouring premises. Other incidents on the highway may give rise to tort problems, such as obstructing the movement of traffic or access to a business.

If you are neither at home nor on the highway when you are injured, you must be on someone else's property. Ever since 1866 when an employee of the gas company fell into an unfenced vat in a sugar factory,[34] accidents on private property have received special attention from the law. Nowadays the Occupier's Liability Act 1957 lays down in some detail the 'common duty of care' owed by the occupier to his 'visitors', persons invited, allowed, or entitled to be there; unwelcome entrants such as burglars and errant children (a perfectly absurd conjunction) are owed a slightly lower duty under the Occupier's Liability Act 1984. If the scene of the accident was a factory or other workplace, the chances of the injured workman recovering damages are very high. This is because breaches of the very numerous safety regulations which the occupier is bound to heed have long been held to give rise to liability. Often, of course, the occupier of the workplace is also the victim's own employer, whose duty for the safety of his employees may be even higher than that of the occupier towards his visitors.

Other places rife with accidents are hospitals, schools, and holiday resorts. As to the latter, Brussels, ever conscious of the wants of tourists while reducing the attractions of travel abroad, has greatly stiffened the liability of package tour operators, and it may be possible to sue them here. Nor does one have to return to the scene of the injury if one is run over in the street while abroad: thanks to the Fifth (!) Motor Insurance Directive (2005), the foreign motor insurer is bound to maintain a claims representative in Britain and can be sued here.

---

[34] *Indermaur v Dames* (1867) LR 2 CP 311.

Even for physical accidents the place of occurrence is not always relevant: a person injured by a defective chattel can sue the producer no matter where the injury took place. In the economic torts, including misrepresentation and most forms of professional liability, it will be the transactional rather than the physical context of the wrong which is most important.

HUMAN AND OTHER BODIES

Only human beings can suffer personal injury or death, the harms traditionally in issue in a tort claim. Property damage and financial harm, on the other hand, can be suffered by merely legal persons, which, if not inhuman, are certainly not human. It is worth emphasizing the fact that the legal world contains two quite different kinds of players, individual human beings on the one hand and, on the other, firms, companies, governmental units, quangos, all those (non)entities called 'bodies'— rather oddly, seeing that they have no body at all. It is a serious mistake to suppose that a trading company, for example, is really its human employees and shareholders (many of the shareholders, such as pension funds, being themselves merely legal). A legal person is by no means just human beings in a group, and one must resist the temptation to think it is. Companies do not exist naturally in the way people do: they are *deemed* to exist by lawyers and economists. This fact is rather obscured by the anthropomorphism unavoidably rampant in legal discourse: even in this book companies are treated, spoken of, believed in, *as if* they were people. The fiction is taken for fact. This is not to deny that companies, like the square root of minus one, have their uses, but it must always be remembered that they are devices invented by individuals for their own benefit, and occasionally the benefit of others as well. For example, it is established law that only the company itself can sue if the company's assets are diminished by a tort and the actual loss is suffered by the shareholders, even if there is only one of them.[35]

In the contract books companies and other legal persons are very big players, because contracting is an act in law, and in law companies are persons. In the law of tort, however, they sit oddly, because tort law is principally concerned with acts in fact. In the Newtonian world in which we move, physical harm can be caused only by physical force, and while human beings are capable of physical force, companies are not, because

---

[35] *Johnson v Gore Wood* [2001] 1 All ER 481.

they do not physically exist. Companies cannot drive cars or hit people in other ways, but it would be intolerable if they were therefore incapable of liability in tort, for they often have lots of money and can pay (or be liquidated), payment being a legal act of which they are well capable. To ensure that companies can be made liable the law has two devices at its disposal. The first is to impose liability for failure to act (non-existent bodies are very good at *not* doing things, since in fact they can't do anything), as by making the occupier of premises liable for failing to make its visitors reasonably safe, by making the bailee liable for failing to look after the goods properly, and the employer for failing to institute a safe system of work. The second device is to make the employer (normally corporate) pay for the torts committed by its employees (invariably human). This is called 'vicarious liability', and it is a vitally important feature of the law of tort which will be discussed in Chapter 6.

Lawyers tend to prefer clients which are corporate rather than human, because companies don't burst into tears in the office and usually pay the bill. In consequence the law tends to accord to legal persons rights which properly belong to individuals. Companies may sue for defamation, for example, and, perhaps surprisingly, enjoy some of the rights contained in the Human Rights Act 1998. This is explicit as regards the peaceful enjoyment of possessions, but the Strasbourg Court has granted them other rights as well; indeed, one of the first declarations of the incompatibility of a British statute with the Convention was pronounced in favour of a pawnbroking company![36] Brussels, on the other hand, is surprisingly ready to discriminate. Thus a company cannot invoke the Consumer Protection Act 1987 in respect of damage due to a defective product, since the underlying Directive applies only to personal injury, death, and damage to consumer property, not including commercial property. Again, only 'individuals' can invoke the Directive on Unfair Terms in Consumer Contracts.[37] Less obvious, perhaps, is the fact that many important tort claims are simply not available to companies: they cannot in the nature of things complain of stress, shock, or wrongful imprisonment; it is not clear whether or not they can complain of 'harassment' under the Act of 1997, and while a company may certainly protect its confidential information it is doubtful whether it can complain of invasion of privacy as fully as human beings can, for it has neither the 'family life' nor 'home' which 'everyone' is entitled to have respected under Art. 8 of the European

[36] *Wilson v First County Trust* [2001] 3 All ER 229.
[37] *Cape SNC v Idealservice SRL* (Case C-541/99) ECJ.

Convention. Suppose that a vital employee is injured through negligence. Can the company sue? In a case where a star footballer was disabled as a result of bad medical advice, the football club could not sue the doctor, though it regularly paid his bills.[38] Much less can a company sue if an employee is killed, for only human relatives are qualified to sue under the Fatal Accidents Act 1976. Companies can, of course, sue for damage to, or deprivation of, their property, and they are in the forefront of claiming damages for economic loss, whether caused by competitors or by others. Indeed, the damages awarded to companies tend to dwarf those awarded to human beings: in one famous case in Texas, Pennzoil obtained an award of $11,120,976,000 against Texaco, which had allegedly horned in on Pennzoil's purchase of Getty Oil.

INSURANCE COMPANIES

One kind of company is especially significant in the tort world. That is the insurance company. The characteristic of insurance is that whereas most other contracts envisage reciprocal profit or mutual advancement, the insurance contract is designed not for the profit of the customer— indeed, from most kinds of insurance he is not permitted to profit—but to protect him against loss or liability, that is, precisely the central concerns of tort law. Insurance companies are involved much more often than is evident in the law reports. This is because an insurance company is frequently lurking behind either the claimant or the defendant and sometimes both, so that what seems to be quite interesting litigation between individuals is really a dispute between insurers of very little moment. Take a standard highway accident, appearing in the reports as *Smith v Jones*. Jones will certainly be insured against liability, since as everyone knows, those who use a motor vehicle in a public place are required by law to have a policy of insurance against the risk that they may be held liable to those they injure. Such 'liability insurance' protects careless motorists from being bankrupted and ensures that their victims get paid. If Smith's claim is for damage to his car, his own insurer may also be involved, for sensible people insure their own cars, although they are not bound to, since after all one's car may be damaged without anyone's fault but one's own. This kind of 'property insurance' benefits claimants, and is often called 'first party insurance'.

Although insurance companies of both types are involved in almost every lawsuit about property damage, neither is ever mentioned in court.

---

[38] *West Bromwich Albion Football Club v El-Safty* [2005] EWHC 2866 (QB).

As was said in the House of Lords as recently as 1994 'At common law the circumstance that a defendant is contractually indemnified by a third party against a particular legal liability can have no relevance whatever to the measure of that liability.'[39] Although in England one can sue the tortfeasor's employer directly, without joining the tortfeasor himself, it is only in the case of traffic accidents (and then only because of an intervention from Brussels) that one can sue the tortfeasor's insurer without suing the tortfeasor first. In many cases, therefore, the tortfeasor's liability insurer (who is usually in complete control of the defence) goes unmentioned. There is also a coy silence about the claimant's property insurer. This has a different explanation, namely that the insurer which has paid out on its policy is entitled by law to use the insured's own name in order to exercise any rights the insured may have had to claim compensation for the insured damage or loss. The reason for this is that since both property insurance and tort damages are designed to compensate the insured victim, but not to overcompensate him, he cannot be permitted to keep both the proceeds of the insurance and the tort damages, so in order to prevent his being unjustly enriched the insurer is able to claim back out of the tort damages the amount it paid him under the policy.

The technical name for this chicanery is 'subrogation': the insurer is 'subrogated' to the rights of the insured. Not only is the property insurer subrogated to the rights of the insured victim against the tortfeasor but the tortfeasor's liability insurer is subrogated to the tortfeasor's right to claim contribution from any other person liable for the same damage, even though the tortfeasor himself, being insured, would never have exercised that right. So again you never know for sure whether the named human party is acting for himself or is merely a puppet whose strings are being pulled by his insurance company. At least two foreign systems have laid down the sensible rule that if insured property is damaged by negligence, only the insurer is liable: the negligent tortfeasor is not. Note, however, that subrogation benefits only property and liability insurers: it does not apply to personal accident insurance, where you pay a premium to an insurer in return for its promise to pay you certain sums if you suffer accidental bodily injury. Thus if Smith suffers personal injury he may keep both the proceeds of such a policy and any damages he can obtain from the tortfeasor (or his liability insurer)—another indication that victims of personal injury are preferentially treated by the law.

---

[39] *Hunt v Severs* [1994] 2 All ER 385 at 395.

PUBLIC AND PRIVATE BODIES

Insurers and other trading companies operate in the private sector, but many bodies are public in one sense or another. Fluid though the distinction was even before the (semi)privatisation of public services, it is important, because public and private law have different procedures and qualities. On the one hand, it might be said that public bodies, set up for the public good, should behave better, more responsibly, than private ones, which are out to make a profit; on the other, when a private body is held liable only its shareholders suffer, whereas making a public body pay damages may reduce its ability to perform its services to the public. Thus hospital trusts which have to pay damages out of their normal budget have less money available for the cure of the sick. It was therefore nothing short of outrageous that for many years, until stopped by the House of Lords,[40] our courts made them pay the cost of bringing up a perfectly healthy child born as a result of their negligence: it was robbing sick Paul to pay healthy Peterkin.

Salmon LJ once said: 'The doctrine that the executive is subject to extraordinary legal liabilities is dangerous. It is but a short step from that doctrine to the doctrine that the executive may enjoy corresponding extraordinary legal rights. This is entirely contrary to one of the fundamental principles of the common law, namely that it regards all men indifferently. The cabinet minister by virtue of his office has no greater legal rights or liabilities than his humblest constituent. All are equal before the law. This surely is one of the pillars of freedom'.[41] His Lordship was objecting to the decision of the House of Lords in 1964 that a public official might be liable in punitive damages when a private actor would not.[42] His objection was unavailing. Indeed, the differential treatment has increased since then. Only 'public authorities' are expressly subjected to the duty to respect the rights contained in the Human Rights Act 1998; only public bodies, as emanations of the state, are bound by EC Directives which the government has failed to enact properly; only officials can be guilty of the tort of misfeasance in public office. It is clear, therefore, that the nature of a body as public may lead to increased liability.

If special liabilities attach to public bodies, do they enjoy special immunities also? The matter is very controverted and complex. Of course officials are given special statutory powers to invade the basic rights of

---

[40] *McFarlane v Tayside Health Board* [1999] 4 All ER 961.
[41] *Broome v Cassell & Co* [1971] 2 All ER 187 at 204.
[42] *Rookes v Barnard* [1964] 1 All ER 367.

the citizen—policemen may arrest where a citizen may not, and numerous civil servants are empowered to enter premises to rummage about in search of incriminating matter—and they are protected from liability in trespass if they can establish that they exercised these powers reasonably and within the conditions laid down by statute. But most of the powers granted to public bodies are to do acts which are not trespassory at all, such as those which cause merely economic loss, and certainly it is not *trespassory* to fail, however negligently, to do what one should have done, though a public authority may be liable under the Human Rights Act 1998 if it fails to protect one citizen from an invasion of his rights by another. The courts are very conscious that in granting powers to bodies, Parliament intended the body (and not the courts) to be free to decide how to use them—within limits, of course, which it necessarily fell to the courts to determine in the context of the enabling legislation. As a matter of administrative law a decision was apt to be quashed only if it was extremely unreasonable (*'Wednesbury* unreasonable'), that is, downright irrational, but even then damages might not be available, for as Lord Goff said 'in this country there is no general right to indemnity by reason of damage suffered through invalid administrative action'.[43]

In private law, however, simple unreasonableness of conduct suffices to constitute a breach of duty, supposing that a duty of care exists, so when the tort of negligence expanded to cover omissions which led to merely economic harm, as it did in 1978, life became very difficult for public bodies and their staff. One technique employed to protect them was to deny the existence of a common law duty of care as regards the exercise of statutory *powers* (i.e., what statute allowed, but did not require, the body to do). It could be held that it was not 'fair, just and reasonable' to impose such a fetter on the exercise of discretionary powers. Thus it was held by the House of Lords that the police owed no duty to anyone as regards their activities in investigating crime,[44] and that a local authority owed no duty to exercise its powers to protect children who were being abused at home.[45] This device had the advantage (for the public body) of protecting it not just from liability but also from any investigation into what it had actually done or, more commonly, failed to do, though the value of the device was later weakened when the courts held that though the body itself was under no duty it could be made liable for negligence

---

[43] *Factortame Ltd v Secretary of State (No 2)* [1991] 1 All ER 70 at 119.
[44] *Hill v Chief Constable* [1988] 2 All ER 238.
[45] *X v Bedfordshire CC* [1995] 3 All ER 353.

on the part of those to whom it delegated its role.[46] A greater bodyblow came in the form of a decision in Strasbourg which held that English law must, on pain of being held defective, provide a remedy where a public authority had culpably failed to protect the Convention rights of a person from invasion by a third party. By qualifying as 'unlawful' all acts and failures to act of public authorities which infringe the Convention rights of the individual, the Human Rights Act might seem to bridge the gap between administrative and tort law.

Nevertheless there remains a difference as regards remedies, for the 1998 Act provides that damages are to be awarded only if necessary to afford the claimant just satisfaction, and our courts follow Strasbourg in holding that a declaration of the unlawfulness of conduct may constitute 'just satisfaction'.[47] Still, it seems that damages are appropriate when a living claimant has suffered actual harm, though we surely need not follow that court in awarding damages to the relatives of persons into whose death no adequate inquiry has been held, especially since at common law there is no duty to hold any inquiry.[48] The upshot is that the courts are now readier to impose liability in damages on public authorities whose unreasonable exercise of statutory powers causes harm to an individual, and are indeed extending the kinds of harm which they regard as adequate, such as educational impairment. Indeed it seems that it is only budgetary decisions which the courts will treat as 'non-justiciable'.

The matter is treated slightly differently where the authority has been charged with a duty. Normally a breach of duty is an actionable wrong, but the general tendency of the courts is to deny that Parliament, in creating the duty, intended it to confer a right to damages on the victim of its breach, especially if any other remedy is available. Consider highway authorities. The Highways Act 1980 imposes on them a duty to 'maintain' the highway (s. 41). This duty (which did not, until recent corrective legislation, include keeping it clear of snow and ice) certainly generates a claim for damages on breach, but the 'duty to promote road safety', which the Act also imposes on them (s. 39), has been held by the House of Lords to be a 'target' duty such that not only is a breach of it not actionable as a breach of statutory duty but no common law duty of care should be annexed to it.[49] Rather like the reluctance to hold that a body with power to act is under a common law duty to act, the reluctance to hold that

---

[46] *Phelps v Hillingdon LBC* [2001] 2 AC 619.
[47] *R (Greenfield) v Secretary of State* [2005] UKHL 14.
[48] *In Re McKerr* [2004] UKHL 12.
[49] *Gorringe v Calderdale MBC* [2004] UKHL 15.

breach of statutory duties generates a claim for damages certainly benefits public authorities, though it is not confined to them.

Parliament itself is not a 'public authority' for the purposes of the Human Rights Act 1998. It can freely enact statutes which are incompatible with Convention rights, and if the statute cannot be construed so as to make it compatible, the courts must apply it, and cannot sanction the Minister who implements it. The consequence is that the United Kingdom will be held liable in Strasbourg. European Union law is different. Our Parliament cannot validly enact statutes which conflict with Community law or the rights it grants, nor may the courts apply such enactments; indeed, they must hold the State itself liable for Parliament's shortcomings, if sufficiently serious.[50] So much for the sovereignty of Parliament, if sovereignty means, as it does, the power to enact laws that your courts will enforce!

NUMBER OF CLAIMANTS

A theme which runs throughout the law is a concern to restrict the number of persons who can complain of any particular conduct. In contract this was done by the rule ('privity') that only the promisee himself could sue the promisor, that is, only the buyer could sue the seller, not the person for whom the goods were intended, a rule only slightly modified by recent legislation. In property law only a person with a precise right in the property can claim, as we shall see in the tort of nuisance (land), conversion (goods) and even negligence (both). Even clearer is the rule in the tort of public nuisance: the person who blocks the highway is guilty of a common law offence, but the only possible claimants are those who have suffered a 'particular' harm, not the generality who have been seriously put out. Again, in order to claim under the Human Rights Act 1998 you have to be the 'victim', according to the jurisprudence of the Strasbourg Court. In public law, too, there are problems about 'locus standi' or standing to complain. We shall see the force of this viewpoint in the law relating to financial harm and nervous shock resulting from a clear act of negligence, where foreseeability is not enough, precisely because too many people may foreseeably suffer such harm as a result of a single incident: we may have to distinguish between 'primary' and 'secondary' victims.

---

[50] *R v Secretary of State, ex p Factortame* [1999] 4 All ER 906.

2

Negligence

A history of tort law would doubtless start off with the venerable, though still vital, tort of trespass, or possibly nuisance. Those torts will be dealt with later, but today the tort of 'negligence' is so dominant and pervasive, controlling traffic accidents, professional liability, and so much else, that it must be dealt with first. It is indeed a relatively recent arrival on the scene, for though there had long been certain specific situations not covered by trespass where liability was imposed if the claimant could prove that the defendant's misconduct had caused him harm—for example, if he was the patient of a careless doctor, or the victim of injury on the defendant's premises, or the owner of a thing damaged while in the defendant's possession—one could not properly speak of a coherent tort of negligence until these instances were generalised. *Enfin vint Lord Atkin* who said in 1932: '. . . in English law there must be, and is, some general conception of relations giving rise to a duty of care, of which the particular cases found in the books are but instances', and he proceeded to state: 'You must take reasonable care to avoid acts or omissions which you can reasonably foresee would be likely to injure your neighbour. Who, then, in law is my neighbour? The answer seems to be—persons who are so closely and directly affected by my act that I ought reasonably to have them in contemplation as being so affected when I am directing my mind to the acts or omissions which are called in question'.[1]

Neighbourhood principle

THE DUTY QUESTION

The question which Lord Atkin had to answer was whether the manufacturer of a bottled drink 'is under any legal duty to the ultimate purchaser or consumer to take reasonable care that the article is free from defect likely to cause injury to health'. Rather than asking when there is *liability* for carelessly poisoning people (which is what we are really interested in), he is inquiring about the existence (in a very odd sense) of a

---

[1] *Donoghue v Stevenson* [1932] AC 562 at 580.

legal *duty* to take care not to poison them. This emphasis on duty is a characteristic of English common law, not found in other systems. As another judge put it: 'In most situations it is better to be careful than careless, but it is quite another thing to elevate all carelessness into a tort. Liability has to be based on a legal duty not to be careless. . .'[2]

The duty concept has been said to be unnecessary, in the sense that all cases could be decided just as well in terms of fault and/or remoteness of damage, but it has proved useful and in any case it is now ineradicable, since it is used not only by the courts but also by Parliament. It was therefore quite daring of counsel recently to argue before the House of Lords that the duty concept be jettisoned in favour of concentrating on the question of breach (*alias* negligence!), and quite surprising that two of their Lordships seemed to warm to the suggestion.[3] Lord Bingham 'would regard that shift as welcome, since the concept of duty had proved itself a somewhat blunt instrument for dividing claims which ought reasonably to lead to recovery from claims which ought not . . .', and Lord Nicholls, who decided against its use in negligence claims generally, nevertheless said that 'This approach . . . is not without attraction. It is peculiarly appropriate in the field of human rights.'

This last point is significant. Although rights and duties may be in some sense correlative, emphasis on rights does tend to diminish emphasis on duties. After all, in cases of trespass, where liability depends on the invasion of rights, we do not use the notion of duty, nor do we use it in cases of deceit, where telling lies is as manifestly unlawful as the Human Rights Act 1998 declares invasions of Convention rights to be. The sticking point, however, will surely prove to be those cases where the public body is charged not with a positive unlawful act but with failure to prevent invasions by others: here it seems very difficult to avoid the notion of duty, as it would be if you sought to extend liability in deceit from positive lies to mere non-disclosure. In any case we must not let human rights cases wag the dog of tort. The corrective can be found in the speech of Lord Rodger, which should be mandatory reading for anyone starting out on the law of negligence.[4]

Lord Rodger demonstrates how useful the duty device is when we wish to hold a careless defendant liable to A but not to B, though damage to both is equally foreseeable. Thus while one owes a duty to a pedestrian to

---

[2] *Moorgate Mercantile Co v Twitchings* [1976] 2 All ER 641 at 659.
[3] *D v East Berks Community Health NHS Trust* [2005] UKHL 23 at 49 and 92.
[4] *Ibid.* 97 to 119.

take care not to run him over, one owes none to his widow who has a fit when, quite foreseeably, she hears of his death (it is different if she actually witnesses it). So, too, when young delinquents damaged a yacht in their attempt to escape from their island camp while their warders slept, the warders were held to owe a duty to the yacht company, but only because the yacht was in the 'immediate vicinity', no duty being owed to owners of property further away. Generally, indeed, a person who carelessly damages property is in breach of duty only to those who own or possess it, not to others adversely affected, however foreseeably, such as the insurer of the property or the charterer of a vessel or anyone with merely a contractual liability or right in relation to the physical damage. Again, a shareholder cannot found on breach of a duty owed to the company. And in the very case where counsel made his daring suggestion the decision was precisely that while doctors and social workers who stupidly suspected that a child had been abused owed a duty to the child they owed none to the father.

Yet the duty notion has perhaps become overstrained, in that any discussion of duty now tends to involve consideration not just of the relationship of the parties and the nature of the defendant's conduct, as one would expect, but also of the nature of the harm involved and the link between the conduct of the harm, that is, all the focal points we have identified as relevant in any tort case. It is no longer just the existence of the duty which is crucial, but also its 'scope'.

Whatever the aesthetics of discussing cases in terms of duty, breach, causation or remoteness, it is still the law that before we can hold a careless person liable for the damage he has caused we must find that he owed the claimant a duty of care. Note that the 'duty' question is one of law: it is a matter of argument, not proof. In the distant past, when it was for the jury to decide whether the defendant had misbehaved and how much he should pay, the requirement of duty was useful since it permitted the judge to prevent the case reaching the jury at all by ruling that on the facts there was no duty in law. Even after the demise of the jury in negligence cases, the duty question could still be treated as a preliminary issue to be decided before any actual facts were proved, as in *Donoghue v Stevenson* itself. A negative decision on the duty question is very useful to defendants, for it does away with the need for a trial, since even if it could be shown that the defendant was careless and the harm a foreseeable result of such carelessness, there would, for want of any duty in law, be no liability.

In such a case defendants faced no public inquiry into their actual conduct, and were spared the trouble and expense of pretrial paperwork, sending witnesses to court, and so on. Thus when the courts held that advocates were under no duty of care to their clients as regards matters in court, advocates could calmly proceed to be equally helpful to the next client,[5] and when the House of Lords held that it was contrary to public policy to hold that the police were under any duty of care to the potential victims of crimes they were investigating, the effect was that the police never had to lead evidence of what they actually did or did not do. In deference to a very negative reaction in Strasbourg to any suggestion of an 'immunity', our courts not only abandoned the rule about the immunity of the forensic lawyer and modified their view of police liability but also altered their useful practice of 'striking out' a claimant's pleadings on the ground that they disclosed no duty owed to him by the defendant. Instead they now say that the question of 'duty or no duty' cannot properly be decided until the actual facts are known. Of course this destroys the utility of the duty concept in the respect under discussion, but a compromise has perhaps been reached: if the case asserted by the claimant has no real chance of succeeding in the light of the evidence provided by the affidavits before the court, summary judgment can be given in favour of the defendant without exciting the ire of the judges in Strasbourg who seem to think that tort litigation is an effective and costless way of ascertaining the actual facts.

As Lord Rodger made clear, the notion of duty is useful in allowing us to hold the defendant liable to one person and not to another. It also makes it possible to hold that the duty is owed to the claimant only in some particular capacity: when auditors circulated to shareholders an allegedly negligent report on their company and the claimant shareholder proceeded to take it over, the issue was whether the accountants owed the claimant a duty of care (a) in his capacity as potential investor, and (b) in his capacity as actual shareholder.[6] This comes close to holding that the duty can be restricted to certain kinds of harm, and it is certainly true that a duty to take care to avoid causing physical harm by no means entails a similar duty regarding harm which is purely economic, even if both types of harm are suffered by the same person in the same incident.[7] A recurrent phrase is 'the scope of the duty'. Thus in the auditors case Lord Bridge said: 'It is never sufficient to ask simply whether A owes B a

---

[5] *Rondel v Worsley* [1967] 3 All ER 993.
[6] *Caparo Industries v Dickman* [1990] 1 All ER 568.
[7] *Spartan Steel v Martin & Co* [1972] 3 All ER 557.

duty of care. It is always necessary to determine the scope of the duty by reference to the kind of damage from which A must take care to save B harmless'. Or as it has been put more recently: was there 'a duty in respect of the kind of loss which in the event was suffered'?[8] One can accordingly rationalise the holding that the manufacturer of a defective product is not liable to the consumer whose loss is purely financial by saying that the scope of his duty of care does not extend that far.

But the 'scope of duty' approach can lead to oddities. In quite a simple case where the defendant motorist collided with a pedestrian who suddenly stepped out from behind a parked vehicle which blocked the defendant's vision, the trial judge held that though the defendant was negligent in driving too fast, her negligence did not cause the injury. The Court of Appeal correctly dismissed the claimant's appeal, but held that the judge had given the wrong reason: the right reason, forsooth, was that the motorist owed the pedestrian no duty![9] In fact the trial judge was quite correct. Although the defendant was driving faster than was safe in the circumstances, the accident could only have been avoided if she had been driving much more slowly than proper care required; accordingly her excess speed did not contribute to the injury, for it would have occurred had she been driving quite properly. To decide the case on the ground of 'no duty' rather than, as the trial judge did, on causation, is decidedly peculiar.

The duty question tends to come first in the books: this is natural enough, since it has often been a preliminary question in the courts and is always a precondition of liability in negligence. But though it is an important question, it is not one very commonly raised in court. In fact, the duty question is raised only in novel cases where it is plausibly arguable that there should be no liability even if the harm was foreseeable and the defendant was careless in causing it. In the great majority of cases, the existence of the duty of care is taken for granted. It is quite unnecessary to argue or state that persons using the highway owe each other a duty to take care not to injure them or their property, that the occupier of premises owes his visitors a duty to look out for their safety, or that the person in possession of another's goods must do his best to guard them from damage and loss. Glimpses into the obvious should be avoided: where the answer is self-evident or well established by authority, the question of the existence of the duty does not arise.

---

[8] *Corbett v Bond Pearce* [2001] 3 All ER 769 at 780.
[9] *Sam v Atkins* [2005] EWCA Civ 1452.

FORESEEABILITY

The leading case on when a duty to take care exists is the 1932 case from which we have already quoted.[10] The facts alleged were that Mrs Donoghue went to Minchella's café with a friend who bought her some ice-cream in a glass and a bottle of ginger beer to pour over it. After the effervescence had abated, Mrs Donoghue emptied the bottle into her glass and found to her horror that a decomposed snail, obscured by the opacity of the bottle, had been lurking within. She alleged that the presence of this noxious foreign body and the harm she had suffered in consequence were due to the negligence of the producer. The Court of Session in Scotland had held that a manufacturer owed a consumer no duty in law not carelessly to injure her, but this decision, so inimical to consumer protection, was reversed by a bare majority in the House of Lords, led by Lord Atkin.

Two features in the facts alleged were rather underemphasised by his Lordship. The first relates to the harm suffered, and the second to the defender's conduct: Mrs Donoghue supposedly suffered actual personal injury—indeed she was poisoned—and the defender was guilty of a positively dangerous act. This last point is often misunderstood. When asked what Stevenson did wrong, students usually say 'He failed to keep the snail out of the bottle' or 'He didn't wash the bottles carefully enough' or words to that effect, always using a negative formulation, focussing on what Stevenson didn't do. But in truth one can keep as many snails in bottles as one likes (subject to the rules about cruelty to animals). What one must not do is send out into the highways and byways of commerce a bottled snail masquerading as wholesome ginger beer. And that is what Stevenson did. He added a danger to life: he didn't just fail to save Mrs Donoghue from the snail, he inflicted the snail on her.

Lord Atkin's views on the existence of a duty are thus appropriate in cases where the tortfeasor's positive act has caused physical harm to a foreseeable victim, but quite possibly distinguishable where either the tortfeasor's conduct was not positive or the claimant's harm was not physical, or both. As Lord Hoffmann said in a later case: 'Omissions, like economic loss, are notoriously a category of conduct in which Lord Atkin's generalisation . . . offers limited help'.[11] Yet it was precisely in a case of omission causing economic loss that Lord Wilberforce sought to

---

[10] *Donoghue v Stevenson* [1932] AC 562.   [11] [1996] 3 All ER 801 at 818.

improve, nearly 50 years later, on Lord Atkin's formulation. In *Anns v Merton London Borough Council* he said: '. . . the question has to be approached in two stages. First one has to ask whether, as between the alleged wrongdoer and the person who has suffered damage there is a sufficient relationship of proximity, or neighbourhood such that, in the reasonable contemplation of the former, carelessness on his part may be likely to cause damage to the latter, in which case a *prima facie* duty of care arises. Secondly, if the first question is answered affirmatively, it is necessary to consider whether there are any considerations which ought to negative, or to reduce or limit the scope of the duty or the class of person to whom it is owed or the damages to which a breach of it may give rise'.[12] He proceeded to hold a local authority liable for failing to exercise its powers to prevent a jerry-builder putting up an unstable house which the plaintiff later purchased to his financial detriment. The case therefore involved pure economic loss resulting from an omission— both the points on which *Donoghue v Stevenson* is unauthoritative. It is accordingly less than very surprising that the decision was dramatically overruled by an afforced House of Lords eleven years later as 'impossible to reconcile . . . with any previously accepted principles of the tort of negligence'.[13]

PROXIMITY

In between times some doubt had been cast on Lord Wilberforce's formulation, which seemed unduly to extend liability for purely economic loss. In the accountancy case already mentioned Lord Bridge said this: '. . . in addition to the foreseeability of damage, necessary ingredients in any situation giving rise to a duty of care are that there should exist between the party owing the duty and the party to whom it is owed a relationship characterised by the law as one of "proximity" or "neighbourhood" and that the situation should be one in which the courts considers it fair, just, and reasonable that the law should impose a duty of a given scope on the one party for the benefit of the other. But . . . the concepts of proximity and fairness embodied in these additional requirements are not susceptible of any such precise definition as would be necessary to give them utility as practical tests, but amount in effect to little more than convenient labels to attach to the features of different specific situations which,

---

[12] [1977] 2 All ER 492 at 498.
[13] *Murphy v Brentwood DC* [1990] 2 All ER 908 at 936.

on a detailed examination of all the circumstances, the law recognises pragmatically as giving rise to a duty of care of a given scope.'[14] This is commonly referred to as the *Caparo* test for the existence of a duty of care.

Proximity, which is after all just Latin for closeness, relates to the physical world, and it is not an easy notion to apply figuratively, any more than the cognate notion of 'neighbour'. Indeed Lord Goff has said that 'Once proximity is no longer treated as expressing a relationship founded on foreseeability of damage, it ceases to have an ascertainable meaning, and it cannot therefore provide a criterion for liability'.[15] Quite so, but since it is now clear that the foreseeability of harm is not in itself enough to impose a duty to take care to avoid it, 'proximity' must somehow be dealt with. If it resists analysis, its application can perhaps be exemplified. In one case, the police were aware that there was a serial rapist on the loose, but knew neither who he was nor who his next victim might be; there was no proximity between the police and the eventual victim.[16] In another case the police knew the identity of both the person threatening violence and his intended victims, but did not have him in custody; there was probably sufficient proximity between the police and the known victim.[17] In a third case, a tape on which the police had recorded sensitive information given in confidence by the plaintiff was stolen from a police car and came into the hands of the suspect; there was clearly proximity between the police and the claimant (though at trial it was found that the police had not been negligent).[18]

ASSUMPTION OF RESPONSIBILITY

Those were all cases of physical harm. Where the harm is purely economic, rather more may be required, and it is here that one comes across the phrase 'assumption of responsibility'. Now if the defendant personally has as good as said to the claimant personally 'You can rely on me to do this, or to do it properly'; then if he is paid (consideration) he will be contractually bound, and obviously liable for failure to act, and even if he is not paid he may be held to be under a tort duty to act with care, if he acts at all, perhaps even under a duty to act. Indeed as early as 1793 we

[14] *Caparo Industries v Dickman* [1990] 1 All ER 568 at 574.
[15] *Leigh & Sillivan v Aliakmon Shipping Co* [1985] 2 All ER 44 at 74.
[16] *Hill v Chief Constable* [1988] 2 All ER 238.
[17] *Osman v Ferguson* [1993] 4 All ER 344.
[18] *Swinney v Chief Constable* [1996] 3 All ER 449.

find the following in a case where the defendant gratuitously undertook to effect insurance on behalf of the plaintiff and failed to do so effectively: 'That though there was no consideration for the plaintiff's undertaking to procure an insurance for another, yet where a party voluntarily undertook to do it . . . but did it so negligently or unskilfully, that the party could obtain no benefit from it, that in that case he should be liable to an action'.[19] Here we have an undertaking on the side of the defendant and reliance on that undertaking on the side of the claimant.

Assumption of responsibility and reliance were key features in the second most important case in the law of negligence, namely *Hedley Byrne & Co v Heller and Partners* in 1963.[20] The letter which the defendant bank wrote in response to an inquiry about the solvency of a common customer, though not actually inaccurate, misled the plaintiff into continuing to afford credit to the customer, who quickly went bankrupt. The lower courts held that there was no duty to take care what one said, as opposed to what one did, and that in consequence inaccurate statements were not actionable unless deliberately false or warranted true, and here there was no deceit and, because the information was provided gratuitously, no contract. The House of Lords nevertheless held that, but for the letterhead which excluded liability, the defendants might well be under a duty to take care what they said, notwithstanding that the only harm apt to ensue from the plaintiff's reliance was purely economic.

The five speeches, unanimous in the conclusion that there might well be a duty to take care of another's merely financial interests, varied in their terms. Leading notions were whether there was a 'special' relationship between the parties (described by Lord Devlin as 'equivalent to contract'), whether the defendant was an expert, whether he knew or should have known that the recipient of his information would rely on its accuracy (as is apt to be the case if the recipient asked for it) and whether, by responding when he was under no duty to do so, there had been a 'voluntary assumption of responsibility' by the defendant for what he was saying (this being the point on which the defendant in the case escaped liability, since his disclaimer showed that he was not assuming responsibility).

But 'reliance' is a weasel word. It can be used very loosely, as in Lord Nolan's speech in *White v Jones*: 'If the defendant drives his car on the highway, he implicitly assumes a responsibility towards other road users,

---

[19] *Wilkinson v Coverdale* (1793) 170 ER 284.
[20] *Hedley Byrne & Co v Heller and Partners* [1963] 2 All ER 575.

and they in turn implicitly rely on him to discharge that responsibility'.[21] This is to rob the idea of all utility, but it does indicate the connection between assumption of responsibility and reliance, properly understood. In its strictest denotation it refers to the case where A takes action in the belief that things are as they have been made to appear. Indeed if A wishes to persuade the court that B's representation *caused* him loss, he will usually have to demonstrate that he relied on it in this sense.

Two-party cases are relatively simple to understand, for there the assumption of responsibility is *towards the claimant*, and the claimant has relied on the defendant's undertaking. The addition of a third party makes for complications, as usual. Must the undertaking be by the defendant personally to the claimant personally, or is it enough that the claimant was affected by the defendant's undertaking towards a third party who relied on it, or that the claimant relied on an undertaking made by the defendant to a third party?

In *Harris v Wyre Forest District Council* the plaintiff purchased a modest house with the aid of a loan from the first defendant, the local authority, to which their employee, the second defendant, had negligently reported that the house was in better condition than was the case. The report was not shown to the plaintiff, but the local authority made the loan. It was held that *both* defendants were liable, that is, both the local authority for implicitly representing the value of the property and their employee who effected the erroneous valuation. It is fair to say that no argument was addressed to their Lordships to the effect that the employee should not be held liable.[22]

In that case, at any rate, the plaintiff, by proceeding to buy the house, had relied on the representation, as did the plaintiff in *Hedley Byrne* (where, however, there was no discussion of whether the director or secretary who drafted or signed the misleading banker's reference was personally liable). It was, however, far from obvious that the employee who did the actual valuation had assumed responsibility towards the plaintiff purchaser, as well as to the local authority, and it was certain that the plaintiff was not relying on any such assumption of responsibility by the employee, of whom he knew nothing whatever. Perhaps that is why Lord Griffiths said 'I do not think that voluntary assumption of responsibility is a helpful or realistic test for liability . . . the phrase "assumption of responsibility" can only have any real meaning if it is understood as referring to circumstances in which the law will deem the maker of a

---

[21] [1995] 1 All ER 691 at 735.   [22] [1989] 2 All ER 514.

statement to have assumed responsibility to the person who acts on the advice'.[23] Those circumstances were of course present in *Hedley Byrne* in which the notion of assumption of responsibility played a prominent part, if we ignore the disclaimer, a like disclaimer having been held void as unreasonable under the Unfair Contract Terms Act 1977 in a case decided concurrently with *Harris*.

Notwithstanding Lord Griffiths' observations, the idea of assumption of responsibility as the source of a duty to take care was resuscitated with vigour by Lord Goff in what has been the most extreme case so far (and by far), where a solicitor failed to execute his client's instructions to draw up a will in favour of the client's two daughters, and was held liable to them.[24] Lord Browne-Wilkinson was of the opinion that merely by undertaking to do a job one assumed responsibility to anyone apt to be affected by its non- or misperformance (thereby in effect extending *Donoghue v Stevenson* to omissions causing economic loss). This manifestly goes too far, and it is agreed that Lord Goff's view represents the ratio of the decision. His Lordship accepted that the *Hedley Byrne* decision could not itself 'give rise on ordinary principles to an assumption of responsibility by the testator's solicitor towards an intended beneficiary' but held that since solicitors were professionals and legacies were important to individuals, it was only just that careless solicitors should be liable to disappointed legatees, and that this could be done by extending 'to the intended beneficiary a remedy under the *Hedley Byrne* principle by holding that the assumption of responsibility by the solicitor towards his client should be held in law to extend to the intended beneficiary who (as the solicitor can reasonably foresee) may, as a result of the solicitor's negligence, be deprived of his intended legacy ...'. Lord Mustill's powerful dissent explained why *Hedley Byrne* could not, consistently with principle, apply (as Lord Goff accepted) but denied that justice required its extension (as Lord Goff proposed). The difficulty was that the disappointed legatees could in no sense be said to have relied on the solicitor's acting promptly: they may well not even have known that he had been instructed to act, but in any case they took no action in reliance on his acting: there was no 'mutuality' between the legatees and the solicitor, between plaintiff and defendant, and mutuality was, according to Lord Mustill, of the essence of *Hedley Byrne*. On the other hand, there was clearly 'proximity', since the solicitor knew perfectly well for whom

---

[23] *Smith v Eric S Bush* [1989] 2 All ER 514 at 534.
[24] *White v Jones* [1995] 1 All ER 691.

the legacies were intended: indeed he must have written their very names down on his note of instructions.

Lord Goff's espousal of the concept of 'assumption of responsibility', which had the further advantage of making it easier to impose liability for failing to act, as in the case at hand, has not rendered it immune to criticism. Lord Slynn has subsequently said that 'The phrase means simply that the law recognises that there is a duty of care. It is not so much that responsibility is assumed as that it is recognized or imposed by the law'.[25] In between times, however, it had been emphatically relied on with the approval of a unanimous House. The case was one where a firm had sold the plaintiffs a franchise for a health food store after sending them, on the firm's writing paper, an inaccurately optimistic forecast of the profits likely to be achieved. The actual source of this misinformation was the managing director, with whom the claimants had no personal dealings, but who was sued by them when the firm was wound up. The House of Lords, reversing the Court of Appeal, dismissed the claim: it was the firm, not the managing director who owned the firm, on whom the plaintiffs had relied, and the managing director had not undertaken responsibility towards them. Lord Steyn, with whom Lord Goff and the others agreed, said 'The test is whether the plaintiff could *reasonably* rely on an assumption of personal responsibility by the individual who performed the services on behalf of the company'.[26]

Lord Steyn described *Harris v Wyre Forest District Council*, as 'decided on special facts'. There, it will be recalled, liability was imposed not only on the local authority which represented the value of the property but also on the employee who made the actual valuation on its behalf, in a report which was not shown to the plaintiffs. The conflict between this holding and the reasoning in the health food case is clear, and came before the Court of Appeal in another valuation case. The building society sought from the Plymouth branch of a firm a valuation of a property which the claimant wished to buy. The valuation was negligently effected by Mr Babb, an employee, who signed his report and was sued by the claimants when the firm which employed him went bankrupt. The Court of Appeal by a majority held the employee personally liable; they quoted the depreciatory remarks of Lord Griffiths and Lord Slynn about assumption of responsibility and decided to follow *Harris v Wyre Forest District Council* rather than the health food case, ignoring the rule that a

[25] *Phelps v Hillingdon London Borough Council* [2000] 4 All ER 504 at 518.
[26] *Williams v Natural Life Health Foods* [1998] 2 All ER 584.

case is not authoritative for a point which was not argued.[27] It is a pity that the House of Lords refused leave to appeal, for while the individual valuer in *Harris* would certainly have been indemnified by the local authority which employed him, Mr Babb's employer's insurance policy, which would have covered him, had been cancelled by the trustee in bankruptcy (whose personal liability to Mr Babb might be difficult to establish).[28]

It is to be noted that in the *Harris* case Lord Templeman spoke of it as concerning 'negligence in circumstances which are akin to contract'.[29] When a creditor suffers a financial loss because the firm with which he has contracted has failed to perform or has performed badly, the breach is generally due to the fault of one of its employees, or even the deliberate decision of a director. There can be no question of rendering the employee or even the director liable for the breach of contract. There should equally be no question of rendering them liable for the financial loss suffered by the creditor by allowing him to invoke the law of tort, in particular the case of *Hedley Byrne* which depends upon there being between the parties a relationship described by Lord Devlin in that case as 'akin to contract'. While contract looks to the firm which is to be paid, tort looks to the individual at fault and although, as we shall see, the principle of vicarious liability in tort renders the firm liable for the harm done by its employee, it seems wrong in the transactional area to render the employee liable in addition to the firm.

FAIR, JUST, AND REASONABLE

But even foreseeability of damage, proximity and arguably assumption of responsibility may not be enough. Note that in the quotation from *Caparo* given above, Lord Bridge said that in addition to proximity it must be 'fair just and reasonable' to impose a duty (meaning, to impose liability for unreasonably harmful conduct). This criterion, apparently (but only apparently) less objective than the others, was used in a case of considerable interest.[30]

A vessel carrying the plaintiff's goods was en route to the Black Sea from Chile and Peru when it sprung a leak in the Gulf of Mexico and put in to Puerto Rico. The owners of the vessel were keen for it to proceed to a port where major repairs would be cheaper, and managed to persuade

[27] *Merrett v Babb* [2001] QB 1174.   [28] *Burns v Shuttlehurst* [1999] 2 All ER 27.
[29] [1989] 2 All ER 520.   [30] *The Nicholas H* [1995] 3 All ER 307.

the surveyor of the defendant classification society, whose permission was essential for the maintenance of the vessel's insurance, to agree that it could sail on if temporary repairs were effected on the spot. As matters turned out, the surveyor should have insisted that permanent repairs be effected then and there, for the vessel sank with the plaintiff's cargo on board. The question put to the House of Lords was whether the classification society owed the plaintiff a duty to take care not to endanger its cargo (the real question being whether the defendant would have to pay if the surveyor were shown to have acted unreasonably). The House held that although the harm was perfectly foreseeable and there was probably proximity between the surveyor and the cargo-owner (the surveyor had, after all, been fully aware of the existence of the cargo and must indeed have inspected the hold in which it lay), nevertheless it would not, in all the circumstances, be fair, just, and reasonable to impose a duty on the society, that is, to make it liable for unreasonably causing foreseeable damage to the cargo.

One can hardly dissent from the proposition that the courts should refrain from imposing liability where to do so would be unfair, unjust, or unreasonable (or all three, supposing there is any difference between them), but the question whether, in a particular case, it would indeed be unfair, unjust, and unreasonable to apply the traditional rules of liability in negligence may provoke quite divergent views. Indeed, it did so in this case, for Lord Lloyd dissented very vigorously. 'All that is required', he said, 'is a straightforward application of *Donoghue v Stevenson*': the defendant had sent the vessel forth to its doom when he should have realised it was unsafe to do so and had thereby caused foreseeable physical harm to the cargo owner, just as a careless ship-repairer might have done. His Lordship asserted (correctly) that theretofore the 'unfair unjust unreasonable' mantra had been developed to deal with cases of merely economic harm, not physical harm due to dangerous conduct, which was the present case.

Nevertheless, *in the particular circumstances of this case*, which involved not only the surveyor and the cargo-owner, but also the shipowner, who was under a strict contractual duty to the cargo-owner, it *would* have been unfair, unjust, and unreasonable to hold the defendant liable. Most of the relevant considerations militating against liability were laid out in the majority opinion of Lord Steyn. He emphasised that to impose liability on the defendant, one of a mere handful of classification societies world-wide, which was acting for the public good in seeing to the safety of vessels, would render the resolution of cargo claims more complex and also put up the price of surveys to the shipowners (who would pass on the extra cost to the cargo-owners). His point that the defendant did not *directly* cause the harm is, as Lord Lloyd showed, less persuasive, but he was surely right to say that there was no ground for 'voluntary assumption of responsibility', given that it was the shipowner who relied on the surveyor, and not the cargo-owner, who knew nothing about what was going on.

Two other factors which justify this decision were not mooted. The first, a point of which the law has not yet overtly taken account and which counsel would not dare to raise, is that the plaintiff's loss had already been met by his insurer (all cargo afloat is in fact insured, as it must be if it is for sale), so that it was not really the owner of the sunken cargo that was making the claim, but its insurer, which had suffered only an economic loss, and that, too, as a result of its own undertaking, for which it had been paid. Secondly, if Lord Lloyd had had his way and the defendant had been held liable, it would have ended up paying 95% of the total value of the cargo (over six million dollars) although it was the shipowner that was primarily at fault in putting to sea in a leaky vessel in breach of its contract with the cargo-owner. Now when two parties are liable for the same damage, as the shipowner and the defendant would have been had the defendant been held liable, they usually share the loss in proportion to their responsibility for it (see Chapter 7 below), but where the liability of one of them to the victim is limited by contract or statute, as was the shipowner's liability in this case, that limitation also applies to the claim for contribution.

Two questions invite consideration. First, if the defendant had been held liable for the cargo, must he also have been held liable for the vessel, equally at the bottom of the Sargasso Sea? And given that the defendant was held not liable for the loss of the cargo, would he also have been held not liable to the crew if injured and their widows if drowned? Note that the crew would not be insured (and if they had been, their damages if injured could be cumulated with the insurance proceeds, which would in any case be neglected in a suit by their widows) and the contribution problem would not arise since in the case of injury to crew members the shipowner's liability is not subject to any limit. There would therefore be no difficulty in holding that it would be quite fair, just, and reasonable to hold the surveyor and his employer liable to the crew and their widows.

If Lord Lloyd's view is correct that this was a straightforward *Donoghue v Stevenson* case of unreasonable conduct causing foreseeable physical harm, the decision is one which sidesteps the normal rules of negligence law for reasons of policy. If we move from the high seas of commerce to the oasis of the family home we find another instance of this. When a doctor, who had been retained to conduct a sterilisation operation on a husband, carelessly certified that the operation had been successful and that normal marital relations could be resumed, a healthy child was born. The parents' claim for the cost of bringing up the child was dismissed by the House of Lords.[31] True, the claim was for pure economic loss, but there was a special relationship between the parties, let alone a direct misrepresentation *à la Hedley Byrne*, designed to be relied on, and the harm complained of was not just foreseeable, it was the very thing that the defendant was retained to prevent. Bog-standard negligence law would make the defendant liable, but the House was unanimous that the claim must fail, and though the reasons given varied widely, it is quite clear that they were policy-driven rather than strictly juridical. Three years later the House, invited to overrule the decision, unanimously decided not to do so, but by a bare majority ruled that in similar cases the claimants should be awarded a lump sum of £15,000, a decision so odd as to suggest the unease their Lordships felt at sending the involuntary parents empty away when the actual law was on their side.[32]

PROPERTY DAMAGE AND PERSONAL INJURY

As it happened, the question of the applicability of *The Nicholas H* to personal injury arose shortly afterwards in a case where an amateur aviationist built a light aircraft from a do-it-yourself kit but installed a non-standard gearbox which was incompatible with the propeller. The aircraft required a certificate of airworthiness and the defendant provided it, though he should have realised that the aircraft was not airworthy, as was proved on the test flight when it nose-dived and injured the plaintiff passenger. The defendants naturally invoked *The Nicholas H*, but in vain. Hobhouse LJ in particular was scathing about importing into personal injury cases doctrine applicable to cases of economic loss: this would represent 'a fundamental attack upon the principle of tortious liability for negligent conduct which had caused foreseeable personal injury to others'.[33]

We may conclude, therefore, and without any surprise, that one is more

---

[31] *McFarlane v Tayside Health Board* [2000] 2 AC 59.
[32] *Rees v Darlington Memorial Hospital NHS Trust* [2003] UKHL 52.
[33] *Perrett v Collins* [1998] 2 Lloyd's Rep 255 at 257, [1998] TLR 393.

likely to be held liable for causing personal injury than for causing property damage (especially when it is insured), and that this fact is reflected in the apparently neutral discussions regarding the duty of care. It may be instructive in this context to consider the differential treatment of fire brigades sued for property damage and ambulance services sued for personal injury. Of several claims brought by owners of premises against the fire services which had allegedly allowed them to be burned to the ground when they could have been saved, the only one where the claim succeeded was where the fire brigade had actually made the situation worse by turning off the sprinkler system: the distinction was drawn between acts and omissions, and it was held that there was no liability simply for failure to put out the fire even when that could easily have been done.[34] Shortly thereafter, however, an ambulance which had been called for an emergency took so long to arrive that the patient suffered a serious attack which would probably have been prevented by timely arrival. The ambulance authority was held liable.[35] Despite the fact that in the latter case there was more reliance on the arrival of the ambulance (because if one is told that an ambulance is not coming there is something one can do about it), it is difficult not to attribute the differential treatment to the fact that in one case property only was involved (though people are often burnt in burning houses) and in the other a sick person, and perhaps also to the fact that premises are almost invariably insured against fire (and that consequently the actual plaintiffs in the fire cases were probably insurance companies in disguise).

PURELY ECONOMIC HARM

If in the law reports, unlike the statute book, the differential treatment of personal injury and property damage is only a matter of inference, the distinction between physical damage of either kind and purely economic harm is quite openly accepted. Some cases could not be clearer. In one case highway engineers carelessly dug up an electric cable they had been told about and thereby cut off the power to the steelworks close by. The result was that the iron ore actually being smelted was destroyed and further smelting was delayed for three days until the power was reconnected. The steelworks recovered damages for the spoilt ore (including the profit they would have made from that particular ore), but not for the

---

[34] *Capital and Counties plc v Hampshire CC* [1997] 2 All ER 865.
[35] *Kent v Griffiths* [2000] 2 All ER 474.

profits they would have made during the three days standstill, for that was pure economic loss not consequent on damage to any property. Since the nature of the defendant's conduct and the foreseeability of the harm (as well as directness, if necessary) were identical as to the two items of loss, the only difference was the nature of the harm—the economic loss was 'the wrong kind of harm'. But this was not quite what Lord Denning said. He said: 'Sometimes I say "There was no duty". In others I say: "The damage was too remote". So much so that I think the time has come to discard those tests which have proved so elusive. It seems to me better to consider the particular relationship in hand, and see whether or not, as a matter of policy, economic loss should be recoverable'.[36] Of course the policy decision will continue to be expressed in terms of duty and/or remoteness. It should be noted that it was no novelty to hold that there might be recovery for physical damage but not for pure economic loss suffered in the same incident: a century earlier it had been held that when the defendant flooded a building site the builder could recover for damage to his property but not for the loss suffered under his fixed price contract by reason of the ensuing delay.[37]

Between the workmen on the highway and the steelworks on the hill there was no 'particular relationship', but in *Muirhead v Industrial Tank Specialities*[38] the relationship was that of manufacturer and consumer, a relationship already described as 'special' in *Donoghue v Stevenson*. The plaintiff hoped to make money by buying lobsters in the summer when they are relatively cheap and selling them in the winter when they fetch a great deal more. But if lobsters are to be kept alive, they must be kept in moving water of the correct salinity, so Muirhead obtained a circulating pump manufactured by the defendant. It worked poorly, and not only did the lobsters already purchased die, but no further lobsters could be kept. As in *Spartan Steel* the defendant was held liable for the property damage (the dead lobsters) but not for the profits foregone through the inability to buy and keep further lobsters. This is correct, but it was not obvious to the trial judge who was so confused by pronouncements in the House of Lords that he held that since lobsters were unforeseeable sort of creatures, no damages could be awarded for their death, but that some commercial use of the pump was foreseeable, so that lost profits were recoverable!

---

[36] *Spartan Steel and Alloys v Martin & Co* [1972] 3 All ER 557 at 562.
[37] *Cattle v Stockton Waterworks* (1875) LR 10 QB 453.
[38] *Muirhead v Industrial Tank Specialities* [1985] 3 All ER 705.

Financial harm is often suffered by one person (Y) as a result of physical harm caused to another (X). Where X dies as a result of suffering *personal injury* and Y loses money as a result, Y has a claim only if he is a human being and his relationship to X is one specified in the Fatal Accidents Act 1976. Where X survives his injuries and Y suffers a loss by looking after him, perhaps giving up a job to do so, Y has no claim against the tortfeasor but X may claim a reasonable sum in respect of Y's care and holds this sum for Y.[39] Where the tort causes damage to *property* in X's possession, Y may claim for his own loss only if he also had a property interest in it. Thus although the charterer of a vessel stands to lose if it is damaged in a collision, and may be the only person who stands to lose, he cannot claim against the ship which negligently collides with it since he has only a contractual right to the use of the vessel, which remains in the shipowner's possession through the master and crew.[40]

The fact that purely economic interests are less well protected against mere negligence than are physical interests in person and property is perhaps unsurprising, given that the only rights protected by its ancestor tort of trespass were physical. Indeed, for 30 years after *Donoghue v Stevenson* it was thought that the only duty actionable in negligence was a duty to take care to avoid physical damage, that is, to refrain from acting dangerously, and that one could never recover in negligence (as opposed to deceit or contract) unless there was physical damage. That changed in 1963, in *Hedley Byrne v Heller*, a case already considered, but it occurred in a curious way, for the case involved not only harm which was not physical but also conduct which was not action, but speech. Doubtless because of the arguments of counsel, their Lordships concentrated less on the nature of the harm caused than on the means by which it was caused—the defendant's conduct rather than the victim's harm—though manifestly both were crucial.

The reaction of one of the first judges on whom this decision was pressed was to say that '. . . that case was very much nearer contract than tort',[41] and there is no doubt that we are here concerned with transactions rather than with actions, since it is commonly by transactions that money is lost. As is shown by the cases of the iron ore and the circulating pump the decision was not extended across the whole area of negligence: financial harm was not simply equated with physical harm. At first almost all

---

[39] *Hunt v Severs* [1994] 2 All ER 385.
[40] *The Mineral Transporter* [1985] 2 All ER 935.
[41] *The World Harmony* [1965] 2 All ER 139 at 155.

the cases involved statements, whether representations of fact or advice. Especially important was the holding that it applied to statements made in negotiations for a contract (though special statutory provision was made in 1967 for the case where a contract was actually reached between the parties). The great expansion came when it was decided that it applied not only to statements but to commercial and professional services in general: solicitors, for example, became liable to their clients in tort for professional negligence.[42] This being so, the question arose whether the tort claim could concur with a claim for damages for breach of contract, contracts for professional services normally involving an undertaking to use due care. In *Henderson v Merrett Syndicates*[43] the House of Lords held that claims in tort and for breach of contract did indeed concur, with the result that almost every breach of a professional's contract could be treated as a tort by his client (and possibly others, since this was not a contractual claim), an untidy position which other systems have had the good sense to avoid.

Then the question arose whether this liability could be expanded to cover non-performance of an undertaking as well as misperformance, and it was so held in the case already discussed, where intended legatees were allowed to sue a solicitor for failing to follow the testator's instructions to draw up a will reinstating them.[44] It remains to be seen whether the move from misperformance to nonperformance will be matched by a movement from misrepresentation to silence. If so, persons negotiating a contract had better watch out, for hitherto the courts have been chary of requiring persons to divulge information when dickering for a deal other than insurance.

Most cases of misrepresentation, like *Hedley Byrne* itself, involved a communication made directly by the defendant to the plaintiff, but as was seen in *Harris v Wyre District Council* it has been held that a person who makes a statement to A may be under a duty to B who predictably relies on it. In such cases the misrepresentation (or the assumption of responsibility for it) is the source of the duty, but a misrepresentation to A may constitute a breach of an independent and antecedent duty owed to B, and if A relies on it to B's detriment, B may well have a claim for damages. It was so held in a case where an ex-employer gave a possible future employer a needlessly disparaging report on the plaintiff.[45] In the absence

---

[42] *Midland Bank Trust Co v Hett Stubbs and Kemp* [1978] 3 All ER 571.
[43] [1994] 3 All ER 506.　　　[44] *White v Jones* [1995] 1 All ER 691.
[45] *Spring v Guardian Assurance* [1994] 3 All ER 129.

of such a duty the subject of the statement would have to prove malice, just as the addressee, in the absence of a duty of care owed to him, would have to prove fraud.

PSYCHIATRIC HARM

Although in an extreme case financial collapse may lead to suicidal stress, it may be thought eccentric to juxtapose purely economic harm and psychiatric damage, which seem to be at opposite ends of the spectrum of misfortunes. Different though they are, they nevertheless pose similar problems to the lawyer, one of legal technique, one of social value-judgment. The technical difficulty is to keep the number of claimants within manageable limits, a recurrent problem in the law. Where physical harm is in issue this is done for us by the restrictive physical law of inertia. In other cases one needs devices of a legal nature. Foreseeability alone is certainly unduly inclusive in cases of economic or psychiatric harm, for just as B may be impoverished by damage to A's property, so B may go into a decline out of grief or shock at A's death or injury, as where A is President Kennedy or Princess Di.

The other reason is one of value-judgment. Just as money, though important, is less important than health (we do not have a National Wealth Service—indeed, we have the very opposite, in the form of HM Revenue and Customs!), so, it is widely if unfeelingly felt, mental harm is less significant than physical harm, inability to cope through neurosis less serious than inability to walk by reason of amputation. Admittedly this is much controverted; there is no doubt that clinical depression is a serious affliction and that it is not only wounds which cause pain, but we do distinguish psychiatrists and surgeons, we do have special mental wards in hospitals and we do have a Mental Health Act which does not apply to patients with broken limbs. However this may be, it is at present clear that special obstacles have to be overcome by those who, without being exposed to physical danger, seek compensation for the psychiatric harm they suffer owing to the negligence of the defendant.

The bulk of recent cases arose from the dreadful disaster at Hillsborough in Sheffield in April 1989 when the police allowed a crowd of excited football fans into an already overcrowded enclosure and chaos ensued. Ninety-five people were crushed to death. Those on the other side of the football field could actually see this happening, and thousands more were at home watching an edited version on television. The situation was very grim and gruesome, and many spectators, television viewers, and even policemen were shocked in varying degrees. The trauma had the usual consequences—loss of sleep, recurrent nightmares, inability to cope, feelings of helplessness and anger, and a claim for damages.

Damages were awarded to all those physically injured but to very few of those merely shocked, although there was nothing unforeseeable about the shocking nature of the event, since it was precisely to avoid such a crush that the police should have kept the fans out. Claims by those watching television were dismissed because even if they were closely related to the primary victims, they were not close to the actual scene; claims by those actually in the grounds were dismissed unless they were very closely related to one of the primary victims;[46] claims by the policemen were dismissed although they were helping with the rescue operations and were employed by the defendant whose fault it was.[47] None of these plaintiffs had been themselves at physical risk; had they been exposed to such a risk, they could have recovered for psychiatric harm. In this way the range of *possible* physical harm is used to limit the number of possible claimants unrelated to the principal victim. While practical enough, this rule is barely rational except where the shock results from the fear of such harm, and it is rendered even more irrational by a very dubious decision of the House of Lords that a person at any physical risk may recover for psychiatric harm even if the foreseeable physical harm did not occur and the psychiatric harm, due to the plaintiff's ultrasensitive predisposition, was entirely unforeseeable.[48]

The current rules are much criticised as irrational and unsympathetic, but the problem cannot properly be resolved by saying that psychiatric harm is simply personal injury (as several statutes seem to proclaim) and that therefore all that is required is that the harm be real and foreseeable as likely to be suffered by a normal person. Indeed, one of the prime difficulties in this area is that normality is hard to ascertain, given that people vary very much more in psychological resilience than in physical robustness.

Attempts by the courts to widen liability have actually made things worse. When the Court of Appeal suggested that only spouses and parents should be entitled to sue (a practical rule adopted in other systems, and indeed by our own legislation as regards bereavement damages) the

---

[46] *Alcock v Chief Constable* [1991] 4 All ER 907.
[47] *White v Chief Constable* [1999] 1 All ER 1.
[48] *Page v Smith* [1995] 2 All ER 736.

House of Lords substituted a requirement that the plaintiff must prove that he was in a close loving relationship with the primary victim. Is it really helpful to require a person allegedly suffering from shock to dwell on the intensity of their love for the dear departed? Again, there was a rule that the plaintiff must actually have witnessed the shocking event. This rule the House of Lords modified by holding that it was enough if the plaintiff happened upon the 'immediate aftermath' of the event, as if it was just as easy to say that a person was nearly there as that he was actually there. This is surely an area in which it is best to adopt rules that are clear, even if artificial, since the claimants will inevitably (unless lying) be in a disturbed state which is sure to be worsened by prolonged uncertainty about the outcome of their claim.

The Law Commission has naturally made proposals for reform in this area. They are unlikely to be enacted and most unlikely, if enacted, to improve the situation. One proposal is that A should be able to sue B if A is shocked by what B does to himself. It is quite true that a housemaid coming to work may be shocked by finding that the householder has hanged himself in the hallway, but the proposal goes too far. Indeed, a judge has subsequently held that a fireman who was called to the scene of a motor accident and was shocked to discover his own son injured and unconscious at the wheel of the car he had been driving had no claim against the son (actually the Motor Insurers' Bureau, since the son was driving uninsured as well as negligently).[49]

Two further points should be made. First, where the victim has himself suffered physical injury there has never been a problem about awarding him damages for the psychological consequences, if adequately proved, just as there is none about awarding him damages for consequent financial harm. Secondly, the law awards no damages for grief. The reason for this is that no claim whatever lay at common law when someone else had been killed, and when a remedy was introduced by statute the judges held (contrary to its terms) that it covered only economic loss and therefore not human harm, such as grief. It is no answer to say that everyone suffers grief (see Queen Gertrude's admonition to Prince Hamlet), for not everyone suffers disabling grief; nor is it an answer to say that grief is immeasurable: it is no more immeasurable than pain, for which the courts award damages every day.

Most litigated cases of psychiatric harm have involved a claimant shocked by injury to someone else. In a sense such claimants are

[49] *Greatorex v Greatorex* [2000] 4 All ER 769.

secondary victims (though they are called 'primary' if they are in the zone
of physical risk). But is a shocking event necessary? Must there be a
trauma preceding the stress? Certainly industrial injury benefit cannot be
claimed for the mere fact of suffering stress from being engaged in a
stressful occupation,[50] but under the Law Commission's proposals 'It is
not a condition of the claim's success that the illness was induced by a
shock', and in fact we are increasingly seeing cases where there is no
physical trigger to the psychiatric collapse. These include cases of stress
at work, not heeded or alleviated by the employer,[51] the case where the
police failed to warn a volunteer that the interviews she agreed to attend
were to be with a gruesome serial killer,[52] or the case where parents who
had insisted that they would not foster a child abuser were shocked to
find, some time after the event, that the youth sent to them for fostering
had indeed proceeded to abuse their children.[53] In the last-mentioned
case the House of Lords held that the claimants could arguably recover.
In all these cases there was a special relationship between claimant and
defendant, whereas in the mainstream shock cases there is generally no
such relationship. We have seen that in claims for pure economic loss a
special relationship is highly significant, and it might well be the same as
regards psychiatric harm. Certainly the employer's duty to his staff
includes the duty to take care to avoid causing them psychiatric illness
and to help them if they suffer it. May it not be necessary to reconsider
the holding that the Hillsborough policemen got no special consideration
by reason of the fact that their employer was responsible for the situation
which shocked them, even if their Lordships were understandably
reluctant to reward the police while dismissing the claims of the public
they are supposed to serve?[54]

LESS SERIOUS UPSET

Damages for distress falling far short of any pathological harm have often
been awarded by the courts against a contractor who failed to do something known to be important for the customer's peace of mind.[55] In the
light of this, the position as regards the employment contract seems very

---

[50] *Chief Adjudication Officer v Faulds* [2000] 2 All ER 961.
[51] *Hatton v Sutherland* [2002] EWCA Civ 76.
[52] *Leach v Chief Constable* [1999] 1 All ER 215.
[53] *W v Essex CC* [2000] 2 All ER 237.
[54] *Frost (or White) v Chief Constable* [1999] 2 AC 455.
[55] *Farley v Skinner* [2001] 4 All ER 801.

unstable, especially as to dismissal. In 1909 the House of Lords, in a case not yet formally overruled, held that no damages could be awarded for distress caused by a brutal method of dismissal.[56] It is true that compensation may now be awarded by special statutory tribunals if the dismissal is unfair, as is common when the correct procedural steps have not been danced, but the compensation those tribunals can award is subject to a fixed maximum and covers only economic loss (restrictions which do not apply in cases of racial or sexual discrimination). This statutory scheme would be eclipsed if persons dismissed could bring a claim at common law free from those restrictions, so the House of Lords has reached a very uneasy compromise: no claim at all lies at common law in respect of actual dismissal and its consequences, but improper conduct by the employer prior to any dismissal may generate a claim for damages for both economic and emotional harm.[57] The position as regards other contracts is quite established: first, a package holiday company was held liable to a disappointed holiday-maker,[58] then solicitors had to pay for the distress caused to their client by their mismanagement of proceedings to enjoin molestation,[59] so now one could surely claim significant damages from a vet who carelessly killed one's beloved pet.

Distress may also be caused by a stranger, as was the case in *Wilkinson v Downton* where the defendant shocked the claimant badly by telling her as a practical joke that her husband had been injured in an accident.[60] After a moment's doubt, it has now been held that the case does not provide a remedy for distress which does not amount to recognised psychiatric injury, and *if* there is a tort of intentionally inflicting distress by a single act or word (a remedy for repeated misconduct is provided by the Protection from Harassment Act 1997) it must be shown that the defendant really intended to cause such distress.[61] As to liability in the absence of such an intention or a special relationship, the words of Lord Bridge appear to remain good: 'Those trapped in the crush at Hillsborough who were fortunate enough to escape without injury have no claim in respect of the distress they suffered in what must have been a truly terrifying experience.'[62]

---

[56] *Addis v Gramophone Co* [1909] AC 488.
[57] *Eastwood v Magnavox Electric* [2004] UKHL 35.
[58] *Jarvis v Swans Tours* [1973] 1 All ER 71.
[59] *Heywood v Wellers* [1976] 1 All ER 300.   [60] [1897] 2 QB 57.
[61] *Wainwright v Home Office* [2003] UKHL 53.
[62] *Hicks v Chief Constable* [1992] 2 All ER 65 at 69.

OMISSIONS

We have seen that the duty notion is put under some strain in cases of financial or psychiatric harm, and that in the former case some confusion results from the categorisation of the defendant's conduct as either speech or action. The duty notion is also put under some stress when the defendant's conduct consists of an omission rather than an action, where instead of adding a danger to life the defendant has simply failed to protect the claimant. Just as the distinction between words and acts is slightly fuzzy and capable of being confused, so is the distinction between acts and omissions to act. Lord Atkin, it will be recalled, classed them together. Nevertheless the distinction is an important one, as it determines when a person must not only refrain from causing harm to another but must take positive steps, busy himself, to protect that person from harm emanating from elsewhere, be it a third party, some natural phenomenon, or even the victim himself.

In certain special relationships it is well established that one party may be under a duty to act for the benefit of the other party to the relationship: the employer must take active steps to look out for the safety of his staff, the occupier of premises must bestir himself to see that his visitors are reasonably safe there, the bailee of a chattel must positively protect the goods entrusted to him, doctors cannot simply wash their hands, and so on.

If the defendant is in control of the source of a danger, he may well come under a duty to take active steps to prevent its doing damage. Thus the occupier of premises must take reasonable steps to save his neighbour's property from harm emanating from a danger on his own premises, even if it is due to natural causes or the acts of third parties.[63] It is true that in one case it was denied that the occupier of a disused cinema was liable for the destruction by fire of a neighbouring church, the fire having been started by trespassers who broke into the cinema and set fire to film scrap there, but the decision is best seen not as denying the existence of a duty (as Lord Goff held) but as denying the existence of a breach of duty on the facts of the case (as Lord Griffiths did).[64] Of course occupiers of adjoining properties are in a special relationship, but when the House of Lords held that the owner of a yacht damaged by escaping borstal boys could sue the warders for failing to prevent their attempt to

---

[63] *Goldman v Hargrave* [1966] 2 All ER 989.
[64] *Smith v Littlewoods Organization* [1987] 1 All ER 710.

escape from the island on the ground that the yacht was in the 'immediate vicinity', their decision certainly seemed to extend liability for omissions (though the boys were in the defendant's control). However, the decision is now being taken not as an instance of pure omission at all but as turning on the fact that the warders had brought the boys to the island in the first place, and had thus introduced the danger they had then failed to control. That they were not at fault in bringing the boys to the island is irrelevant: one who innocently causes a danger comes under a duty to try to prevent damage resulting from it. For example, a motorist who, entirely without any fault on his part, injures a pedestrian, cannot simply leave the victim lying on the road to be run over by someone else: he must take reasonable steps to protect him from further harm. Likewise, an occupier who knows that a trespasser is lying injured on his premises must surely take steps to alleviate his condition, even if it is not at all the fault of the occupier that he was injured in the first place.

The general question of liability for omissions was fully ventilated in the case of *Stovin v Wise*,[65] though as usual there were other factors in the case which rather obscure the discussion. The principal disturbing factor in the case was the public nature of the party whose liability was in issue, for, as has been noted, the duties of public bodies may not be identical with those of private parties. A further disturbing factor was that the question of the defendant's liability to the victim was raised not by the victim himself, who had already been paid by the motorist's insurer, but by the insurer seeking contribution from the public body towards that payment.

There was an accident at an acute intersection between a minor road from which a motorist was emerging and a major road along which a motorcyclist was proceeding quite normally. The motorist, whose view to the right was obscured by the existence of a bank of earth on private land beside the highway, was held liable. Her greedy insurer now claimed a contribution from the highway authority on the ground that the authority too could have been sued by the motorcyclist for failing to procure the removal of the embankment, as it had statutory power (though no statutory duty) to do, and had originally decided to exercise it.

The question presented in this tiresome manner was therefore whether the highway authority owed a *common law* duty to users of the highway, such as the motorcyclist, to exercise its statutory powers to improve visibility and consequently safety. By a bare majority the House of Lords

[65] [1996] 3 All ER 801.

reversed the decision of the courts below, and held that the highway authority owed no duty at common law to exercise its powers in this respect. Even the leading dissentient in the House agreed that 'the distinction [between act and omission] is fundamentally sound', and Lord Hoffmann gave eloquent reasons for supporting it and applying it in the case before him. The point of division was whether the public nature of the authority and the existence of its statutory powers took it outside the general rule that in the absence of some special relationship or feature there was no duty at common law to act for the benefit of others. The distinction between act and omission was reasserted shortly afterwards in the Court of Appeal when it decided that fire brigades were not liable simply for failing to douse a fire but would be liable if they did anything stupid which made the situation worse, as by turning off the sprinkler system. As we have seen, however, it is difficult to be categorical, since shortly afterwards liability was imposed on the ambulance service which had accepted an emergency call and failed to turn up reasonably promptly.

We must here again advert to the Human Rights Act 1998, for it lays down (for the purposes of the statute only) that 'An act includes a failure to act'. Consequently, a public authority may be held to have acted unlawfully if it fails to protect a citizen's Convention rights from invasion by a third party, himself not bound by the Act. The extent of such liability is very uncertain, and it will be difficult to hold that the idle authority 'acted' unlawfully unless it can be held that it was under a duty to take appropriate protective action.

LEVEL OF DUTY

In one sense the common law duty is higher when it requires a person to take active steps to protect others than when it requires only that he refrain from positively causing an injury, but once it is held that a duty exists, its level is always, apparently, the same: it is the duty to take such care as *in all the circumstances of the case* is reasonable. What is reasonable is the matter discussed in the following chapter, when we shall also consider whether it might not be better for the courts to admit that sometimes they should require that the plaintiff show that the defendant had behaved not just unreasonably, but *very* unreasonably, that is, with *gross* negligence.

3

Breach of Duty

If the existence of a duty of care is a question of law (and it is, even though the duty question is now said to be so heavily dependent on the proven facts that courts are reluctant to strike out a claim on the pleadings), the question whether the defendant was or was not in breach of that duty is surely one of fact. This means that decisions on breach are not citable as *authorities*; they are merely *illustrations* of the application of the indubitable rule that if one is under a duty at common law such care must be taken as is called for in all the circumstances.

Vastly more cases in the courts turn on whether there was a breach than on whether there was a duty, riveting though the latter matter is from the point of view of legal development and of scholars with articles to write. Fortunately or unfortunately, there is not much to say on the question of breach: we do not have exciting matters of policy to discuss, or even the question whether we should discuss them or not. On the breach question, we are not asking whether it would or would not be good to make the defendant liable if he fell below what we are entitled to expect of him, we are asking simply whether he did in fact fall below that standard, the standard being set by the down-to-earth model of the reasonable, alert, mature, and considerate person in his position.

In the days when we had a jury in these cases, it was for them to decide whether the defendant was negligent or not, once the judge had decided that in law there was a duty to take care. The jury gave no reasons, just as it gives no reasons for convicting or acquitting the accused in criminal trials. Judges are obliged to give reasons, even for a correct conclusion, so what they say on the question of breach begins to look like law, but it is still really a 'jury' question, a matter of impression resulting from the consideration and weighing-up of lots of different factors. Jury findings were virtually unappealable, but appeals against similar findings by judges are now quite common. There are restrictions, however. In *Barber v Somerset CC* the Court of Appeal disagreed with the finding of the trial judge that the deputy headmistress had not behaved with sufficient sympathy for the teacher who was claiming damages for stress, but the

House of Lords unwisely held by a majority that the Court of Appeal (with whose view of the law it was in entire agreement) was not entitled to reverse the trial judge's finding of fact.[1]

DIFFERENT DUTIES

There are duties and duties, and they vary in intensity. A 'duty' laid down by statute may prescribe a certain result, so that there is a breach if that result is not achieved and the defendant will be liable even if he is not to blame at all, subject to any defence which the statute may provide. Duties at common law, by contrast, are normally duties to behave reasonably, so that a breach is only established if there is some misbehaviour by the defendant himself. Nevertheless there are some duties, even at common law, such that a party may be put in breach of his duty though he himself is in no way at fault. Duties of this intensity are described as 'non-delegable': it is enough to render the defendant liable if the party to whom he delegated performance of his duty failed to meet the appropriate standard. As has been said, there must be 'due diligence in the work itself'.[2] Among such duties at common law are those of the employer towards his employees as regards the safety of working conditions, and that of the bailee towards the bailor as regards the safety of the goods in his possession. As regards activities which he permits on his land the duty of the occupier of land towards his neighbour's property is probably of this intensity; towards visitors, by contrast, the occupier of premises is not answerable for the faults of his independent contractors, unless he should have realised that they were unreasonably endangering the visitors, in which case he is himself at fault and in breach of his personal duty to take all reasonable steps for their protection.

Concentration on breach of the defendant's duty, whether by himself or by his delegate, must not, however, lead one to suppose that a defendant is necessarily exempt from liability just because no duty incumbent on him was breached: he may well be answerable for someone else's breach of duty, as is the case of the employer whose employee commits a tort in the course and scope of his employment. This 'vicarious liability' calls for detailed consideration in Chapter 6.

---

[1] [2004] UKHL 13.
[2] *Riverstone Meat Co v Lancashire Shipping Co* [1961] 1 All ER 495 at 523.

THE TEST OF REASONABLENESS

Here we shall focus on the normal duty in the tort of negligence, the duty to take such care as is required in all the circumstances to see that the person to whom the duty is owed does not suffer foreseeable damage of an appropriate kind. It is not a duty to *ensure* safety, but a duty to *try*—not, however, just a duty to try one's best, but a duty to reach the proper standard of effort, unavailing though it may prove to be. The critical question is whether the defendant behaved *reasonably*, and in deciding what the answer to this question should be many factors play a role. This is not surprising since the question is whether the defendant behaved reasonably *in all the circumstances*, and the circumstances may vary greatly. In particular, while the duty is constant, the steps to be taken to meet it vary enormously depending on the situation. Consider, for example, how cautiously one should carry a baby and a beach ball respectively. As Sedley LJ has said: 'a ubiquitous duty of care does not imply a uniform standard of care'.[3]

A definition was hazarded in 1856: 'Negligence is the omission to do something which a reasonable man, guided upon those considerations which ordinarily regulate the conduct of human affairs, would do, or doing something which a prudent and reasonable man would not do'.[4] Perhaps Baron Alderson was wrong to prioritise 'omission', for we have seen that when, as it usually is, the duty is to refrain from damaging the victim, the breach of this duty (if one is to be negative) must be a failure to refrain, that is, some positive conduct. As we saw earlier, Stevenson's breach of duty did not consist in failing to keep the snail out of the bottle, but in putting into circulation a bottle which was poisonous owing to his want of care. Viscount Simonds made the point when he said in criticism of the pleadings in a case where a workman had been blinded by the fracture of a metal tool called a drift, '. . . the accident occurred not through a failure to supply a suitable drift—a failure that could result in nothing—but through the supply of an unsuitable drift. Therein lay the alleged negligence . . .'.[5] Omissions constitute a breach of duty only where there is a duty to take positive steps. Such a duty certainly exists at common law in the case of the bailee and the occupier and has recently been extended to certain cases where the defendant can be said to have 'assumed responsibility',

---

[3] *Vellino v Chief Constable* [2001] EWCA Civ 1249, para 45.
[4] *Blyth v Birmingham Waterworks* (1856) 156 ER 1047 at 1049.
[5] *Davie v New Merton Board Mills* [1959] AC 604 at 617.

especially by inducing the victim to rely on his expertise, but generally, in the absence of a special relationship, a breach consists in a positive act, the duty being a duty to avoid causing harm by acting carelessly.

RELEVANT FACTORS

FORESEEABILITY OF HARM

If conduct, duly appraised at the time, appears perfectly innocuous, quite unlikely to cause any harm, it can hardly be called negligent. Thus in one case patients were severely injured because the drug with which they were injected had been adulterated by the antiseptic liquid in which the ampoules were kept. The antiseptic had seeped into the ampoules through tiny invisible cracks. These cracks must have been due to a slight jolting in the hospital, but since no one knew at the time that such a slight jolt might cause invisible cracks through which seepage could occur, the hospital was held not liable.[6] Now that we know better (thanks to that very incident, actually), it would be negligent to use a drug from an ampoule which had been kept in a bath of unstained antiseptic, since the precaution of staining is simple to take and effective to disclose adulteration. Likewise employers are not liable for failure to take precautions against conditions which are not recognised at the time as sufficiently deleterious to workmen's health to require them.[7] Nor, by statute, are producers of a product which only subsequent developments in scientific knowledge have enabled us to recognise as defective.[8]

It is relevant not only whether some harm is likely but also how serious the foreseeable harm is. Even if the harm is not really likely to occur but would be extremely serious in the unlikely event that it did occur, the duty may require one to take precautions to avoid it. The case always cited involved a one-eyed workman in Stepney called Paris, though he was more like the Cyclops than his namesake who preferred Aphrodite to Athene and triggered the Trojan War. Because Paris would be totally blind if his one eye were injured whereas his fellow-workmen if similarly injured would still be able to see, their employer owed Paris a duty to take particular precautions to guard him against such injury.[9] Risk involves not only chance of injury but the seriousness of injury should it occur.

---

[6] *Roe v Minister of Health* [1954] 2 All ER 131.
[7] *Thompson v Smiths Shiprepairers* [1984] 1 All ER 881 at 895.
[8] Consumer Protection Act 1987, s 4(1)(e).
[9] *Paris v Stepney BC* [1951] AC 367.

It must be remembered, however, that although foreseeability of harm is a relevant factor when conduct falls to be evaluated, it is only one factor among others, and the crucial question is whether the defendant behaved reasonably in the light of all the factors. Thus it is eminently foreseeable that people in a demanding job may suffer stress, but as Simon Brown LJ said once, 'It is not easy to make good . . . a claim in negligence for . . . work-related stress . . . Unless there was a real risk of breakdown which the claimant's employers ought reasonably to have foreseen *and which they ought properly to have averted*, there can be no liability'.[10]

OBJECTIVE STANDARD

It is said that the test of negligence is 'objective', independent, that is, of the defendant's own attitude or qualities. Thus a farmer whose stack of wet hay spontaneously ignited and caused a fire was held liable although he sincerely believed that this could not happen.[11] He was not conscious of doing anything dangerous, but most farmers knew better. What if the defendant was not conscious at all? A driver who has a heart attack at the wheel is not liable unless he should have known of the risk,[12] but by contrast, a man who had a stroke but continued to drive, though very erratically, was indeed held liable.[13] Nor is it relevant, if a car is being badly driven, that the driver was just a learner: a provisional driving licence is not a licence to injure.[14] Senility is clearly not a mitigating factor, since even the very old are old enough to know better, but what of infancy? Most of the cases involve kids engaging in childish activities such as fencing with plastic rulers (in class!),[15] and the tendency seems to be to ask what a person of their age could be expected to do. The question comes up more often as regards the feckless child's own claim, which will be discussed in Chapter 8 on contributory negligence.

To be noted is that it is not the defendant's *general* conduct but his conduct with regard to the particular incident which is in issue. If one answers a particular question incorrectly, it is irrelevant that one gave a perfect answer to the previous thousand inquiries. If a particular tree on one's estate would, if inspected, be seen to be dangerous, it is no answer

---

[10] *Garrett v Camden London Borough Council* [2001] EWCA Civ 395 (emphasis added), para 63; and see *Hatton v Sutherland* [2002] EWCA Civ 76.
[11] *Vaughan v Menlove* (1837) 132 ER 490.
[12] *Waugh v James K Allen* 1964 SLT 269.
[13] *Roberts v Ramsbottom* [1980] 1 All ER 7.
[14] *Nettleship v Weston* [1971] 3 All ER 581.
[15] *Mullin v Richards* [1978] 1 All ER 920.

that one was inspecting other trees on the estate and would have reached that tree tomorrow. During the war when many bombed buildings in London were in a state of collapse, a loose pane of window glass fell on the plaintiff passer-by. That pane could easily have been tweaked out, and it was nothing to the point that the agent was admirably busy seeing to other, perhaps more pressing, dangers.[16] On the other hand, a mother cannot be expected to keep her eye on a child, or every child, every moment of the day.

NORMAL PRACTICE

If the defendant has acted in a perfectly normal manner, he is unlikely to be held liable in negligence. Accordingly, if in the area in question there is a normal practice it must generally be shown that the defendant deviated from it. But the normal and the normative are not necessarily congruent, and the courts are ready on occasion to state that what is generally done is not good enough, and conversely to uphold beneficial deviations, for progress always takes the form of deviation from standard practice. In many areas there are Codes of Practice, not binding as law but nevertheless indicative of what people in that group think proper. The Highway Code is just one example, not binding but informative.

But experts may disagree on what is proper procedure. This happened very often when the plaintiff and defendant chose their own experts as witnesses. Recent procedural changes emphasise that a joint report is very desirable, and even permit the judge to appoint a court expert, as is the practice on the continent. But it may be clear that there are two or more quite respectable views about what should be done in particular circumstances. Here the courts adopt the *Bolam* test, originally in medical matters, whereby if the defendant acted in a manner regarded as acceptable by a reputable group of experts, he will not be held negligent even if others in the profession quite plausibly prefer another procedure.[17] To attacks on this position as an improper deference by the judiciary to the medical profession the courts have responded by emphasising that they do reserve the right to disapprove even a widely-held view and treat adherence to it as negligent, as they have done with certain practices of solicitors.[18] On the other hand, courts which impose novel duties, as they have done in the fields of social services and education, seek to allay fears

---

[16] *Leanse v Egerton* [1943] 1 All ER 489.

[17] *Bolam v Friern Barnet Hospital Management Committee* [1957] 2 All ER 118.

[18] *Bolitho v City and Hackney Health Authority* [1997] 4 All ER 771 at 779.

that liability will become rampant by emphasizing that the *Bolam* test applies, and that in consequence findings of breach will be less common than one might suppose. Such comforting and complacent predictions are never supported by evidence, and like most wishful thinking commonly prove false.

UTILITY OF CONDUCT

If some harm is foreseeable, one must ask whether the conduct was at all useful. If the conduct was useless, then a very slight risk of harm will suffice to stamp it as negligent. Thus to spill oil when you are supposed to be filling an oil-tank is certainly negligent: there is nothing to be said in its favour. On the other hand, if the aim of the exercise is praiseworthy, one may be entitled to take the risk of causing harm to others, provided that that harm is either not at all likely, or is unlikely to be serious. The leading case of *Bolton v Stone* needs to be carefully understood.[19] The defendants were a cricket club in Cheetham. The point of cricket, in so far as it has one, is for the batsman to hit the ball out of sight, for which he is awarded extra points. The road outside the cricket ground (there is always a road outside a cricket ground) was not a very busy road, it was a residential district, and very occasionally the bowler was so bad or the batsman so good that a ball was hit out of the ground. On one such occasion when Miss Stone was standing outside her house a ball struck her on the head. The club was held not liable: the ground was sufficiently large and sufficiently fenced—not, certainly, as events had shown, sufficiently to guarantee that there would be no accidents, but sufficiently to reduce the risk of accident to an acceptable level, given the importance of cricket to British manhood. In brief, the harm was not unforeseeable, but it was not unreasonable of the defendants not to guard against it.

COST OF PREVENTION

That point could be put another way. In order to avoid the tiny risk that once in a blue moon someone like Miss Stone might be hit by a really exceptional stroke, the cricket ground would have had to be roofed in like the Astrodome or surrounded by an absurdly high fence. In other words, the precautions one must or need take are those proportional to the risk, provided of course that what one is doing is worth doing in the first place. Shortly after the war the floor of a factory was wet, and a workman slipped on it. It was held at common law that in all the circumstances it

---

[19] [1951] 1 All ER 1078.

would not have been reasonable to close the factory just because it was possible that some such minor accident might occur. In other words one may ask whether it would be reasonable to require the defendant to do what was necessary in order to avoid the risk which eventuated.[20] (Regulations now provide that 'So far as is reasonably practicable, every floor in a workplace and the surface of every traffic route in a workplace shall be kept free from obstruction and from any article or substance which may cause a person to slip, trip or fall'.) This has led to liability in some not very deserving cases: the secretary who tripped over a wastepaper basket, the cleaning lady who fell over a box on the floor of the schoolroom she was cleaning, the fireman who slipped on an invisible layer of dust on the floor. . . .

Just as the Regulations require the employer to do everything that is reasonably practicable, despite the effect on business, other occupiers may be put to expense in taking the required precautions. These may not be the only costs. A social cost may also be involved. Just as one should not forget that contracting parties may have family and creditors who will be affected by the decision *inter partes*, so in tort one should not focus so exclusively on victim and defendant as to ignore the effect a decision may have on the general public. In *Tomlinson v Congleton BC*, for example, the House of Lords emphatically, indeed indignantly, reversed the Court of Appeal which had held, in a claim by a young man who had injured himself in a reservoir where swimming was strictly prohibited but notoriously took place, that the occupier was negligent in not erecting a physical barrier which would have barred access to the water altogether.[21] But why should law-abiding third parties be prevented from having innocent fun paddling and playing with spade-and-bucket just because reckless youths might contrive to injure themselves by flagrant disregard of prohibitions designed to protect them? Very strikingly, we find the Compensation Bill 2005 proposing that 'A court considering a claim in negligence may, in determining whether the defendant should have taken particular steps to meet the standard of care (whether by taking precautions against a risk or otherwise), have regard to whether a requirement to take those steps might (a) prevent a desirable activity from being undertaken at all, to a particular extent or in a particular way, or (b) discourage persons from undertaking functions in connection with a desirable activity.' This has been criticised as merely restating the law, but sometimes (as the decision

---

[20] *Latimer v AEC* [1953] 2 All ER 449.
[21] *Tomlinson v Congleton BC* [2003] UKHL 47.

of the Court of Appeal shows) a restatement of familiar aspects of the law is necessary.

In *Tomlinson* it was a prohibition not a warning, but a warning is a precaution which it is usually easy and cheap to take. Even if one cannot defuse a danger, an adequate warning can often prevent damage resulting from it. Accordingly the Occupier's Liability Act 1957 provides that a warning may satisfy the occupier's duty to take reasonable care to see that his visitors are reasonably safe, and failure to give a warning which would probably have avoided the damage may well give rise to liability more generally. Thus in *Al-Kandari v Brown*[22] it looked as if the plaintiff's husband might try to kidnap their children and take them abroad, so the defendant firm of solicitors undertook to prevent him getting hold of his passport. They quite properly took it to his Embassy for processing, but the Embassy staff refused to return it to them, and there was nothing the defendants could do about getting the passport back. They were nevertheless held liable when the man got his passport, beat up his wife and absconded with the children, for they could (and should) have warned the wife so that she could get herself and the children out of harm's way.

We have seen that the courts are reluctant to impose on private citizens a positive duty to protect others from harm extrinsic to their activities. This may be in part because taking precautions may cost money. We have seen, too, that the cost of taking adequate precautions may sometimes justify failure to take them. In this connection the courts should be hesitant to interfere with the budgetary decisions of public authorities, though such considerations are irrelevant when the body is under an actionable statutory duty. On occasion, however, the duty itself is modified. Thus while the occupier of premises must certainly take care that those he permits to enter his land are reasonably safe, and must also guard his neighbour against the adverse effects of activities he conducts or permits to be conducted on his land, if the person injured is not permitted to be there, or the harm results to one's neighbour from natural events on one's land rather than any activity, the duty appears to be modified. In these cases the legislature has laid down that the occupier is liable to a trespasser only if the 'risk is one against which in all the circumstances of the case, he may reasonably be expected to offer . . . some protection' and as to his neighbour the courts have introduced the 'measured duty of care', which prevented a hotel which fell into the sea

[22] [1988] 1 All ER 833.

from getting damages from the (public) occupier of the seaward land for failure to engage in very expensive coastal protection works.[23]

CONDUCT OF OTHERS

Conduct is sometimes risk-free only on the supposition that others will themselves behave reasonably. It *may*, therefore, be negligent in a driver not to look right and left at a junction even if the light is green, especially if it has just changed in his favour. As Lord Uthwatt once observed: 'A driver is not, of course, bound to anticipate folly in all its forms, but he is not . . . entitled to put out of consideration the teachings of experience as to the form those follies commonly take'.[24] Likewise, children are very apt to hurt themselves when adults with more sense would not. It is accordingly appropriate for the Occupier's Liability Act 1957 to provide that 'an occupier must be prepared for children to be less careful than adults'. Contrariwise, if the only persons in the danger area are those who are especially good at looking after themselves, this may modify the precautions required of the occupier. You need not tell experts their business.[25]

But if it may be negligent to act on the supposition that others will act with proper care for third parties and indeed themselves (for their own contributory fault will not neutralise the defendant's carelessness but only affect the amount of damages), what about the case where the intervention is deliberate and exploits the situation created or controlled by the defendant with resulting hurt to the claimant? The difficulties here may sometimes be more conveniently resolved in terms of causation rather than breach, on the basis that the deliberate act of the third party, even if foreseeable, may insulate the defendant from liability for what might otherwise be seen as the consequences of his behaviour, but one may also ask whether it was negligent of the defendant not to take steps to avoid such intervention. In one case an unlocked bus with the keys in the ignition was left outside a pub for hours and hours, which is hardly reasonable, but the bus company was held not liable when the bus was stolen and the thief, whose identity remained unknown, ran over and killed a cyclist[26] (had it not been a regular bus, the claim would have been met by the Motor Insurers' Bureau). We have seen, too, that the owners of a disused cinema were not liable to the neighbour whose property was burnt down when vandals entered the cinema and set fire to some film

---

[23] *Holbeck Hall v Scarborough BC* [2000] 2 All ER 705.
[24] *London Passenger Transport Board v Upson* [1949] AC 155 at 173.
[25] *Ferguson v Welsh* [1987] 3 All ER 777.
[26] *Topp v London Country Bus* [1993] 3 All ER 448.

scraps there: the neighbourhood was not notorious for vandalism, so that the chance of forced entry was slight, and could not be prevented save by having a 24-hour guard, which it would be unreasonable to require in the case of every empty and unalluring building.[27] On the other hand, if the deliberate and damaging act was 'the very thing' that the duty was imposed to prevent, liability may be established. Thus a decorator who had agreed to lock the door of the house and failed to do so was held liable when a thief entered and stole the customer's property; after all, it is against thieves, not rain, that doors are locked.[28] Again, when the police admitted that they had a duty to try to prevent a detainee from committing suicide (there is no duty unless suicide can be foreseen),[29] they were held liable when they negligently failed to prevent his doing so.[30] Note that in both these cases there was a special relationship involving an assumption of responsibility.

EMERGENCIES

Conduct which would certainly be unreasonable in normal circumstances may well not be held negligent if it is a reaction to an emergency. Thus in one case the plaintiffs were proceeding quite normally on the correct side of a four-lane highway when the defendant's lorry crossed the central line and crashed into them, something that manifestly calls for explanation. The defendant established that a car in front of him had suddenly and without warning swerved into his path and he himself had had to swerve in order to avoid a collision. He was acquitted of negligence.[31] So was the shipowner who deliberately offloaded oil from his vessel into the sea, whence it fouled the plaintiff's foreshore; he needed to do this in order to save the lives of the crew aboard. It would have been different had it been the defendant's fault that the emergency arose[32] (there is now strict liability by statute for oil pollution).

DEGREES OF NEGLIGENCE?

One oddity of our law is that if one falls at all below the requisite standard, it is immaterial how far below it one falls. In other words, it apparently doesn't matter how slight or gross the negligence is. This is

---

[27] *Smith v Littlewoods Organization* [1987] 1 All ER 710.
[28] *Stansbie v Troman* [1948] 2 KB 48.
[29] *Orange v Chief Constable* [2001] 3 WLR 736.
[30] *Reeves v Commissioner of Police* [1999] 3 All ER 897.
[31] *Ng Chun Pui v Lee Chuen Tat* [1988] RTR 298.
[32] *Esso Petroleum v Southport Corporation* [1955] 3 All ER 864.

clearly counterintuitive. Other systems operate quite nicely with the concept of gross negligence, without which in certain situations there will be no liability, slight negligence not being enough. In our own system, outside the area of private law, we used to apply an analogous concept. Until very recently the decisions of public bodies were apt to be quashed only if they were '*Wednesbury* unreasonable', that is, very unreasonable indeed. Again, the proposed law against corporate killing specifies that the accused's conduct must fall 'far below' what can rightly be expected. To dispense with so useful a concept in private law is really unjustifiable. The reason it is so repeatedly rejected comes from a quotable quote by a Victorian judge that 'Gross negligence is simply negligence with a vituperative epithet'.[33] It is nothing of the sort: it is no more difficult to say whether a person fell far below the acceptable standard than whether he fell below it at all. There is no real difficulty in saying whether conduct is more or less negligent, and the courts every day apportion liability on the basis of how negligent a party was, whether as between the claimant and the defendant under the Contributory Negligence Act 1945 or between different tortfeasors under the Contribution Act 1978. Particularly in the novel areas of liability, such as those of public bodies as regards social welfare and educational functions, it would be very useful to accept the principle that in order to involve liability misconduct must be really manifest, instead of hiding, as judges do, behind an invocation of the *Bolam* test. Here one may ponder the observation of Lord Bingham, pressed with the suggestion that in cases against public authorities the focus should shift from duty to breach: 'if breach rather than duty were to be the touchstone, no breach could be proved without showing a very clear departure from ordinary standards of skill and care'.[34] The notion of gross negligence would also be useful (and just) in the area of claims for sporting injuries. Indeed, on one view, sportsmen are liable for injuring their opponents only if their conduct constitutes more than an error of judgment and amounts to something really unnecessarily dangerous.[35]

MISREPRESENTATION

Liability in negligence may be imposed not only on those whose dangerous conduct causes physical harm but also, since 1963, on those whose careless speech or other transactional conduct causes merely financial

---

[33] *Wilson v Brett* (1843) 152 ER 737 at 739.
[34] *D v East Berkshire Community Health NHS Trust* [2005] UKHL 23 at 49.
[35] *Caldwell v Maguire* [2001] EWCA Civ 1054.

harm. Speech is subject to a criterion inappropriate to physical conduct, namely accuracy. Being wrong in what one says is not quite the same as doing wrong in what one does, but there is a tendency to suppose that it is enough for liability that what one said was wrong. Indeed the absurd Misrepresentation Act 1967 presumes that if what you said was wrong it was wrong of you to say it: you are presumed from the mere fact of error to have been at least negligent, perhaps even fraudulent! This is grotesque. One may, of course, if paid, guarantee the truth of what one says, and then one will be liable simply because it was not true, but for tortious liability in misrepresentation at common law you must not only have said something inaccurate or misleading, but must have been at fault in saying or believing it.[36]

IDENTIFICATION OF THE BREACH

The next stage of the enquiry being to ascertain whether the tortfeasor's breach of duty contributed to the occurrence of the injury, it is clearly necessary to identify precisely what he did wrong, what he did that he shouldn't have done or didn't do that he should. If there are several aspects of the tortfeasor's conduct which can be criticised, the sensible claimant will pick on one with some causative effect. If a person driving uninsured and without a licence causes an accident by turning right without indicating his intention, it is on the last aspect of his conduct that the sensible claimant will focus rather than his other delinquencies.

The importance of ascertaining exactly in what respect the defendant fell short of what was required can be seen in a case already mentioned.[37] The defendant motorist collided with the claimant pedestrian as she emerged into the defendant's path from behind a stationary transit van. The defendant was driving at 20 miles per hour, which was too fast in the prevailing conditions, but the accident would still have happened if she had been driving at quarter of that speed, which would have been perfectly reasonable. The judge's decision for the defendant (no causation) was upheld, though for the wrong reason (no duty!): since the accident would have happened just the same if the defendant had been driving with reasonable care, her failure to do so did not contribute to its occurrence.

---

[36] *Gooden v Northamptonshire CC* [2001] EWCA Civ 1744.
[37] *Sam v Atkins* [2005] EWCA Civ 1452.

4

Causation

Recent judicial pronouncements in this area of the law have been so dramatic and controversial that one is tempted to suppose that the changes have been deeply radical. Indeed, much of what was written in this chapter in 2002 has had to be revised, though it did not seem very wrong at the time. Nevertheless, it is likely that the basics remain unchanged, so we shall restate the geology and then report on the changes in the landscape.

Damages are (in principle) due to the victim only if the harm was due to the tortfeasor. The harm must be the effect of the defendant's misconduct. Causation must be established. Insurance companies certainly have to pay for losses which they haven't caused, but that is because they promised to pay if such losses occurred. Likewise, the social security office must pay the statutory invalidity benefit, though the state didn't invalidate the recipient, but that is because the statute so provides. But you cannot claim damages from a defendant in tort unless he is responsible for the loss in question, and he is not responsible unless he (or someone for whom he must answer) can be said to have been a cause of the loss. As we have seen, a defendant is not liable in negligence if his conduct was reasonable, or if he was under no duty of care, but even a flagrant breach of duty will not render him liable unless that breach played a part in the occurrence of the harm of which complaint is made. Thus an employer who was clearly in breach of his duty to make safety belts available to his employees was not liable for the death by falling of a steel erector who would certainly not have worn a belt had one been dangled in front of him[1] (the problem arising if he *might* have worn the belt but would *probably* have chosen not to is considered later).

The basic idea is very simple, and is said to be a matter of common sense, though it involves imagining a counterfactual course of events, one which never happened. Would the harm have been suffered just the same *if* the defendant had behaved properly? Did it make any difference to the

---

[1] *McWilliams v Sir William Arrol* [1962] 1 All ER 623.

outcome that he misconducted himself in the way he did? This is commonly called the 'but-for' test. In most cases which come before the courts this test is generally satisfied, simply because one doesn't sue a person wholly uninvolved in a situation. Even so, there are some clear cases of 'no cause'. One is not liable for failing to rescue a man already dead,[2] or not diagnosing an incurable,[3] or giving far too much penicillin to a child when such an overdose is wholly incapable of causing the meningitis from which he subsequently suffered.[4] Nor is one liable for not giving a warning to someone who would have ignored it, or making a misrepresentation to a person who didn't believe it. *Post hoc ergo propter hoc* is not simply a logical fallacy: the subsequent is not necessarily consequent.

In matters of causation, as in other matters, if one wants the right answer, one must ask the right question. It is not right to ask 'What was the cause of this harm?'. That question may be appropriate for doctors certifying the cause of death, but the lawyers' role is to see whether the defendant can be held responsible, an inquiry in which, admittedly, cause plays a great part. Nor is it right to ask 'Did the defendant cause the harm?' or even, more precisely, 'Did the defendant's breach of duty cause the harm?'. The correct question is 'Did the breach of duty *contribute* to the occurrence of the harm?' At all costs one must avoid the easy supposition that a result can have only one cause, or that one must seek out the 'main' cause, relevant though this may be in claims under an insurance policy (where the insurer promises to pay for a loss only if, or unless, it is caused by an event specified in the policy).

CONTRIBUTION

That the correct question is in terms of 'contribution' emerged clearly in *Bonnington Castings v Wardlaw*, where a workman contracted a lung disease as a result of pollution in the air in the workplace.[5] For one of the two pollutants the defendant occupier was responsible, for the other he was not. There was enough of the latter to have caused the disease by itself, so it could not be said that 'but for' the pollutant for which the defendant was responsible, the victim would not have contracted the disease. It was nevertheless held that the 'guilty air' probably made some

---

[2] *The Ogopogo* [1971] 2 Lloyd's Rep 410.
[3] *Barnett v Kensington and Chelsea Hospital* [1968] 1 All ER 1068.
[4] *Kay v Ayrshire and Arran Health Board* [1987] 2 All ER 417.
[5] [1956] 1 All ER 615.

not insubstantial contribution to the occurrence of the disease, and that was enough (a) to make the defendant liable, and (b) to make him liable for the entirety of the claimant's (indivisible) disability. The decision has been both extended as regards (a) and restricted as regards (b).

(a) The extension occurred 16 years later in *McGhee*, where the pursuer developed dermatitis (= skin disease) after cycling home unwashed after each of three days' work cleaning out warm brick kilns.[6] The defendant was not negligent in allowing the plaintiff to get caked with brick dust (kilns cannot be cleaned unless they are still warm), but admitted, curiously enough, that it was negligent in not providing washing facilities. Had such facilities been provided, the plaintiff would very probably have used them, so the question was not, as it was in the case of the steel erector, whether the plaintiff would probably have washed but whether washing would probably have inhibited the onset of the skin disease. On this the evidence was completely equivocal, as the House of Lords admitted, but it nevertheless awarded full damages. Lord Wilberforce suggested that if the defendant's breach of duty increased the risk of the occurrence of the harm in question, that was tantamount in law to contributing to its actual occurrence, as required by *Wardlaw*. This suggestion was held to be wrong in law by the House in a later case, *Wilsher*, where a very premature baby afflicted with several ailments developed a condition which might have been caused by any of those ailments or possibly by the hyperoxygenation, for which alone the defendants were responsible.[7] The House stated that *McGhee* had 'added nothing to the law', and that *Wardlaw's* case was gospel. Then in *Fairchild v Glenhaven Funeral Services*[8] the House unanimously reinstated *McGhee* and held in terms that even if it could not be shown (and especially if it was categorically impossible to show) that the defendant's misconduct had actually contributed to the occurrence of the harm, he could in certain circumstances (but not those of *Wilsher*) be held liable if his misconduct had made it more likely that the harm might occur. The case was one where the claimants had contracted a kind of lung cancer called mesothelioma which is perhaps due to the inhalation of a single asbestos fibre and certainly has a long period of latency before proving fatal. The claimants had all worked for several employers (not including Glenhaven Funeral Services: coffins are not made of asbestos), and while each of them had negligently exposed the claimants to asbestos fibres, the fatal

[6] *McGhee v National Coal Board* [1972] 3 All ER 1008.
[7] *Wilsher v Essex AHA* [1988] 1 All ER 871.   [8] [2002] UKHL 22.

fibre could not be attributed to any particular employer. The Court of Appeal had dismissed the claims, but the House held all the employers liable on the basis that in this case negligent exposure to risk of harm should be treated as equivalent to negligent contribution to its actual occurrence. Note that the House did not say that one can sue just for being put at risk—the Court of Appeal has subsequently held, correctly, that you cannot[9]—it said that *if* the harm does happen one *may* be liable just for making it more likely to occur.

That this decision constitutes a breach in the normal principles of causation is obvious and admitted: after all, each defendant could properly say that the harm could just as well have occurred if he had not been negligent at all, that his negligence was not a 'but for' cause of the harm and had not even been shown to have contributed to it. *Fairchild* has now been reconsidered in *Barker v Corus*.[9a] The *applicability* of the *Fairchild* 'exception' has been clarified: not all the possible contributors to the risk need be tortfeasors, as they were in *Fairchild* itself. Accordingly, when the actual harm is due to physical agent X (asbestos fibre, brick dust, pollution in the air) anyone who negligently increases the risk of its happening is liable, but not if the harm might as well be due to agent Y or Z (as in *Wilsher*).

(b) The *effect* of *Fairchild* has, however, been dramatically reduced. From now on, a defendant whose liability depends on his having contributed to the risk of harm (rather than ot the harm itself) is liable only to the extent of his own contribution, not for the whole of the harm. In technical terms, liability under *Fairchild* is not 'joint and several' but only 'several' The result is that solvent tortfeasors pay only for their own contribution to the risk, not for that of other tortfeasors or indeed of events which involve no tort at all, such as the claimant's own conduct (as held in *Barker*).

Outside *Fairchild* it is still the law—in principle—that if harm is 'indivisible' a defendant whose breach of duty actually contributed to it (rather than just the risk of it) is liable for the full amount of that harm, regardless of any contributions due to other persons or events. The courts have, however, sidestepped this rule by holding that despite all appearances the harm in question is not indivisible, thereby reducing the extent of the defendant's liability. Thus in *Holtby v Brigham and Cowan (Hull)* a case involving asbestosis, a cumulative and progressive industrial

---

[9] *Rothwell v Chemical and Insulating Co* [2006] EWCA Civ 27.
[9a] [2006] UKHL 20.

disease, we find Stuart-Smith LJ adding to his unobjectionable statement that the claimant was entitled to succeed 'if the defendant's conduct made a material contribution to his disability', the revolutionary rider 'but strictly speaking the defendant is liable only to the extent of that contribution.'[10] One can understand unease at rendering a subsequent employer liable for harm already inflicted by a predecessor and readiness to hold him liable only for the aggravation, but it is not the case that harm is divisible simply because it has separable causes. So to decide is not too hurtful for the claimant if all the contributors are solvent tortfeasors, but what if, as now under *Barker*, the other contributory causes invoked to reduce the defendant's liability are not torts at all? For example, the (indivisible) stress suffered by an employee is rarely due exlusively to conditions in the factory or the office: marital and parental problems may well have played a major part. Should only proportional damages be awarded against the careless (uncaring) employer?

In an unreported case cited in *Holtby*, the judge said 'Where there are causes concurrent in time, the likelihood is that a resulting injury will be indivisible; but where causes are sequential in time, it is not likely that an injury will be truly indivisible.' (The adverb 'truly' generally heralds a falsehood.) But it is not the harm they are dividing up, they are distinguishing the causes, measuring and comparing the contributions made, either in intensity or in duration, by the various possible defendants—as if the fact that one can distinguish causes means that the result can be 'truly' divided up. Many industrial afflictions (unlike mesothelioma) are indeed cumulative—the greater the exposure and the longer it lasts, the worse you get—be it deafness, or asbestosis or vibrating white finger, but the victim is complaining that he is now very ill or very deaf or very numb, and he is as ill, deaf or numb as he is, not partly ill or deaf or numb. In the case of death, for example, even if due to 'causes sequential in time' the courts would have some difficulty in dividing it up between those who contributed to it (to which it may be said that Death is Different, as indeed, in many respects, it is).

But in *Rahman v Arearose* this new rule was applied where the faults of the two defendants occurred very close in time.[11] The claimant was attacked and beaten up by thugs one night at the fast food joint near King's Cross of which he was the manager. One of his eyes was quite badly injured. He was taken to the defendant hospital, where the negligence of the eye surgeon made him blind in that eye. Owing to the

---

[10] [2000] 3 All ER 421. [11] [2001] QB 351.

combined effect of the attack (from which the defendant employer should have protected him) and the botched operation the claimant became a total psychological wreck. The court treated his condition as divisible and held each defendant liable for only part of his neurosis. While the hospital was admittedly not responsible for the attack, it should certainly have been held liable, along with the employer, for the claimant's present medical condition to which they had both contributed and which was manifestly indivisible: it is simply nonsense to say that the employer made him half-mad and that the surgeon made him mad as to the other half. Furthermore, was it not the thugs who contributed most? But the court went further into error in holding that the employer was not liable for the deterioration in the claimant's condition due to the medical negligence; as has been subsequently and correctly held, an original tortfeasor is liable for any ordinarily negligent mishaps in the medical treatment he made necessary.[12]

The attempt to divide up a psychological condition is already producing ghastly problems now that a local authority may be held liable for harm suffered by children in care, whether by abuse, neglect, or mismanagement. Such claimants, generally a complete mess at the time of trial, are only taken into care if their home conditions are appalling. Psychiatrists are forever telling us that what happens early in life determines one's condition later, so it is virtually impossible for the courts to say to what extent the fault of the local authority made things worse, how the claimant would have turned out if the local authority had done its job. Thus in one case we read 'It was Mrs G's opinion that 80% of the causation of the difficulty in her adult life lay in her experiences in care. Dr A was at first of the view that her experiences in care were 20% to blame for her problems'.[13] Similar difficulties arise where the local authority is charged with educational malpractice, such as not diagnosing dyslexia. It is permissible to wonder whether the growing tendency to reduce the amount of recovery by making the defendant liable only to the extent of his contribution, even to an indivisible result, may not be due to unease at making him liable at all.

While it is clearly unjust to make a person pay for harm he hasn't caused, we have seen that 'cause', even in its traditional sense, is not the test. The question is, is it unjust to make a defendant pay for the whole of the harm to which he has by his fault contributed? Is it just to give the

---

[12] *Webb v Barclays Bank* [2001] EWCA Civ 1144.
[13] *C v Flintshire CC* [2001] EWCA Civ 302.

claimant only partial damages against him, leaving it up to the claimant to sue others for the balance? One must bear in mind, as regards the claimant (a) that his claim against those others may be time-barred, and (b) that he may well be penalized if he brings another action in respect of the 'same damage'; and as regards the defendant that if he is held liable for the full damage (a) he will be indemnified by the insurance policy he is required by law to have against any liability to his employees that the courts may care to throw at him, and (b) he may claim contribution from others who might have been held liable for the full damage, even if the victim's own claim against them is time-barred, and the quantum of recovery in a contribution claim by a tortfeasor is what is 'just and equitable' which is not at all the test for recovery by the victim. It is true that the right to claim contribution from a fellow tortfeasor is not worth much if he is untraceable or insolvent, and this problem has become more acute as tort liability has increasingly been imposed on defendants who failed to protect the claimant from attack by criminals; but the same is true of the victim's ability to claim damages, and as between the tortfeasor and the victim the risk of not being able to find the other contributors should surely be on the tortfeasor rather than the victim. In any case, even if it is thought that the court is right on the point of justice, it has opened up a can of worms, and one must hope that the House of Lords, in a case which raises the point clearly and is properly argued, will put the lid back on.

If, as *Wardlaw* rightly lays down, 'contribution' to the actual occurrence of the harm is enough, it is evident that there will have been other contributory factors apart from the defendant's conduct. If the other contributory factor is the fault of the claimant himself, then the Act of 1945 reduces the amount of the defendant's liability; this is perfectly just, since one cannot properly claim damages to the extent one's wounds are self-inflicted. Another contributory factor may be the extreme susceptibility of the claimant, who would not have suffered so much harm but for his predisposition. Here the law has long been that the claimant recovers undiminished damages, even for psychiatric harm which normally stolid citizens would not have suffered.[14] What if the susceptibility was due, not to a congenital condition, but to a previous tortfeasor? Here one must apparently distinguish. The second tortfeasor doesn't have to pay for harm which the victim had already suffered, but his tort may well have aggravated the consequences of that harm. If the other contribution

---

[14] *Page v Smith* [1995] 2 All ER 736.

is a subsequent event (as it always is where one is liable for failing to protect the claimant from a danger one did not cause) it may be held to eclipse the causative effect of the original negligence, depending on *novus actus interveniens*, a doctrine shortly to be dealt with.

HARM ECLIPSED?

The cases considered so far involved harm which still existed at the time of trial. What if the harm is already over, or soon will be? *Baker v Willoughby* fascinates not only students but barristers as well, to judge by its citation in court for propositions for which it is not an authority. The plaintiff was injured in his left leg by the negligence of a motorist, and it looked as if he would have a limp for the rest of his life. Not so, for some years later he was shot in that same leg by gangsters and it had to be amputated. For the amputation the motorist was of course not liable, for the gangster's attack was indubitably a *novus actus interveniens*, being both deliberate and unforeseeable. The plaintiff claimed damages from the motorist on the basis of lifelong disamenity, and the House of Lords, reversing the Court of Appeal, allowed his claim (but not for pain and suffering, which had ceased).[15] Part of the reasoning was that as the gangsters would be liable only for damaging a leg already damaged the plaintiff would be out of pocket if he couldn't sue the motorist for life-long disability. The reason was unsound (as well as *obiter*): the gangsters would be liable for what their wrongdoing cost the victim, and that would include the loss of his claim against the motorist.[16] The substantive decision that the motorist was liable for harm which had ceased to exist was much doubted by the House in a later case where the plaintiff, who had suffered a 50% incapacity through an injury due to the defendant's tort, subsequently developed an unconnected disease which totally incapacitated him, as it would have done even if he had not already been partially incapacitated; it was held that the defendant was liable only up to the time the disease eclipsed the effects of the tort.[17]

Such cases are not at all common, and too much should not be made of the puzzle. Meanwhile it is a question whether a distinction is to be drawn depending on whether the subsequent event is a tort or a natural event (unhelpfully called a 'vicissitude' of life), but it is unclear why any such distinction should be made, for it is odd, especially for a judge, to hold

---

[15] [1969] 3 All ER 1528.   [16] *Hassall v Secretary of State* [1996] 3 All ER 909.
[17] *Jobling v ASDA* [1981] 2 All ER 752.

that being torted is not one of the vicissitudes of life. And is it not a vicissitude that one has a thin skull or an egg-shell personality?

PROBABILITIES

It has been seen that before the causation question can be answered it must emerge *exactly* wherein the defendant was at fault, for the question is whether the harm would have happened just the same if he had behaved properly. Classically all that need be shown is that it would *probably* have made a difference if the defendant had not been in breach of duty. Certainty is not required. The essential thing is to persuade the judge that the harm would probably have been avoided if the defendant had acted properly: it does not matter whether he is easily persuaded, because it is obvious, or is persuaded only with difficulty, because the matter is far from clear. The tendency to state the matter in terms of percentages is to be avoided. 'More likely than not' is a matter of per-suasion, not of proof. Statistics are often deployed. There is no reason why they should not be considered, but they cannot be conclusive. Unfortunately, they seem objective. Note this outburst from a normally sensible judge: '. . . it is unjust that there should be no liability for failure to treat a patient, simply because the chances of a successful cure by that treatment were less than 50%. Nor, by the same token, can it be just that, if the chances of a successful cure only marginally exceed 50%, the doctor . . . should be liable to the same extent as if the treatment could be guaranteed to cure. If this is the law, it is high time it was changed . . .'.[18]

The idea that recovery should be proportional to the cogency of the proof of causation is utterly unacceptable, and it was rejected by the House of Lords on appeal. The case was one where a boy fell out of a tree (no one's fault, except perhaps his own) and hurt his hip rather badly. The hospital ignored his hip and X-rayed his knee. Five days of pain ensued, and on the boy's return to hospital they admitted their error but stated (correctly) that his condition was now incurable. At trial they claimed that the injury had always been incurable, so that their admitted misdiagnosis made no difference, but the judge held that there was a one-in-four chance that the boy would have avoided permanent disablement if the proper diagnosis had been made on the first visit, and that the hos-pital's negligence had certainly robbed him of this chance. The judge accordingly granted the plaintiff 25% of the damages he would have

---

[18] *Hotson v East Berkshire Area Health Authority* [1987] 1 All ER 210 at 215.

awarded if, but for the negligence, full recovery had been probable. The House of Lords reversed: the plaintiff must prove that it was more likely than not that proper diagnosis would have prevented the crippling effect of the injury, and he had clearly failed to do so, given that on the evidence it was three times more likely than not that the misdiagnosis had made no difference.[19]

This is quite right, but the decision has caused controversy, because in many cases a claimant is indeed allowed to recover for the loss of a mere chance of obtaining a benefit. The case principally cited is *Chaplin v Hicks* where the defendant wrongly prevented the plaintiff from proceeding to the next round of a beauty competition. The trial judge said that he couldn't possibly tell whether or not she would probably have won, so he awarded nothing. The Court of Appeal sent the case back to him with instructions to decide on the plaintiff's chance of success, and award damages in proportion to that chance, if at all substantial.[20] The defendant's fault in that case was a breach of contract, but the same principle applies in tort also: when a widow sued the person who negligently killed her husband, the trial judge dismissed her claim since she would more likely than not have been divorced for adultery, but the House of Lords said that the true question was whether there were any substantial chance that the matrimonial rift might be healed and her husband continue to support her.[21]

How do these cases relate to the decision in *Hotson*? The explanation is that where the claimant is suing in respect of personal injury or property damage, he must persuade the judge that that injury or damage was probably due to the defendant's tort, whereas in cases of financial harm it is enough to show that the claimant had a chance of gain which the defendant has probably caused him to lose. There is nothing irrational in this, unless one supposes it is sensible to speak of 'loss of a chance' without saying what the chance is of. Losing a chance of gain is a loss like the loss of the gain itself, alike in quality, just less in quantity: losing a chance of not losing a leg is not at all the same kind of thing as losing the leg.

This squares with another point. The judge in *Hotson* was certainly logical, for in a subsequent case where the still-birth of the plaintiff's baby was almost certainly due to the negligence of the defendant hospital he reduced the damages to take account of the faint possibility that the

---

[19] *Hotson v East Berkshire Area Health Authority* [1987] 2 All ER 909.
[20] [1911] 2 KB 786.   [21] *Davies v Taylor* [1972] 3 All ER 836.

baby might have been born dead anyway.[22] This was sternly discountenanced by the House of Lords. In financial loss cases, by contrast, where a benefit which would probably have been gained but for the defendant's negligence or breach of contract (there is now not much difference where the defendant is a professional), the courts reduce the damages to take account of the possibility that the benefit might not actually have been achieved.[23]

The issue was reventilated in *Gregg v Scott* in 2005, the outburst cited above being echoed in the House of Lords by the main dissentient.[24] When the claimant went to the defendant doctor he already had cancer which would more likely than not kill him within 10 years, but he did have (according to the medical boffins) a 42% chance of recovery within that period. Since that chance had slumped to 25% a year later when the correct diagnosis was made, the defendant's negligent misdiagnosis had nearly halved the claimant's chances of living a bit longer. Although no damages can be awarded for the mere loss of time on earth, a claim does lie for the earnings one would have made during that period and for distress at contemplating the accelerated approach of death.

The claim was rejected by the trial judge, and by a majority in both the Court of Appeal and the House of Lords. It should now be clear that in medical negligence cases as in other claims for personal injury the claimant must show that the defendant's breach of duty probably contributed to the occurrence of the harm complained of, and that it is not enough to show that it merely deprived him of a chance of escaping such harm: the claimant must show that he *would* (probably), not just that he *might* (possibly), have been better off if the defendant had acted properly. As Lord Phillips observed 'A robust test which produces rough justice may be preferable to a test that on occasion will be difficult, if not impossible, to apply with confidence in practice.'

Of course even when there are dissents which clarify the point at issue, decisions are never quite as clear as one would wish. One reason why *Hotson* has been held (by those who dislike it) to be inconclusive on the question whether the loss of a chance of a better medical outcome is compensable is that the House affected to hold that the judge's finding that the injury was *probably* incurable meant that it was *certainly* incurable (so that there was no chance of recovery) though the judge had held that it was *possibly* curable (with a 25% chance of recovery). Given this,

---

[22] *Bagley v North Hertfordshire Health Authority* (1986) 136 NLJ 1014.
[23] *Blue Circle v Ministry of Defence* [1998] 3 All ER 385.   [24] [2005] UKHL 2.

the judge in question was surely right, when *Gregg* came before him in
the Court of Appeal, to hold that *Hotson* was indistinguishable. Likewise,
certain peculiarities in the *Gregg* case suggest that it may not have put
paid to adventurous claims: first, the doctors' statistics are all in terms of
living a further 10 years, not, as lawyers think, of living a normal lifespan;
secondly, the fact that the claimant was alive at the time of the hearing in
the House, and in good enough health to attend it, is ample indication
that the statistics in issue were not conclusive in his own case. Of course
Fairchild was put in play by the eager attorneys, but the answer was given
by Lord Phillips 'there is a danger, if special tests of causation are
developed piecemeal to deal with perceived injustices in particular factual
situations, that the coherence of our common law will be destroyed.'

AVOIDANCE OF LIABILITY FOR CONSEQUENCES

Although it is clear that one should not have to pay for harm if one's
breach of duty did not contribute to it at all, it does not follow that one
should have to pay for all its consequences if it did make such a contribution. The law has three ways of letting a defendant off the hook even
though the harm would not have occurred but for his negligence. The three
ways are not entirely distinct, but they may be called rules of remoteness,
intervention, and purpose.

REMOTENESS

In 1921 the Court of Appeal was faced with a case in which the plaintiff's
ship, which had been carrying petrol in open vats, was destroyed when a
workman employed by stevedores retained by the charterer carelessly
knocked a plank into the hold and thereby caused a disastrous and wholly
unexpected explosion. The action by the shipowner against the charterer
was of course, as the very title of the case indicates, based on their very
detailed contract, and could not have succeeded in tort since the workman
was not one of the charterer's employees. The charterer was held liable
on the basis that a negligent defendant was answerable for the physical
consequences which resulted *directly* from his negligent conduct even if
they were quite unforeseeable.[25] Scholars in Oxford were scandalised that
different tests should be applied to determine whether the conduct was
negligent and for what consequences the negligent party was responsible:

[25] *In Re an Arbitration between Polemis and Furness Withy Co* [1921] 3 KB 560.

if foreseeability was the test of negligence, it should also be the test of remoteness of consequences, doubtless on the 'one size fits all' argument. Actually, as we have seen, foreseeability is not the *test* of negligence, but merely a factor to be taken into account in determining whether conduct is unreasonable or not, but this does not seem to have been appreciated by the critics, who were also, apparently, unaware that German lawyers, not greatly given to fatuity, draw a clear distinction between the link which must be established between the conduct and the initial harm and the link between the conduct and the ulterior harm for which claim is made. Be that as it may, the Privy Council 40 years later categorically and dog-matically disavowed the reason underlying the Court of Appeal's decision and held that it is only for the foreseeable consequences of his conduct that a negligent person can be held liable: it accordingly dismissed the claim of the owner of a wharf in Sydney burnt in a fire on the ground that the fire was unforeseeable, though it was unquestionably and immediately due to the oil which the defendant had negligently spilled into the har-bour.[26] English law is thus formally committed to the rule that 'negligent parties pay only for the foreseeable consequences of their negligence'. That leaves open the question of what 'foreseeable' indicates in this con-text. And we learn without much surprise that once a party has been held negligent in the light of the harm that might have been foreseen, the consequences have to be really quite exceptional ('Who would have thought it?') for him to escape liability for them.[27] Perhaps one could take some of the stress off the notion of 'foreseeability' by using the concept of 'normality', which is closely connected with it but seems slightly more objective; one would be liable for all but quite abnormal consequences of one's breach of duty.

It is the *type of harm*, not the precise *way* it occurs nor yet its *extent* which has to be foreseeable. There are not very many types of harm, one would think. As we have seen, purely economic harm is different from property damage, but it has been held that there is no difference between psychological injury and physical damage to the person.[28] In the Sydney Harbour case pollution damage was foreseeable but fire damage was not. That was a case of damage to property. Two cases involving personal injury to adventurous youths have been more generous. In the first the pursuer came upon the allurement of an open manhole in an Edinburgh

---

[26] *The Wagon Mound (No 1)* [1961] 1 All ER 404.
[27] *The Wagon Mound (No 2)* [1966] 2 All ER 709.
[28] *Page v Smith* [1995] 2 All ER 736.

street one late winter afternoon. The manhole had a canvas tent over it and a paraffin lamp beside it, left unguarded when the defender's men went off for tea. The youth took the lamp into the hole but dropped it and there was an unexpected explosion in which he was burnt. The Court of Session held that since the explosion was unforeseeable, the pursuer could not recover for his burns, but the House of Lords reversed and held that since it was foreseeable that he might well be burnt and he had been burnt, it was immaterial that it happened in an unexpected way.[29] More recently, a boy was rendered paraplegic when the abandoned boat which he had jacked up fell on him while he was working underneath it in the romantic hope of rendering it seaworthy. The boat, which was rotten, was on the defendant's property and they admitted that they should have removed it, but they alleged that while it was foreseeable that a child clambering on it might put his foot through the rotten timber, it was not foreseeable that boys would do what these boys did, and that the accident was therefore of a quite different kind. The Court of Appeal agreed with this, but their decision was reversed in the House of Lords, and the Borough of Sutton (which had many abandoned cars on the property) was made to pay over half a million pounds, 25% contributory negligence having been taken into account.[30] It was emphasised in the House that it was a sterile activity to compare cases on this point when the rule was clear. But if the rule is clear, it is far from clear how it is to be applied. Suppose a youth tried to lift an abandoned car and suffered a hernia or, as has happened, threw matches into the petrol tank and got burnt?

The German distinction adverted to above actually has a role to play in English law. If I negligently cause actionable harm to a person and he suffers further harm in consequence, the question is not whether that further harm could be foreseen as a consequence of my conduct, but rather whether by harming him I increased the risk of that further harm occurring. Thus if I injure a person I remain responsible for the further harm done to him by a negligent doctor in treating him, since injured people need treatment and treatment involves a risk of iatrogenic exacerbation.[31] If, however, the doctor cuts off the wrong leg or does something really insane, my liability will terminate. It is only the risk of normal negligence, so to speak, which is enhanced: really gross negligence will count as a *novus actus interveniens*. But suppose my victim has

---

[29] *Hughes v Lord Advocate* [1963] 1 All ER 705.
[30] *Jolley v Sutton LBC* [2000] 3 All ER 409.
[31] *Webb v Barclays Bank* [2001] EWCA Civ 1141, paras 52–56.

to be carried away in an ambulance, and the ambulance is involved in a collision in which the patient suffers further harm. Here I shall probably not be liable, for ambulances are not more likely to be involved in accidents than other vehicles. Suppose that while my victim is lying in the highway unconscious he is run over by another vehicle. I shall be liable, but not if his wallet is taken by a thief or he is struck on the head by a falling tile, though the reasons are slightly different.

NOVUS ACTUS INTERVENIENS

It often happens that an act of negligence on the part of X creates a danger which is triggered by the subsequent act of Y, or indeed of the victim himself, with resulting injury which would not have occurred but for the intervention. This was true, for instance, of the youth who tried to prop up the abandoned boat. Of course the harm also would not have happened but for the original act of negligence. So there is a problem of causation.

First, there is no difficulty at all in holding both X and Y liable for the consequences of their combined negligence. As noted already, a result may have several causes. Thus if X's careless driving causes a collision on the highway and Y, a following driver paying inadequate attention, runs into the melee and causes further harm, that harm may well be attributable to both X and Y.[32] It is, indeed, extremely common for more than one party to be liable, for much of the development in the law of tort over the past century has been to provide claimants with extra sources of compensation by imposing on more remote defendants a duty to anticipate or defuse the dangerous conduct of tortfeasors closer to the damage. Reference can be made to the section on liability for omissions (above, p. 54).

Although the defendant's misconduct need not be the sole cause of the eventual harm, nor even the main cause, it may be such a minor cause in comparison with another cause or causes that it can properly be denied any causal effect at all. This is particularly true where the subsequent conduct of another is so deplorable that it would not be right to hold the original tortfeasor liable for the ulterior harm. Consider the following mildly puzzling case.[33] One wet and foggy evening the Mini Minor which X was driving eastwards on the four-lane A45 (as it then was) coughed to a halt. X was held negligent in not pushing the now stationary car off the carriageway (but surely not very negligent, she being a young woman

---

[32] *Rouse v Squires* [1973] 2 All ER 903.   [33] *Wright v Lodge* [1993] 4 All ER 299.

caught in an emergency). Y came tearing along in his articulated lorry at wicked speed and collided with the Mini Minor, injuring X's passenger. So fast was Y going that the collision forced him on to the opposite carriageway into the path of another vehicle calmly proceeding westwards, with fatal results. Y settled with all the victims and now claimed contribution from X on the ground that X also was liable to them. The Court of Appeal made X contribute 10% towards the sum paid to her passenger but nothing towards the sums paid to the other victims: Y's driving was so 'reckless' as to insulate X from liability to those on the other side of the road, although there would have been no accident but for her having left her Mini Minor on the roadway.

Another example is provided by *Knightley v Johns*.[34] X turned his car upside down in the Queensway tunnel in Birmingham, blocking the right-hand lane just beyond the bend on the northbound carriageway. The police were summoned but went to the exit, forgetting the standing order that the entry to the tunnel must first be closed to prevent further traffic entering it. The inspector then told two of his men, including the plaintiff, to get on their bikes and ride back up the tunnel to close it; in so doing the plaintiff was struck and injured by a vehicle driven quite carefully by the unsuspecting Z. The trial judge held that this was all the fault of X, and held him solely liable. The Court of Appeal reversed, held the police inspector liable for failing to obey standing orders and endangering his men, and—this being the significant point—further held that this negligence was so extreme and unforeseeble that X should be held not liable for the injury to the plaintiff.

The explanation of the *novus actus* cases in terms of foreseeability is perhaps not entirely convincing. After all, wickedness and laziness are not less foreseeable than negligence and clumsiness, yet it is clear that deliberate acts of the intervener tend to insulate the prior tortfeasor more effectively than merely negligent ones, and positive acts more effectively than omissions. Perhaps it can be suggested that since it is clear that there must come a moment when the party originally responsible for a dangerous situation ceases to be liable for its ulterior effects one might ask whether the 'buck has passed' from the original tortfeasor to the intervener. This seems to happen in particular when the danger comes to the notice of a person who can and should defuse it and prevent the danger causing harm or more harm, as was the situation of the police inspector in *Knightley v Johns*, (where the plaintiff was his fellow-employee and not a

[34] [1982] 1 All ER 851.

stranger such as another motorist). This is possibly also the explanation of the decision in *McKew v Holland and Hannen and Cubitts*.[35] The pursuer had suffered an injury to his left leg owing to the fault of his employer, and had been paid for it. Not long thereafter, when he was fully aware that his leg might 'go away' from under him, he was coming down some steep and worn stone stairs in a Glasgow tenement where there was no banister when his leg 'went'. In order to avoid falling, he jumped down on to the half-landing, and broke his right leg. His claim was dismissed, and though controversial (many commentators think he should have received damages reduced for his carelessness) the decision is surely right. The pursuer was now in control of the situation, he knew his gait and balance were impaired, and it was up to him to take account of the injury for which he had been paid. Considerations of foreseeability and reasonableness are not entirely apt in the circumstances. The question really is whether at the relevant time the intervener was in control and free to act, rather than still reacting to an emergency triggered by the defendant.

It is to be noted that these considerations apply only where the conduct alleged to insulate the defendant from liability for ulterior consequences actually *intervenes*, that is, *comes between* the defendant's conduct and the occurrence of the harm. Prior acts of negligence are not intervening acts, and cannot, on causal grounds, excuse subsequent negligence (though they may cause an emergency or crisis such that an unfortunate reaction by a person caught up in it is not to be regarded as negligent at all).

One must therefore distinguish the cases where, because the victim was especially sensitive or vulnerable, the defendant's conduct causes much more harm than could have been expected. Here one trots out the saying 'The tortfeasor takes the victim as he finds him' and holds the defendant liable. This is dubious policy where the claimant is physically susceptible: there is no good reason why the accident-prone should increase the liability of normal people, and it is really unacceptable in the case of the neurotic who has fits at the drop of a hat. Yet it was so held in *Page v Smith*, where a driver involved in a minor collision which did him no physical harm whatsoever took to his bed in shock and obtained damages on the basis that he would never be able to work again.[36] Should an employee really be able to claim damages when the position to which they sought promotion proves more stressful than they are able to cope with? It is, however, true

---

[35] [1969] 3 All ER 1621.   [36] [1995] 2 All ER 736.

that before the 'thin-skull' rule applies, with the effect of holding a defendant liable for unforeseeable consequences, it must be shown that the defendant was indeed negligent. The point can be seen as between neighbours: you need not curtail your activities because your neighbour is ultra-sensitive, but if you make so much noise that a normal person would be distressed, you will be liable if, being very sensitive, he suffers much more than could have been expected.

PURPOSE

In one case the plaintiff's sheep were being carried on the defendant's vessel and were washed overboard, a fate they would have avoided had the defendant penned them in as statute required. The court held that in imposing the duty to pen the beasts Parliament's purpose was to prevent contagion, not drowning. The claim was consequently lost: the harm was doubtless caused by the infringement but it was not the kind of harm which it was the purpose of the provision infringed to prevent.[37] One must not be too precise about the purpose, however: the provision that the roof in a coal mine must be kept secure was held to cover not only the obvious risk that a piece of it might fall on a miner but also the risk that an accident might be caused to a miner by a piece which had already fallen.[38] On the continent, where all basic law is legislative, it is a widespread principle that in order to be compensable the consequence of negligence must be such as it was the purpose of the rule infringed to avoid. For example, in a German case, when the noise of a vehicular collision on a country road caused pigs on a nearby farm to panic and kill each other the farmer could not invoke the Traffic Act, which was held not to have such consequences in mind.

Common lawyers can apply this teleological approach to statutory duties quite nicely, as we have seen, but they have much more difficulty with duties which arise at common law, since we do not think of such duties as having been laid down by someone with some inferable purpose in mind for future cases. A useful substitute is to speak in terms of the 'scope' of the duty. That is what Lord Hoffmann did in a case where the plaintiff lender would not have lent money at all but for the erroneously high valuation which the defendant had negligently placed on the property which was to act as security for the loan. The borrower failed to

---

[37] *Gorris v Scott* (1874) LR 9 Exch 125.
[38] *Grant v National Coal Board* [1956] 1 All ER 682.

repay, and the security was doubly inadequate because the property market had collapsed. The lender was not allowed to recover his full loss, but only the amount by which the defendant had overstated the value of the property. His Lordship said that the plaintiff 'must show . . . a duty in respect of the kind of loss which he has suffered' and that 'Normally the law limits liability to those consequences which are attributable to that which made the act wrongful'.[39] His Lordship gives an interesting example. A doctor consulted by a patient who proposes, if he gets a clean bill of health, to go on a climbing expedition negligently certifies the knee as fit when it is not. The patient is injured on the mountainside, say in an avalanche or because of his colleague's failure to belay properly. Although he would not have been on the mountain at all 'but for' the doctor's negligence, the doctor will not be liable. Likewise it is negligent for a parent to give an adolescent a gun, but this is because he may shoot someone with it; the parent will not be liable if the boy clumsily drops the gun on a friend's foot.

At this point it is necessary to deal with the third of the trilogy of contentious decisions in the matter of causation rendered by the House of Lords in the past few years. In *Chester v Afshar* the very experienced defendant surgeon advised the claimant patient to undergo an operation on her spine but omitted to inform her, as it was his duty to do, that there was a small risk (less than 2%) that she might end up worse than before. Had he so informed her, she would probably have taken a second opinion and had the operation later. Unwarned, she had the operation right away and it went wrong without any operational fault on the part of the defendant surgeon.[40]

Was she entitled to damages? The Court of Appeal had held that she was. Indeed the case seems perfectly clear: her injury was due to the surgeon's operating on her when he should not have done so, and the harm would probably not have been suffered had he given the warning, since the chance of its occurring in a later operation (though identical) was virtually negligible. Wherein is the problem?

The minority in the House, who would have reversed the decision for the claimant, were of the opinion that one is not liable for harm unless one's negligence increases the risk of that harm occurring. This was asserted to be 'conventional' causation law. It is far from clear that this is so. It is almost as if the dissentients were inferring from *Fairchild* that if

---

[39] *SAAMCO v York Montague* [1996] 3 All ER 365, 370 at 371.
[40] [2004] UKHL 41.

you are liable for increasing the risk of harm without actually causing it, you cannot be liable for the harm you cause unless you increased the risk of it. But tort is about harm rather than risk.

The alarming aspect of the case, however, is that even the majority, who favoured the claim, seem to have believed that their decision deviated from standard causation lore and was justified only in order to give effect to the doctor's duty to warn. Yet is this extract from the speech of Lord Hope not consistent with 'conventional' causation lore? : 'It can be said that Miss Chester would not have suffered her injury "but for" Mr Afshar's failure to warn her of the risks, as she would have declined to be operated on by him on 21 November 1994. . . . If she had been given the warning she would have avoided the risk, and the chances of her being injured in that way if she had had the operation later would have been very small—between 1 and 2% . . .'. What more can be required?

The claimant's injury was certainly bad luck, but it was not a coincidence: the harm was within the scope of the duty, unless by scope we mean purpose. The purpose behind the duty to warn is doubtless to enable the patient to make up her mind, but it is surely not necessary to ignore consequences of a breach just because it was not the purpose of the duty to prevent them.

Note, however, that the purpose analysis may have the effect of rendering the defendant liable when otherwise he would not be. In a case already mentioned, the police were held liable for not closing the flap on the door of the cell of a remand prisoner who used the opening to tie his shirt to and strangle himself: the very purpose of keeping the flap closed was to prevent the prisoner from using it to kill himself.[41] Likewise a painter was held liable for theft from premises he had undertaken to keep locked, precisely because the purpose of locking the door was to prevent theft, which otherwise would have rated as a *novus actus*. This was 'the very thing' the obligation was designed to prevent.[42]

[41] *Reeves v Commissioner of Police* [1999] 3 All ER 897.
[42] *Stansbie v Troman* [1948] 1 All ER 599.

5

Strict Liability

We have seen that there is a general principle, of a sort, to the effect that one is liable for the foreseeable harm due to one's unreasonable conduct unless it would be unfair, unjust, or unreasonable to impose such liability. Where the harm is caused without any provable fault, however, there is certainly no such general principle. True, trespass, defamation, and conversion are torts of 'strict liability', but those are torts where the law is much more concerned with the vindication of rights than with compensation for harm. What of harm caused by a person who is not to blame at all?

COMMON LAW

Whereas strict liability is said to be axiomatic in contract law (though actually obligations to try are nearly as common as warranties of success), instances in the common law of tort are distinctly rare. The famous example is the decision in *Rylands v Fletcher* in the mid-nineteenth century.[1] In that case an entrepreneur who had retained reputable contractors to build a reservoir on his land was held liable when water from it leaked into the plaintiff's mineworkings nearby and flooded them. It was said to be enough that the entrepreneur had brought on to his land something likely to do damage if it escaped, at any rate if his use of the land was 'non-natural', and it had escaped and done damage. Explosives are certainly unnatural and likely to do damage if they (or rather the blast waves from them) escape, and in *Read v J Lyons & Co* almost a century later there was an explosion in the defendant's munitions factory. The plaintiff was not, however, a neighbour complaining of property damage but a visitor, a person working on the premises, complaining of personal injury. There was no allegation of negligence, and her claim was dismissed.[2] It was emphasised that nothing had escaped from the defendant's land, but the significance of this point is that the House of Lords

[1] (1868) LR 3 HL 330.   [2] [1946] 2 All ER 471.

was drawing a distinction between an occupier's liability to visitors on the one hand, and an occupier's liability to his neighbour on the other, perhaps also between a claim for personal injury on the one hand and a claim for damage to property on the other. At any rate if, as appears to be the case, strict liability under *Rylands v Fletcher* is a feature only of the law between neighbours, this is perhaps justified by their long-term mutual exposure, and if it does not cover personal injury, this is not because we regard property damage as more important than personal injury, but because citizens must be treated equally as regards their bodily integrity and we would not be treating them equally if we made the protection of their person depend on their property relations. *Read v Lyons* is a very important case: it can be seen as the corollary of *Donoghue v Stevenson*, for if the latter says that negligence is normally sufficient for liability, the former says that it is normally necessary.

It is not everything that escapes from the defendant's land on to the claimant's which generates liability: escape from domestic installations does not count, even from a large water-pipe serving a high-rise apartment block,[3] but the escape of industrial chemicals, however commonly used, makes for liability provided that the harm was a foreseeable consequence of the escape, which need not itself be likely or due to any negligence.[4] *Rylands v Fletcher* has been slightly extended in the United States to cover cases of extremely hazardous activities, whereas in Australia it has been wholly repudiated and is now regarded as an instance of a nondelegable duty of care, or liability for independent contractors. In 2003 the House of Lords was pressed to follow the Australian example, but it elected unanimously to retain *Rylands v Fletcher* in English law as a ground of tortious liability, independent of fault either in the introduction onto one's land of something not properly there or its escape and doing damage to the property of one's neighbour.[5] It is now clear beyond even undergraduate fantasies that it cannot be prayed in aid by the victim of personal injury, even if suffered by a neighbour on his own land.

Animals provided another instance of strict liability at common law. If your 'cattle' escaped and trespassed on neighbouring land you were strictly liable, as you were for damage done by a nasty foreign animal you kept, or even a native animal with a nasty disposition you knew about. Both of these have been replaced by statutory liabilities in the Animals

---

[3] *Stockport MBC v British Gas* [2001] Env LR 44.
[4] *Cambridge Water Co v Eastern Counties Leather* [1994] 1 All ER 53.
[5] *Transco plc v Stockport MBC* [2003] UKHL 61.

Act 1971, the former, significantly, by covering only damage to property, and the latter by a provision whose effect on the law was uncertain, thanks to a degree of opacity exceptional even in the products of the Law Commission, of which this was the first example. The uncertainty has now been resolved (erroneously) by a bare majority of the House of Lords which has been pleased to hold that one may be liable for the damage done by a perfectly normal pet which reacts in a perfectly normal way to abnormal circumstances even if one had not the faintest idea that such abnormal circumstances actually existed.[6]

STATUTORY LIABILITY

If strict liability is rare at common law, it is relatively common by statute. Sometimes the enactment imposes liability quite explicitly, but often, as we shall see, it imposes a duty or creates an offence instead. When the harm is due to something under the defendant's control strict liability is quite often imposed explicitly, as it is, for example, on the owner of an aircraft when it or anything from it falls on a groundling, on the operator of a radiation complex for the physical harm done by the escape of radioactive material, on the water authority for the escape of water from a mains, on the ship-owner for oil pollution, and on the producer of products which prove to be defective. These are all statutory claims for compensatory damages, usually in respect of physical harm only, where the quantum of damages is worked out in the normal way. Thus when a dwelling was rendered virtually unsaleable owing to ionising radiation emanating from the nuclear plant at nearby Sellafield, the owners failed to recover under the Nuclear Installations Act 1965 because no physical damage had been done to their property.[7] Everything depends on the precise terms of each statute, for it will be recalled that statutes are never applied by analogy.

PRODUCT LIABILITY

Of these statutory liabilities we here consider only the liability for damage done by defective products under the Consumer Protection Act 1987, based on the more readable EC Directive of 5 July 1985. Whereas the claimant under *Donoghue v Stevenson* has in principle to prove that the

---

[6] *Mirvahedy v Henley* [2003] UKHL 16.
[7] *Merlin v British Nuclear Fuels* [1990] 3 All ER 711.

manufacturer was at fault, the claimant under the Directive need show
only that the product was defective and caused appropriate damage. The
application of the Directive is controlled by the Court in Luxembourg,
which somewhat hesitantly rejected the Commission's challenge to the
Consumer Protection Act 1987 as not adequately reflecting the Directive,[8] now amended (thanks to mad cow disease) to include primary
agricultural products.

For the first ten years after its enactment, the Directive seems to have
generated no litigation in England, and rather little elsewhere. The calm
is now over. Lawsuits have involved polluted water, a leaking condom,
breast implants, sheep-dip, combined contraceptive pills, the MMR vaccine and hot coffee, as well as contaminated blood and a baby blanket,
shortly to be considered. Quite a number of these claims have failed, on a
finding either that the product was not defective (hot coffee) or that the
defect did not cause the condition complained of (sheep-dip).

Suit lies against the apparent or actual manufacturer/importer into the
EU, or any intermediate supplier who fails to identify them or his own
supplier. The claimant must prove that the product was defective, that is,
was less safe than people generally are entitled to expect, given the way it
was presented, the use to which it was likely to be put, and how long ago
it was produced (rights are extinguished ten years after the producer first
put the item into circulation). In other words, the defect must render the
product dangerous. Not all defective goods are dangerous or vice versa: a
sharp knife is dangerous but not defective, a blunt knife is defective but
not dangerous, a sharp knife with a wonky handle is both.

The claimant must also prove that the defect caused damage of the
defined variety, namely, personal injury, death, or damage to personal (not
commercial) property above a certain amount. Damages are reduced
where the fault of the claimant, though not that of a third party, contributes to the harm, but the only important complete defence for the producer is that of 'development risks': if at the time of circulation it was
quite impossible, owing to the state of current knowledge, to ascertain the
respect in which, as we now know, the product was defective, the producer
is not liable. It is not a negligence liability based on what the producer
should reasonably have known, but a strict liability with a defence that he
could not possibly have known.

Two cases show the Act/Directive in operation. In one case the product was blood which had infected the recipients with hepatitis C, a disease

---

[8] *European Commission v United Kingdom* [1997] All ER (EC) 481.

not usually disabling, but occasionally serious and sometimes fatal. At the time of the transfusions, the medical authorities were aware of the risk of such infection but had no technical means of ascertaining whether any particular batch of blood was so contaminated. The judge held that persons generally were entitled to expect that the blood provided would be 100% safe, not just as safe as technically possible; by this very strict test, the blood was held defective. The defendants therefore raised the development risks defence. This the judge disallowed on the ground that the risk was known to the medical profession, even if they had no means of countering it. To hold that the blood was defective because consumers did not know of the inherent and unavoidable risk and that the defendants had no defence because they did know of it is to apply consumer protection with a vengeance.[9]

Another case involved 'Cosytoes', a sleeping bag which was to be attached to an infant's pushchair by means of elastic straps and a metal buckle. In trying to attach it, the 12 year old claimant lost hold of the strap; the taut elastic flew back and the buckle hit him in the eye. 'Cosytoes' had been in production for ten years, no such accident had ever been known, and the experts were agreed that no reasonable manufacturer could prior to this accident have been aware of the risk of its occurrence. Nevertheless the court held that 'Cosytoes' was unnecessarily dangerous, and therefore defective: a non-elastic method of attachment would have been possible, or a warning should have been issued[10]—as if a 12 year old could manage strings or heed a warning. The holding seems very dubious. After all, zips can catch quite painfully where flybuttons would not, but surely that doesn't mean we must abandon the zip. In the United States, where the idea of strict product liability in tort originated (it has always existed in contracts of sale), a distinction is drawn between manufacturing defects, where the product does not meet the producer's own standards (snail in bottle), and design defects, where, as in Cosytoes, the whole range of a product is impugned: in the latter case the test is whether the design was, objectively, a reasonable one. If the Court of Appeal is right, the failure of the Directive to distinguish these two types of defect has resulted in a wider liability here than there; indeed, in the case of the infected blood, the judge held the distinction inapplicable.

The manufacturer of Cosytoes, held strictly liable, was not negligent, since no accident could reasonably be foreseen. Does this mean that

---

[9] *A v National Blood Authority* [2001] 3 All ER 289.
[10] *Abouzaid v Mothercare (UK)* [2001] TLR 136.

Donoghue v Stevenson, under which the manufacturer had to be shown at fault, has no further role to play? No: it depends on the nature of the harm. Since the Directive covers only personal injury and death, plus damage to private property, the common law of negligence continues to apply where the claim is for damage to commercial property, in respect of which we can expect the courts to be more exigent in finding a breach now that personal injury is covered by statute. If the harm due to the defect is purely economic, whether to an individual or to a company, there will be no liability at all in the absence of a contract, even if the producer is shown to have been careless, as the *Muirhead* case shows.[11]

INEXPLICIT STATUTES

The statutes mentioned so far impose civil liability explicitly and in terms. About such liability there can be little debate. We now address a different question: when will the courts hold that Parliament has *implicitly* affected civil liability, or, to put it another way, when will the courts impose liability on the ground that the defendant's conduct contravened a statute which does not mention civil liability at all? The question of the civil liability of the offender is dealt with under the heading of 'breach of statutory duty', but the heading is not very apt, since the word 'duty' may well not figure in the statute at all. Statutes vary so enormously in purpose and draftsmanship that general statements about them are almost bound to be misleading, but for present purposes we can distinguish two main types, those directed to private persons and those addressed to public bodies.

Statutes which lay down what private persons must or must not do generally impose a penalty for contravention, and provide no other sanction or remedy. The question is whether the victim of an offence can claim damages from the offender on the ground simply that he committed an offence. Can one say 'You broke the law and I got hurt in consequence so you owe me'? Generally not. Bad people pay more, of course, and offenders sound like bad people, but not all punishable conduct is wicked: a person may be fined although he is not at fault in any real sense. It would be a strict liability if he were then made liable in damages, and the courts dislike strict liability. It is not as odd as it sounds to say that those who break the law are not necessarily liable to those who are injured by their illegal conduct, for if the defendant has behaved unreasonably

---

[11] *Muirhead v Industrial Tank Specialities* [1985] 3 All ER 705.

and caused foreseeable physical damage he will almost certainly be liable at common law, though admittedly the burden of proof may well be greater.

Statutes addressed to public bodies, on the other hand, usually attach no sanction such as a fine, but rather expressly impose a duty to act in a certain way. This is perhaps because there are measures in administrative law whereby a public body, unlike a private individual, may be compelled actually to do its duty (which is what we want). Breach of the duty by no means always entails liability in damages. For example, local authorities are under a statutory duty to 'secure that accommodation is made available' to certain classes of homeless persons, and though a Court of Appeal in 1979 had eccentrically held that a qualified applicant could claim damages if accommodation was not provided, the House of Lords overruled this decision in 1997[12] and noted that breach of a duty to provide a benefit would rarely give rise to a damages claim, especially as judicial review of the decision would be available unless some special statutory appeal procedure was laid down, as it is in cases of refusal to pay a social security benefit.[13] The claim in the earlier case of *Cutler v Wandsworth Stadium*[14] was less meritorious: a bookie claimed damages for the profits he would have made at the dog races had the local authority, which occupied the track, provided him, as required by statute, with space in which to ply his trade—a claim for damages so hopeless that it is surprising to find the case so frequently cited as an authority.

In addition to duties imposed on them, public bodies often have powers conferred on them to act in certain ways. Here, too, the phrase 'breach of statutory duty' is inappropriate, since powers ('you may') are distinct from duties ('you must'). It is, however, open to the courts to hold that there may well be a common law duty to exercise such powers reasonably, unless to impose liability would be inconsistent with Parliament's presumed intention to leave the matter to the body in question, but even if they are disinclined to impose on the authority any duty at common law to exercise its powers reasonably, they can frequently reach the same result by holding that the authority must answer for any negligence on the part of those to whom it has entrusted the execution of its powers.[15]

---

[12] *O'Rourke v Camden LBC* [1997] 3 All ER 23.

[13] *Jones v Department of Employment* [1988] 1 All ER 725.

[14] [1949] 1 All ER 544.   [15] *Phelps v Hillingdon LBC* [2001] 2 AC 619.

STATUTORY OFFENCES

In the private sphere, where traffic and industrial accidents give rise to the bulk of tort claims, owners of vehicles and employers alike are guilty of an offence if they do not have the requisite insurance cover against liability to their victims and employees. Rather surprisingly, the courts have held that while the uninsured owner of the vehicle is liable to the unpaid victim of a permitted motorist's negligence,[16] the unpaid employee has no claim against the director of an uninsured employer, although he is equally guilty of an offence.[17] This is all the odder in that the courts readily impose liability if an employer, though not negligent at all, is in punishable breach of safety regulations, but steadfastly refuse to grant damages to the victim of a non-negligent traffic offence: the illegal nature of a motorist's driving or parking may interest the police, but the courts are concerned only with whether or not it was unreasonably dangerous, the only apparent exception being where a motorist runs over a pedestrian on a pedestrian crossing.

Thus in a case from 1923 the plaintiff's van was damaged in a collision with a lorry belonging to the defendant. The plaintiff could not show that the lorry driver was negligent, but did prove that the lorry was in an illegal condition such that the defendant could have been fined. His claim was dismissed, the court stating it as the 'general rule' that where a remedy was provided (here the fine) Parliament should be taken not to have intended to confer a civil remedy by way of action.[18] Contrast this case. A postman fell off his bike when it suddenly seized up owing to a latent structural defect. The defect being undetectable, the employer was not liable for breach of his common law duty to take care regarding the safety of the equipment provided for his workforce, but he was nevertheless held liable under a statutory instrument which provided that 'Every employer shall ensure that work equipment is maintained in an efficient state', efficient working order and in good repair'.[19] For over a century the courts have held that breach of such safety regulations triggers not only a fine but also a liability in damages towards the person protected, here the employee. Indeed, the Health and Safety at Work Act 1974 itself now provides that specific regulations regarding the safety of equipment, workplaces and so on—regulations largely responsive to

---

[16] *Monk v Warbey* [1935] 1 KB 75.   [17] *Richardson v Pitt-Stanley* [1995] 1 All ER 460.
[18] *Phillips v Britannia Hygienic Laundry* [1923] 2 KB 832.
[19] *Stark v Post Office* [2000] ICR 1013.

the 20-odd Directives from Brussels—give rise to liability even if the general statutory duties of the employer (and the workmen themselves) do not.[20]

Industrial injuries apart, it may be said that in general a defendant will rarely be held liable in damages just for contravening a statutory prohibition unless the statute so provides. Such provision is made, for example, in the Environmental Protection Act 1990, s 73 where the defendant has dumped waste illegally, and in the investment field a private person may claim damages from an authorised operator who contravenes a rule laid down under the Financial Services and Markets Act 2000, s 150. Damages may also be awarded against an undertaking which has infringed either of the statutory prohibitions contained in the Competition Act 1998—abusing a dominant position in a market or being party to an agreement which distorts or restricts competition. The original provisions on the 'civil liability of an undertaking for harm caused by infringement', which were extremely coy, have been beefed up by the Enterprise Act 2002, which permits the Office of Fair Trading to award damages to individuals or representative bodies.

STATUTORY DUTIES

Neither of these last two enactments are in terms of 'duty'—the Human Rights Act 1998 makes conduct 'unlawful' and the Competition Act says what is 'prohibited'—but as an example of a duty expressly imposed on public bodies we may instance the Highways Act 1980, s 41: 'The highway authority are under a duty to maintain the highway'. For many years there was acute disagreement in the courts about the scope of this duty. Did 'maintain' mean simply 'keep in repair' or did it include 'remove obstructions [such as snow and ice] from? The House of Lords resolved the dispute in the former sense,[21] but Parliament then laid down that the authority's duty did extend to the removal of snow and ice (but presumably not, given that statutes cover only what they specify, the removal of mud or slurry). The duty under s 41 as so extended is strict in that the claimant need not show that the authority was at fault, but the statute provides a defence in s 58 if 'the authority had taken such care as in all the circumstances was reasonably required to secure that the part of the highway to which the action relates was not dangerous for traffic.' It is not

---

[20] Health and Safety at Work Act 1974, s 47.
[21] *Goodes v East Sussex CC* [2000] 3 All ER 603.

uncommon for such defences to be provided by statute and quite common for them to fail in the courts.

The Road Traffic Act 1988 also imposes 'duties' on local authorities: they 'must take such measures as appear to the authority to be appropriate to prevent . . . accidents' (s 39). Describing this as a 'target' duty which leaves a fair discretion to the authority, the Court of Appeal was able to dismiss an impertinent complaint by a motorist that there were only two 'Give Way' signs on the minor road from which she emerged with insufficient care.[22] The observation *obiter* that the authority might well be liable at common law if the exercise of its discretion was unreasonable was subsequently discountenanced by the House of Lords when it dismissed another claim by a motorist that her injuries were due to inadequate (but not misleading) signage.[23]

REMOTENESS

As regards the damage for which compensation may be recovered where statute is involved, the common law test of its foreseeability may be inapplicable, for where the statute imposes liability, the only question is whether its requirements have been met. Take the claim under the Fatal Accidents Act by relatives of a person tortiously killed. Since they have no claim at all unless the deceased himself could have sued the defendant for his injuries, it must be shown that the deceased's injuries were the foreseeable result of the defendant's tort, unless of course the defendant was under a strict statutory liability to him. Once this requirement is met, however, the statutory claim of the relatives kicks in and foreseeability falls out of the picture: they can claim whatever the death cost them, however unforeseeable their loss, or even their existence. Likewise, if a workman is injured because the workplace is not safe (in the sense that some injury might be foreseen—foreseeability in general being implicit in the notion of 'danger'), it is no answer to say that *that* particular injury could not have been foreseen.[24]

In other cases, as we have seen, where the courts hold that the victim of an offence can sue at all, a teleological or purpose test may be applied: was the harm such that Parliament must have intended it to be guarded against? This is illustrated in the case already mentioned where the

[22] *Larner v Solihull Metropolitan Borough Council* [2001] RTR 32.
[23] *Gorringe v Calderdale MBC* [2004] UKHL 15.
[24] *Millard v Serck Tubes* [1968] 1 All ER 598.

claimant's sheep were washed overboard: since it was to prevent contagion, not drowning, that they were to be kept penned in, the claimant lost his claim.[25] To give a more recent instance: one winter's day a driver spent hours digging his milk tanker out of the snow, and icy water leaked into his protective boot through a tiny unobserved and virtually unobservable hole where the reinforced toe-cap joined the sole. He suffered frostbite in his little toe, but got no damages when a divided House of Lords upheld a divided Court of Appeal, on the ground that the boots were not designed to protect him from frostbite.[26] We get more 'risk' talk from Lord Hoffmann: 'Mr Fytche claims that because his boots were designed to protect him against a risk of his employment, his employers are liable in damages because they were inadequate to protect him against an injury which was not a risk of his employment.' Frostbite may not have been a risk of his employment, but he was harmed in his employment and was harmed because the boot was defective. Readers may prefer the powerful and lucid dissenting judgment of Baroness Hale.

[25] *Gorris v Scott* (1874) LR 9 Exch 125.
[26] *Fytche v Wincanton Logistics* [2004] UKHL 31.

6

Vicarious Liability

Although most torts are committed by individuals, almost all damages are paid by companies, usually employers or insurers: individuals are rarely worth suing unless they are either employed or insured. Insurance against liability is compulsory for motorists and also, in respect of injury to their workforce, for employers. This deals with two of the main sources of tort claims, traffic and industrial accidents. Furthermore, people often take out liability-insurance of their own accord and for their own protection: employers generally have insurance against liability to the public, and many householders have policies which cover them and sometimes also the members of their household against liability to third parties. This helps to explain the frequency of claims under the Occupier's Liability Acts. There is one important distinction between employers and insurers as regards their liability: whereas the employer can be sued directly at common law and his liability is regarded as part of tort law, the victim has no common law claim against the tortfeasor's insurer and has a statutory claim only if he has first obtained judgment against the tortfeasor himself, though there is now an exception, thanks to Brussels, in the case of traffic accidents, when suit may be brought against the motorist's liability insurer right away. In other cases, the tortfeasor's insurer, though conducting the case, is invisible and its role is often overlooked.

VICARIOUS LIABILITY

We have seen that, in principle, a person is not liable in negligence unless he is in breach of a duty owed by him to the claimant. Quite often, however—indeed very often—a person who is not in breach of any duty incumbent on himself is nevertheless liable, and strictly liable, for torts committed by someone else. His liability is then said to be 'vicarious'. The word is unfortunate in suggesting that this liability is a substitute for that of the person actually at fault; in fact it is additional, and the employee remains liable even if he has made his employer vicariously liable for what he did wrong. A few countries may have begun to absolve the employee of personal liability if the employer is solvent, as public bodies usually are, but this has yet to occur in England, except in certain cases of local government and the health services. In England, indeed, an employer who is held vicariously liable is entitled to sue the careless employee.[1] Where the employee has acted very badly, as where a police constable had harassed and fondled a blameless citizen, the employer's claim for an indemnity is perfectly acceptable.[2]

For many years, indeed, suit was brought against the humble employee rather than his wealthy employer. This occurred when the claimant was a customer of the employer and the contract between them contained a clause which exempted the employer from liability. The courts were too feeble to invalidate such clauses between the parties to the contract and resorted to the rather indecent expedient of allowing suit against the careless employee, who was prevented by the doctrine of privity (!) from invoking the exemption clause in his employer's contract even if it expressly purported to protect him.[3] Now, however, exemptions from liability for personal injuries negligently caused are entirely invalid (Unfair Contract Terms Act 1977), and where property damage is in issue, the employee can usually rely on a reasonable exemption clause in his employer's contract (Contracts (Rights of Third Parties) Act 1999).

The principal instance of vicarious liability is that of the employer for his employees. Various rationales have been offered for this—that he has the kind of control over them which frequently leads to liability (compare the keeper of animals and the occupier of premises); that he profits from them, and perhaps those who profit should bear concomitant losses; that by giving his staff tasks to do he increases the risk of their doing them badly; that he is richer, and so on. There is no point in discussing the matter, for two reasons: (a) the scope of the rule is not determined by the preferred rationale, and (b) all Western legal systems have this rule (though in Germany the employer can escape liability by proving that he did all that could be expected of him by way of selecting, training, and supervising his staff). In any case it is not only employers who have to answer for what others do for them, so the underlying principle, if any, may well be that you are liable for what you get people to do for you unless doing it is actually their own business or someone else's. It may

---

[1] *Lister v Romford Ice and Cold Storage Co* [1957] 1 All ER 125.
[2] *KD v Chief Constable of Hampshire* (Tugendhat J, 23 November 2005).
[3] *Adler v Dickson* [1955] 1 QB 158.

therefore be useful to distinguish between the different classes of helper and the different types of thing they are asked to do.

EMPLOYEES AND OTHER CONTRACTORS

Those who do what someone else asks them to do are either paid for it or they are not. People who do things for pay are in law contractors. Some contractors are in business on their own and are paid a fee for their services, often a one-off job; others slave away for ages in the business of their paymaster, and receive wages or a salary. The former are called 'independent contractors', while the latter are employees. Independent contractors are more often firms than individuals and have lots of customers, while employees are *invariably* human beings who usually have only one employer on whom, one assumes, they are taken to be 'dependent'. The distinction is fundamental for legal purposes, for while the employer is vicariously liable for his employees, the customer/client/ punter is not vicariously liable for his independent contractor or his contractor's employees. Given that while all employees, being human, are usually employed by a firm and that independent services are very commonly provided by firms to individual consumers, this rule has the desirable effect of rendering firms liable for individuals and not vice versa. A further effect is that the employee's victim knows whom to sue, since the tortfeasor has only one employer, whereas a firm has as many customers as it can get. Thus if the driver of a bus carelessly injures a pedestrian, it would be absurd to think of making the passengers liable, even though they are paying to be driven and even put the fare into the driver's hand; the bus company which pays wages to the driver is liable and the passengers who pay fares to the company are not.

NON-CONTRACTORS

People who do something for nothing are neither employees nor independent contractors, since they are not contractors at all. Nevertheless, you may well be answerable for the misconduct of those you ask to do you a favour. This was seen when Murphie asked his friend Ormrod to drive Murphie's fancy car to Monte Carlo where Murphie was to take part in the rally, and shortly after setting off Ormrod carelessly drove it into a bus.[4] Ormrod was obviously not Murphie's employee, but he was said to

---

[4] *Ormrod v Crosville Motor Services* [1953] 2 All ER 753.

be Murphie's 'agent' in driving the car and this was enough to render Murphie liable for the damage Ormrod carelessly caused while doing what he was asked to do. The use of the word 'agent' in this context is confusing, for it is more commonly used to denote a person who on request does an act-in-law, such as negotiating a contract, rather than an act-in-fact, such as driving an Austin Healey. To illustrate the difference we may say that the airline which flies you to your destination is doing an act-in-fact while the travel-agent does an act-in-law in getting you the ticket.

AGENTS

An agent in the technical sense, who may not be a contractor at all, since the test is not whether he is paid but whether he was authorised, may be either a firm (and therefore an independent contractor) or an employee. The booking-clerk in a hotel is both agent and employee, and in consequence binds his principal in contract if he takes a booking for the wedding suite (act-in-law) and renders his employer liable in tort if he drops an inkstand on the foot of the bride who is doing the booking (act-in-fact). But note a difference: if the bridal suite is not provided or the bed in it collapses, the booking clerk is not liable, since it is the hotel through him, and not he himself, that contracted to provide it, whereas he, as a tortfeasor, remains liable for the bride's broken toe and renders the hotel company additionally, though only vicariously, liable.

'Agency', properly speaking, is mainly dealt with in the contract books, but the extension of the tort of negligence so as to embrace negligent misrepresentations during negotiations for a contract (which in the case of a company are necessarily conducted by agents, since companies cannot speak) has made it necessary to reconcile the rule that employees render their employer liable for what they do in the course and scope of their employment with the (not terribly different) rule that the agent binds his principal only if he is acting within the scope of his authority, actual or apparent.[5] Yet the notion of 'authority' has cropped up in tort cases with unfortunate results. In one case where an enraged bus conductor used his employer's ticket machine to lambaste a passenger, the Privy Council rejected the liability of the bus company on the idiotic ground that 'there was no evidence that would justify the ascription of the act of the conductor to any authority, express or implied, vested in

[5] *The Ocean Frost* [1986] 2 All ER 385.

him by his employers'![6] Fortunately the House of Lords has now disavowed the notion of 'authority' in connection with the employer's vicarious liability in tort for the deliberate acts of its employees.[7]

JOINT ENTERPRISE/PARTNERSHIP

Completeness requires us to add that you may be liable for those engaged in a joint enterprise with you, whether as fellow conspirator, partner in a firm, or just someone helping you look for a gas leak with the aid of a candle,[8] but since actual employment is by far the commonest case of vicarious liability in tort, we shall concentrate on it here.

BASIC RULES

The twin and complementary rules are that you are liable for your employees and not for your independent contractors. The terminology is tiresome. For no good reason lawyers insist on calling the person who pays an independent contractor his 'employer', although the contractor is certainly not his employee. No plumber would dream of calling his customer his 'employer'—the plumber probably has an employer of his own unless he is in business for himself: the plumber would call his customer his customer, and so should the law, unless it is determined to confuse students, just as it does with its loose usage of the term 'agent'.

The employer's vicarious liability for his employee depends on the connection between (a) the parties themselves, and (b) their actions or activities: the tortfeasor must be the defendant's employee, and the tort must have been committed in the 'course and scope' of his employment.

WHO IS AN EMPLOYEE?

Whether or not a particular person is an employee is a question which has given the courts (and students) some difficulty. This is rather surprising. After all, most people know whether they are employed or unemployed or freelance (self-employed), whether their remuneration is called wages or salary (the hallmark of employment) or something else. And the taxman certainly knows. Part of the difficulty, indeed, may be that the same

---

[6] *Keppel Bus Co v Sa'ad bin Ahmad* [1974] 3 All ER 700.
[7] *Lister v Hesley Hall* [2001] 2 All ER 769.
[8] *Brooke v Bool* [1928] 2 KB 578.

question—employee or not?—is raised in quite different contexts, which do not necessarily call for the same answer. For example, an employer owes particular duties to his employees as regards their safety, but there seems to be no good reason why the group entitled to such attention should be precisely the same as the group whose members render the employer liable to third parties for their misdoings. Again, employees have very extensive rights as such, under the Employment Rights Act 1996, for example. Should this necessarily involve that all those so entitled, and only they, render their employer vicariously liable? One case commonly cited for the test of who is an employee concerned the question of whether the alleged employer was entitled to copyright in the works written by the alleged employee—which has nothing to do with vicarious liability.[9] Another arose from an attempt by a cement firm to avoid payroll tax by turning its drivers into independent carriers;[10] the attempt was successful, but does this really mean that if one of the drivers had carelessly tipped his load of cement on to the vehicle behind him, the company, which continued to provide the cement, would escape liability in tort?

As to the relatively rare cases in tort when it is a problem whether an individual is an employee or not (agency workers, the building and catering trades), suffice it to say that it is no longer a question simply of whether the boss controls the way the work is to be done, but that several factors are taken into account in addition to, or despite, what the parties have agreed to call their relationship—whether the human being provides his own equipment, whether he works for several people or just one, whether he determines his own hours, and so on. That policemen are not employees at all is a peculiarity of English law: they are amusingly said to be the servants of the public (as a man of religion may be the servant only of God[11]), but this is immaterial since the Police Act 1996 empowers the Chief Constable to use public funds to pay those whom his lesser constables have torted.

WHOSE EMPLOYEE?

Once it is determined that the tortfeasor is an employee one must ask whether the defendant was his employer. Again this is not difficult. Employees are not traded or handed over like Pokemon© cards, though if

---

[9] *Stevenson Jordan & Harrison v Macdonald and Evans* [1952] 1 TLR 101.
[10] *Ready Mixed Concrete (South East) v Minister of Pensions and National Insurance* [1968] 1 All ER 433.
[11] Doubted in *Percy v Church of Scotland* [2005] UKHL 73.

an undertaking is transferred the employee may assert as against the transferee his contractual rights against the transferor. Normally you remain the employee of the firm that employed you until you get your P45, and this is true even if in the course of your employment you are doing a job for someone else: after all, the man delivering the pizza does not become the customer's employee. Nor is the person in a firm who can tell you what to do necessarily your employer: contrary to what both of them might think, a secretary is not employed by her boss or line manager—they are both employed by the firm that pays them. Though not many people are employed by more than one employer, it appears that more than one defendant may be liable for an employee's negligence. In a rather surprising rereading of a House of Lords decision in 1947 which had always been supposed to decide the contrary, the Court of Appeal held in 2005 that where a careless handyman was under the supervision of two persons employed by different employers both employers were liable.[12] But the next year this decision was not followed: instead it was held that where X provided employees as security officers for a nightclub and one of them assaulted a patron, the nightclub was the 'temporary deemed employer' and X was not liable at all![13].

COURSE OF EMPLOYMENT

More difficult and interesting is the question whether the tort committed by the employee was 'in the course and scope' of his employment. Both words, 'course' and 'scope', are quite appropriate. The employer need not pay for what the employee does in his spare time, or, less clearly, for what he does during working hours for his own amusement or profit and against the interests of his employer. In the latter context the charming Victorian words 'frolic' and 'detour' are as useful as any criteria. One could ask 'Was the tortfeasor "on the job" at the time?', bearing in mind that an employee may exploit for his own purposes the time he should be devoting to his job. In one case the employee of a cleaning firm used the customer's telephone to make long distance calls to his friends.[14] The cleaning firm was held not liable, but if the call had been made to ask for more cleaning materials it would have had to pay for the cost. The purpose of the tortfeasor is a relevant consideration here.

---

[12] *Viasystems (Tyneside) v Thermal Transfer (Northern)* [2005] EWCA Civ 1151.
[13] *Hawley v Luminar Leisure* [2006] EWCA Civ 18.
[14] *Heasmans v Clarity Cleaning* [1987] IRLR 286.

The cleaner's act in phoning Yokohama or wherever was deliberate, not negligent. So, too, was the conduct of a school warden who sexually abused the boys in his charge. In holding the school liable, the House of Lords, in a decision which will be discussed again shortly (see p. 112), explicitly altered the test of when conduct is in the 'course of employment.'[15] For over a century the test cited as gospel was that laid down by Sir John Salmond: apart from acts actually authorised by the employer, an act only fell within the course of employment if it was 'a wrongful and unauthorised mode of doing some act authorised by the master'. Now 'attention should be directed to the closeness of the connection between the employee's duties and his wrongdoing and not to verbal formulae' (Lord Millett), and 'The question is whether the warden's torts were so closely connected with his employment that it would be fair and just to hold the employers vicariously liable' (Lord Steyn). In the light of this, it may be a little difficult to maintain the traditional view that an employer is not liable if the employment merely provided the occasion for the tort: what would the decision be if the cleaner case recurs?

An act which has been explicitly forbidden by the employer can hardly fall within the Salmond formula as an unauthorised mode of doing what was authorised, but it has long been clear that an employer does not escape liability simply by forbidding the employee to do the act in question. The case generally cited for this proposition (as well as for the view that the employee's purpose is relevant) is a little odd. Although milk roundsmen had been formally forbidden by their employer to enlist the services of children, Milkman Plenty allowed Master Rose to help him deliver the milk and carelessly injured the boy by driving the milk float too close to the kerb while the boy's foot was dangling over the side.[16] The discussion centred on the question whether, despite the prohibition, Milkman Plenty was in the course of his employment in getting Master Rose to help him in his job. It was held that he was. But enlisting Master Rose was no tort, though it was doubtless a breach of contract justifying instant dismissal, and Master Rose was certainly not complaining of it: the tort was the careless driving, and that was assuredly in the course of his employment. The problem would not have arisen had it been a motor vehicle rather than a milk-float: the driver would then have been covered by the employer's mandatory liability insurance, and the insurer would have been liable even if the employer were not.

---

[15] *Lister v Hesley Hall* [2001] UKHL 22.   [16] *Rose v Plenty* [1976] 1 All ER 97.

OTHER GROUNDS OF EMPLOYER'S LIABILITY

The defendant will not, in his capacity as employer, be vicariously liable if either the tortfeasor was not his employee or, if he was, was not acting in the course and scope of his employment. But this does not mean that the employer is not liable at all, for he may well be liable vicariously on some other ground or personally liable because he is in breach of a duty owed by himself. As to the first possibility, if, during a rail strike, an employer asks employee Bill to drive employee Ben to work and Bill injures Ben by bad driving en route, Bill is not in the course of his employment (for driving to work not normally in the course of employment), but the employer will nevertheless be liable on the basis that he had asked Bill to do him a favour, and thereby made Bill his 'agent' in addition to being his employee.[17] The same would be true where a boss asks his secretary to do something special for him outside her normal duties, like buying presents for his mistress.

The second possibility is exemplified by a case where a notorious prankster who kept tripping up his fellow-employees thereby caused an injury to the crippled plaintiff. As the prankster was doubtless 'frolicking', their employer was not *vicariously* liable, but he was held *personally* liable for breach of his own duty to the plaintiff employee to provide a safe system of work.[18] For this, however, the claimant has to prove fault in the employer, for though vicarious liability is strict, the employer's personal duty is one of reasonable care, as was shown in an even nastier case: two apprentices used their employer's compressed air to blow up a colleague during working hours, and the employer was held not liable at all since he had no reason to suppose that such a thing might occur.[19]

Although the duty of the employer to his workforce is expressed in terms of reasonable care, it is a high duty of the non-delegable variety. In this it is paralleled by the duty of the bailee (warehouseman, borrower, hirer) to the owner of the chattel in his possession. If one of the bailee's employees steals the goods, the thief cannot easily be said to be in the course of his employment, but if he was the very employee to whom the bailee had entrusted the goods, that is, delegated his own personal duty to take care of them, then his employer will be liable for breach of his own duty as bailee.[20] That this is the correct analysis is indicated by the fact

[17] *Vandyke v Fender* [1970] 2 All ER 335.
[18] *Hudson v Ridge Manufacturing Co* [1957] 2 All ER 229.
[19] *Smith v Crossley Bros* (1951) 95 SJ 655.
[20] *Morris v Martin and Sons* [1965] 2 All ER 725.

that the bailee would be liable even if the delegate were an independent contractor, such as a security firm.[21] By contrast, the occupier of premises is not answerable to his visitors for the harm done by his independent contractors unless he should have been aware of the danger they had caused. Thus in order to determine whether a defendant is put in breach of his duty by the misconduct of another, one must consider the relationship between claimant and defendant personally as well as the relationship between tortfeasor and defendant, which is all-important where claimant and defendant are total strangers.

The difficulty in these cases arises from the fact that three parties are involved. Legal obligations are usually bipolar, with just one relationship in issue, but where there are three parties there are three relationships, here claimant/defendant, claimant/tortfeasor and tortfeasor/defendant. The claimant may be saying to the defendant 'You owed me a duty and you were put in breach of that duty by X to whom you delegated its performance' or he may be saying 'X torted me so you are liable, since he is your employee and he was acting in the course and scope of his employment'. There are, after all, two ways round a triangle, and the situation here is triangular.

These distinct analyses were not kept properly apart in an important decision of the House of Lords, reversing the Court of Appeal, that a school for difficult boys was liable when the warden it employed to manage its hostel serially abused them.[22] Here of course the tort was not just negligence but a trespass to the person of a criminal nature, but this is not important in itself since vicarious liability applies to all torts, including defamation. While the speech of Lord Steyn stated that what was involved was vicarious and not personal liability (the school not being at fault), he nevertheless invoked the bailment cases (which are clearly cases of delegation) and observed that here 'the employers entrusted the care of the children. . .to the warden'. It seems evident (as should have been the case where the bus conductor assaulted the passenger) that the special relationship between the claimant boys and the school which employed the warden was an important factor. Yet while making mention of the employer's duty towards the victim and indicating that the employee must have been the employer's delegate, the speeches also stress the connection between the employee's conduct and the job he was employed to do. But what is it that the employer can have delegated? Surely only

---

[21] *British Road Services v Crutchley* [1967] 2 All ER 792.
[22] *Lister v Hesley Hall* [2001] 2 All ER 769.

the performance of his duty towards the victim. But if so, the delegate's misconduct will place the employer in breach of his own duty to the victim, and his liability will not be purely vicarious at all. Lord Hobhouse alone puts his finger on it, in saying that this 'is a situation where the employer has assumed a relationship to the plaintiff which imposes specific duties in tort upon the employer and the role of the employee (or servant) is that he is the person to whom the employer has entrusted the performance of that duty'.[23] This explains why, if the gardener had seized the opportunity of the boys' proximity to abuse them, or if the warden had brought a boy off the street and abused him at the school during working hours, the employer would not be liable. Likewise if the nurse poisons the patient, the hospital will be liable, not if the cleaner does so, though it would be liable if the cleaner carelessly pulled the plug on the drip in order to attach the vacuum cleaner.

The importance of the relationship between claimant and defendant can be seen in *Williams v Hemphill*.[24] The defendants agreed to transport a party of boys back to Glasgow from their summer camp in Benderloch in Argyllshire. Their driver should have followed the direct Western route but at the instigation of the boys went East instead, and was well off the proper route and still going in the wrong direction when there was an accident owing to his negligence and one of the boys was badly injured. The defendant was held liable, and rightly so, but not on the ground given, that the driver was in the course of his employment (which was the sole ground argued), but because the driver was the defendant carrier's delegate. If the lorry carrying the boys had run into a pedestrian on a 'detour' so far off the driver's proper route, his employer would not have been liable (though his insurer would be).

Notwithstanding (or perhaps because of) the confusion in the *Hesley Hall* case between vicarious liability and personal liability for breach by a delegate of a non-delegable duty, the actual decision is clearly having an effect in extending liability, especially for the deliberate acts of a subordinate. Take club bouncers, for example. In 1962 it was held that though the club would be liable if the bouncer ejected a patron with undue force it would not have to pay if he chased the ejected patron down the street in a rage and thumped him again.[25] But in *Mattis v Pollock (t/a Flamingo's Nightclub)* in 2003 the Court of Appeal, reversing the trial

---

[23] *Lister v Hesley Hall* [2001] 2 All ER 769, 789.
[24] [1966] 2 Lloyd's Rep 101.
[25] *Daniels v Whetstone Entertainments* [1962] 2 Lloyd's Rep 1.

judge, held the club liable when its bouncer, after an altercation with a patron, went home to fetch a knife and stabbed him with it.[26]

EXCLUSION OF VICARIOUS LIABILITY?

Given that the relationship between the victim and the employer can extend the latter's liability for the misdoings of his delegates and employees, can it equally exclude the employer's vicarious liability? One obvious case is where the claimant has a contract with the defendant which exempts him from liability for harm negligently caused. Such a clause is invalid as regards personal injury and death, but may be valid, if reasonable, as to property damage. If so, it is clear that the defendant will not be responsible even if his employee negligently caused the damage in the course and scope of his employment. Indeed, after the Contracts (Rights of Third Parties) Act 1999 a properly drafted clause can protect the employee himself. This is satisfactory, especially since much of the property for which the employee might otherwise be liable will be covered by the owner's insurance, and it would be intolerable to let the insurer, by subrogation, sue an uninsured workman, as was once permitted by the House of Lords: when a workman allegedly ran over his father at work, his employer's insurer paid the father and was allowed to sue the son, on the ground that the employer could have done so (though of course he wouldn't).[27] The question may also arise where property belonging to a trespasser on the defendant's land is injured owing to what would be normal negligence on the part of an employee: the occupier's 'no duty' under the 1984 Act should not be sidelined by arguments of vicarious liability.

The dubious view that vicarious liability is a principle of invariable application has led to an oddity in the vexed area of the liability of public authorities for faulty exercise of their discretionary powers. Although it had been held and was accepted that an education authority owed no duty to a pupil as regards the exercise of its discretionary powers, the House of Lords has held that it is vicariously liable for the torts of the personnel it employs or retains to exercise its powers: 'Since the authority can only act through its employees or agents, and if they are negligent vicarious liability will arise, it may rarely be necessary to invoke a claim for direct liability'.[28] Yet if it is not fair, just, and reasonable to make the authority

---

[26] [2003] EWCA Civ 887.
[27] *Lister v Romford Ice and Cold Storage Co* [1957] 1 All ER 125.
[28] *Phelps v Hillingdon London Borough Council* [2000] 4 All ER 504 at 522 per Lord Slynn.

directly liable, it can hardly be so to render it vicariously liable for those through whom alone it can exercise its powers.

DOES THE LIABILITY OF THE EMPLOYER ENTAIL THAT OF THE EMPLOYEE?

Most breaches of contract by a company (and companies are the commonest contractors) are due to some fault on the part of some individual on the company payroll. If physical damage results, the employee's liability under *Donoghue v Stevenson* is clear in principle, but the extension of liability in negligence to cover the case where purely economic harm is due to failure to act (the typical breach of contract) has highlighted the question of the liability of an employee whose laziness or incompetence puts his employer in breach of contract with the claimant. This is especially important where the employer is now insolvent. In one case, already considered, plaintiffs who wanted to run a health food store bought a franchise from a company after receiving from it certain representations as to probable profits which proved unreasonably optimistic. When the franchising company became insolvent, the plaintiffs sued the individual who had in fact drafted the advice in question, actually the managing director. It was held that the managing director was not liable, since the plaintiffs had not relied on any undertaking of responsibility by him: the forecast of profits had been on the company's headed paper.[29] This valuable decision will protect negligent secretaries whose mistyping, uncorrected by a superior, causes a damaging misrepresentation to go forth to a client from the company office. In a subsequent case, however, when an employed (and uninsured) surveyor drew up an overoptimistic report on a dwelling for the mortgage company which had commissioned it from his employer, he was held liable to the purchaser of the house although the purchaser had had no dealings whatever with the defendant personally and had not even seen his report. The authority of the franchising case was disregarded in a rather cavalier manner by the majority of the Court of Appeal—surely no distinction could be made on the basis that the franchisees had a contract with the defendant's employer whereas the purchaser of the house did not?—but in any case the House of Lords refused leave to appeal.[30]

---

[29] *Williams v Natural Life Health Foods* [1998] 2 All ER 577.
[30] *Merrett v Babb* [2001] QB 1174.

7

Contribution Between Tortfeasors

The previous chapter featured the victim who could sue not only the tortfeasor but also, under certain conditions, his employer as well. Employee and employer in such circumstances, like conspirators, are called 'joint tortfeasors': there is only one tort but two persons liable. But there may be several different torts contributing to the same harm and several persons liable for what they have independently done, since in principle, as we have seen, everyone whose tortious conduct has contributed to the occurrence of harm is liable to be sued for the full amount of that harm, provided it is indivisible and not too remote. This 'joint and several liability', as it is unattractively called, is rational, because if two people by independent torts kill a third, each of them has killed the victim, and it is also fair, in that the victim will be paid in full even if one of the tortfeasors is insolvent, untraceable, or in gaol. Even the Law Commission has decided that no major reform of this rule is required; the attack on it is coming, as we have seen, from judges seeking to reduce its incidence by claiming to divide the indivisible (as if physical damage were just money) and thereby introduce proportionate liability.

Once again, as with vicarious liability, we have a triangular situation, with a victim (V) and two tortfeasors (T1 and T2). It is clear law that if V suffers damage to which both T1 and T2 have tortiously contributed and obtains full compensation from T1, whether by judgment or agreement, V can no longer sue T2, since his harm has already been made good. It used to be the law that T1, whose payment to V had released T2 from liability, could nevertheless not claim anything towards that payment from T2: after all, T1 was himself a tortfeasor, his claim would be for purely economic loss, and in the old days the defence of contributory negligence would bar a careless victim's claim even where the harm was physical. The common law solution seemed unfair to the Law Reform Committee, so in 1935 T1 was given a statutory claim against T2 for 'contribution'.[1] This is not a claim for damages in tort (T1's harm is

---

[1] Now Civil Liability (Contribution) Act 1978.

purely economic and T1 and T2 may be total strangers), but rather a claim in restitution for debt, to prevent T2 being unjustifiably enriched at T1's expense by being released from his liability to V. T2 is liable to contribute to T1 only if he could have been sued by V for the 'same damage' as T1, but he remains liable to pay contribution even though V's claim against him has lapsed, whether because V's claim against him has become barred by lapse of time or by V's receipt from T1 of payment in full. The amount of the claim is what is 'just and equitable having regard to the extent of . . . responsibility for the damage'.

Though the underlying idea of the statutory scheme is fair enough, its practical operation is far from unproblematical. The simple case is where V is a passenger in a car negligently driven by her husband T2 and is injured in a collision with an oncoming car being driven equally negligently by T1. V will probably want to sue the stranger T1 rather than assert that her husband was negligent, but T1's insurer will certainly bring in T2 in order to recover contribution from T2's insurer, and the question whether T2 was negligent, the very question V wanted to avoid, will muddy the waters of her claim against T1, although it will not diminish her damages. Perhaps there is nothing much wrong with that, given that both drivers are bound to be insured against liability. But consider the case where T1, solely to blame for a collision in which V, a child, was badly injured, was allowed to claim contribution from V's mother, a passenger, as well as V's aunt, the driver, on the ground that the child was inadequately secured by a seat-belt.[2]

To pursue the matter, take the case that a little girl is able to run into the street and be run over by a careless motorist only because her mother carelessly let go of her hand. The child would never sue the mother, who is most unlikely to be insured against liability, but the motorist's insurer will have no compunction in claiming contribution from her and thereby diminishing the family funds—a result so unsatisfactory that in order to avoid it the New York Court of Appeals has been led to hold that a mother owes her child no duty to look after it![3] Or take another case, a depressingly frequent one. A motorist emerges from a side-road without proper care and collides with a motorcyclist driving quite properly on the main road. Of course the motorist will be liable, but his insurer will, by way of subrogation, try to claim contribution in his name from the highway authority on the ground that it also was to blame for the accident,

---

[2] *Jones v Wilkins* [2001] TLR 89.
[3] *Holodook v Spencer* 324 NE 2d 338 (NY 1974).

whether because the sightlines were poor[4] or the road was not properly maintained or the signage was defective or whatever else they can dream up. It is surely quite wrong for the liability-insurer to be allowed to put part of the loss, which it has itself agreed to bear, on to the public, and put the local authority to the trouble and expense of defending a claim which the victim would never have brought.

Yet another case occurred in days gone by when the purchaser of a badly built house could sue the local authority for failing to prevent its erection.[5] At that time the negligent architect was also liable to the purchaser for the same damage so the statute gave him a contribution claim against the local authority. When it came to deciding on the amount of this claim, the court granted the architect 25%, saying coyly that perhaps the policeman should bear less responsibility than the thief he failed to catch![6] A statute which lets the thief sue the policeman for not catching him is not without regrettable effects. A further effect of the Act as presently drafted is that T1 who has bona fide settled with the victim remains liable to contribute to T2, even if the latter denied liability right up to judgment. And our system professes to encourage settlements!

A tortfeasor who is sued and wishes to claim contribution would be well advised to bring any other supposed tortfeasor into the victim's suit. Likewise, the victim should sue every plausible tortfeasor, because if he brings a second action in respect of the same damage he risks being penalised in costs, and if he loses against one defendant and succeeds against another, he will get all his costs paid by the latter. Indeed, if T1 and T2 both negligently cause an accident in which T1's passenger and he himself are injured, and T1 wishes to claim contribution from T2 towards the damages he has paid to his passenger, T1 *must* join his own claim for damages (subject to his contributory negligence) to his claim for contribution, for if he does not, he may be barred from claiming for his own injuries. This is the astonishing result of a decision of the Court of Appeal, holding that the driver's claim for personal injury damages against the local authority was barred because the claim had not been joined to his insurer's claim for contribution (yes, it was another case where a motorist's insurer was trying to get its snout into the public trough; but why expect a liability insurer to care twopence for the

---

[4] *Stovin v Wise* [1996] 3 All ER 801.
[5] *Anns v Merton LBC* [1977] 2 All ER 492.
[6] *Eames London Estates v North Herts DC* (1980) 18 BLR 50.

insured's personal injury claim anyway?), the Court actually saying of the rule it was applying 'it is a salutary rule ... important for insurance companies'.[7] This decision was not formally denounced, as it should have been, when the House of Lords reviewed the doctrine of 'abuse of process'.[8] So bringing a contribution claim (or having one brought by your insurer) may lose you your claim for damages. Nice work, Parliament! Well done, the courts!

The area of application of the Act was greatly increased in 1978 when contribution claims were allowed not just between tortfeasors but between all persons liable for the same damage suffered by the victim, whether their liability arose from tort, breach of contract, breach of trust(!), or whatever. Although this extension was rendered less momentous by subsequent decisions which effectively held that every negligent breach of contract was also a tort, even though it caused only economic harm, it led to an eccentric result in the following case. D1 negligently certified to P that P owed money to D2, and P duly paid D2. P thereupon became entitled to claim that money back, as paid under a mistake, but brought a suit for damages against D1, who negligently caused that mistake. D1 sought to bring in D2 in order to claim contribution from him. The trial judge correctly held that no such claim lay, but the Court of Appeal under Auld LJ reversed.[9] This is absurd: a claim lies only between persons liable in respect of the same damage, and here D2 was not liable in respect of damage at all, any more than a person liable to pay the price for goods sold and delivered is liable in respect of damage to the seller. The correct solution is that if P has recovered the money from D2, his damages claim against D1 is reduced to that extent, because his loss is thereby reduced; and if P has not yet recovered from D2, the question will be whether his claim against D1 is to be reduced under the rule that a claimant must seek to mitigate his loss by all reasonable means, for example by suing another person whose payment would reduce the damage. It should be noted that in a suit by P against D2 for his money back, it could not possibly be relevant that P had a damages claim against D1.

To grant a tortfeasor who had paid the victim a claim against another tortfeasor who was released by that payment no doubt seemed a good idea at the time, but it is clear that the enactment has had baleful effects. It

[7] *Talbot v Berkshire CC* [1993] 4 All ER 9 at 15.
[8] *Johnson v Gore Wood & Co* [2001] 2 All ER 481.
[9] *Friends Provident Life Office v Hillier Parker* [1995] 4 All ER 260.

permits a party who should bear the loss through his liability insurance to throw this loss or part of it onto a person, public or private, who would never have been sued by the primary victim. The notion that the primary victim will have been actuated by caprice or malice in deciding which tortfeasor to sue is quite unrealistic: victims have legal advice and will sue the party whose liability is most easily established and who is most likely to be able to pay, and that should be the end of the matter. Indeed, it *is* the end of the matter so far as tort law is concerned, but the dog of tort has a tail of restitution and the tail is now distortingly wagging the dog. The fact that T1 can bring T2 into the lawsuit initiated against him by V not only complicates the lawsuit contrary to V's interests but also greatly delays the process of settlement.

An extreme example of dog-wagging occurred in the Court of Appeal recently. A young man who had been beaten up by thugs at work was taken to hospital and lost an eye during treatment there; he became a total nervous wreck in consequence, and sued both the employer who had failed to protect him and the surgeon whose carelessness had blinded him. In this fairly straightforward tort case the *very first* question the Court of Appeal asked was whether the Contribution Act applied, and because, as they held (erroneously) it did not, they gave separate judgments against the defendants, each for their part, rather than a single judgment against both for the harm for which both were responsible.[10] It hardly needs to be said that the application of the Act is a consequence, not a determinant, of tort liability. In this case, as it happened, both defendants were solvent, but even so this solution operated against the interests of the victim, for whom the law of tort exists; had one of the defendants been unable to pay (as the thugs doubtless were) the injustice would have been manifest.

It is worth considering the effect of the two doctrines based on 'equitable' considerations, namely subrogation and contribution. Both of them interfere with the proper operation of the law of tort. Thus the person who causes damage to insured property has to pay the insurer although the insurer has suffered only a financial loss and can claim only through the insured, a party already satisfied.[11] The claimant in contribution is also a party whose loss is purely financial and who could certainly not bring a tort claim for that loss. The outcome is that the only people who can claim for financial loss caused to them by a stranger are the insurer,

---

[10] *Rahman v Arearose* [2001] QB 351.
[11] *Simpson v Thompson* (1887) 3 App Cas 279.

who has promised to pay for that loss, and the tortfeasor, who has himself caused it. The peculiarities are compounded when one notes that not only is the property-insurer subrogated to the insured victim's claim in tort but that the liability-insurer is subrogated to the insured tortfeasor's claim in contribution!

8

Contributory Negligence

It used to be the rule at common law that if your own carelessness had contributed to your injury, your claim in negligence was completely barred, even if the defendant's fault and contribution were much greater than your own. This rule was very harsh, since most accidents, especially those at work, would be avoided if the victim had been more careful, and even if the accident itself cannot be prevented, the harm resulting from it can be reduced by sensible precautions, such as wearing a seat-belt or a hard hat. In 1945 this vicious old rule was replaced by statute.[1] Nowadays damages for an injury are to be reduced to the extent that the claimant's fault contributed to it. 'Contributory negligence' is thus only a partial defence—it affects the claimant's quantum of recovery rather than the defendant's liability—but it is raised very frequently, and has a great impact on the operation of the law. Note that while in the United States 'contributory negligence' refers to the old rule, now generally replaced there by 'comparative negligence', in England 'contributory negligence' denotes only the negligence of the claimant himself, not that of a third party whose negligence contributes to the occurrence of the harm.

According to the 1945 Act the claimant's damages are to be reduced 'to such extent as the court thinks just and equitable having regard to the claimant's share in the responsibility for the damage'. When both parties have been careless, there is no real difficulty, but what if the defendant is either strictly liable and not careless at all, or else worse than careless, that is, deceitful or wicked? The courts apply the Act in the first case but not in the second. As to the case where the defendant is strictly liable, the argument has been heard, and sometimes accepted in other systems, that if the defendant's fault is irrelevant to his liability, the claimant's fault should be irrelevant to his recovery: in France, indeed, this has led to the abolition of any reduction of damages in traffic accidents (unless the claimant was himself at the wheel), and in the United States to problems where a thoughtless consumer is injured by a defective product. The

[1] Law Reform (Contributory Negligence) Act 1945.

question does not seem to bother our courts, who operate on the basis that since the defendant would be liable in full had the victim not contributed to the harm, one simply docks the victim's damages by the amount of his contribution. As to the case where the defendant was very wicked, the courts hold that damages are not to be reduced:[2] the con-man can hardly complain that it was stupid of his dupe to be taken in.

It is not only under the Act that a claimant's conduct may affect his claim. If his conduct was voluntary, one must consider the possibility that it constitutes a *novus actus interveniens* which 'breaks the chain of causation' with the result that the defendant, though at fault, is not liable at all. Thus when a person broke his right leg by jumping downstairs when his left leg, defective owing to a prior injury which the defendant had paid for, 'went' under him, the House of Lords dismissed his claim.[3] The House has been criticised for not awarding reduced damages under the 1945 Act, a criticism quite in line with the tendency to resort to the Act in order to split the difference between the parties rather than adopt the 'all or nothing' approach characteristic of the common law. Indeed, if we ignore the established doctrine of mitigation of loss and the unorthodox concept of 'proportional damages' embraced by the Court of Appeal, the Act provides the only means by which a court can award reduced damages. Accordingly, when judges feel diffident about awarding either full damages or none at all they increasingly resort to the Act, however inappropriately.

One cannot really object to the use of the Act to reduce the damages of the victim of exposure to asbestos whose continual smoking of cigarettes contributed to his early demise from lung cancer.[4] There the defendant's breach of duty actually contributed to the harm, but where liability arises only under *Fairchild* (for contributing to the risk of harm rather than to the harm itself) the Act is inapplicable since the defendant now pays only for his own contribution to the risk, not for the whole harm less the claimant's contribution to it.[5] But in other cases the invocation of the Act has been very objectionable. In one case a burglar, shot but not aimed at by the defendant occupier, was awarded reduced damages, whereas his claim should have been dismissed altogether on the grounds that he was a criminal,[6] especially as the House of Lords had held that damages

---

[2] *Standard Chartered Bank v Pakistan National Shipping Corp* [2001] QB 167.
[3] *McKew v Holland and Hannen and Cubitts* [1969] 3 All ER 1621.
[4] *Badger v Ministry of Defence* [2005] EWHC 2941 (QB).
[5] *Barker v Corus* [2006] UKHL 20.
[6] *Revill v Newbery* [1996] 1 All ER 291.

were not to be reduced just because the claimant was trespassing, but only if he should have realised that he was exposing himself to danger.[7] In another case, Sedley LJ indulged in a cadenza to the effect that the Act should always be applied in claims by criminal claimants because it produces a fairer result.[8] Again, suppose that by assaulting you, I provoke a fist-fight and you go beyond self-defence by striking me with a knuckle-duster: do I get full damages or should they be reduced? The courts have split on this issue.[9] Another unresolved question is whether damages may be reduced by 100% under the Act. This also arises from a reluctance to award nothing: 20% is doubtless fairer (and carries entitlement to costs!).

The House of Lords has even contrived to hold that it was contributory negligence for a detainee to commit suicide, the occasion for which was presented by the very slight negligence of the police.[10] The case was remarkable in that in the Court of Appeal one judge would have made no reduction at all, another would have reduced the claim to zero, and the third opted for a reduction of 50%, which was upheld by the House of Lords. Such unpredictability as regards quantum is unsatisfactory, for although the outcome of a lawsuit is never certain, it is important to reduce the uncertainties as far as possible, and there is no doubt that if an increasing number of careless claimants win nowadays, it is less clear how much they will receive. If litigants are quite unable to predict what damages may be awarded, they can hardly settle their differences, and they are encouraged to settle, not least by the rule that if an offer is made and rejected which later proves adequate, the costs of the unnecessary trial and expenses incurred after the offer was made must all be borne by the party unwise enough to reject it, even though the eventual decision on liability was in his favour.

One effect of this is that since far more turns on a successful appeal than simply the amount by which the trial judge's award may be increased or diminished, appeals on apportionment are brought quite frequently. The Court of Appeal keeps saying that it will rarely interfere, but in fact it does so quite often. On one day it increased from 50% to 75% the reduction made in the damages awarded when a pedal cyclist travelling in the wrong direction was struck by a motorist emerging from his driveway[11]

---

[7] *Westwood v Post Office* [1973] 3 All ER 184.

[8] *Vellino v Chief Constable* [2001] EWCA Civ 1249.

[9] *Murphy v Culhane* [1976] 3 All ER 533.

[10] *Reeves v Commissioner of Police* [1999] 3 All ER 897.

[11] *Chappell v Imperial Design* (CA, 31 October 2000).

and lowered to 50% the reduction in the damages awarded to a 13 year old boy who filched a drum of waste solvent put out for collection and, despite warnings from his friends, set fire to it and was burned in the ensuing explosion.[12] Generally the courts are fairly tender to silly young victims,[13] but they have not followed the recommendation of the Pearson Commission in 1976 that no reduction should be made if a child injured in a highway accident is as young as 12.

THIRD PARTIES

The presence of a third party on either side leads to the usual complications. The claimant is affected by the contributory fault of anyone for whom he would have been vicariously liable. Thus in the case where Murphie's Austin Healey, being driven to Monte Carlo at his request by Ormrod, was damaged in a collision with a bus, any claim Murphie might have had against the bus company would have been reduced to the extent of Ormrod's negligence.[14] That would have been a case of property damage, unusual in that the party vicariously liable was an individual, and not a corporate employer. The principle is generally inapplicable in claims for personal injuries, for the fault of the driver is not imputable to an injured passenger, unless the driver is his 'agent', nor, contrary to what one might expect, is the fault of a parent imputable to a child injured through the parent's failure to look after him.[15] By contrast, however, if a person's own fault contributes to his death, his relatives' claim under the Fatal Accidents Act will be reduced, and the person who gratuitously cares for an injured victim will get less if the victim himself contributed to the injury, because it is only in the victim's own claim that any sum for the carer may be awarded.

In cases where more than one tortfeasor is liable for the harm to which the careless victim has himself contributed, the apportionment must be effected between the three parties. Between claimant and tortfeasors the apportionment is done under the Contributory Negligence Act 1945, while as between tortfeasors liable for the same damage it is done under the Contribution Act 1978. Fortunately both statutes provide that the apportionment is to be what is 'just and equitable'. The proper way to proceed is first to ask how much the claimant himself contributed to the

---

[12] *Richards v Quinton* (CA, 31 October 2000).
[13] *Gough v Thorne* [1966] 3 All ER 398.
[14] *Ormrod v Crosville Motor Services* [1953] 2 All ER 753.
[15] *Oliver v Birmingham and Midland Omnibus Co* [1933] 1 KB 35.

harm, as compared with the total contributions of those found liable to him, and to reduce his damages to the extent of his contribution relative to theirs. He then gets judgment for the balance against each of the tortfeasors and can proceed to execute against either.[16] Thus if V is one-third to blame and T1 and T2 are respectively one half and one sixth to blame, V will get judgment against both defendants for two-thirds of his harm. It is true that though V was twice as much to blame as T2, he can claim two-thirds from him; but if T2 pays the two-thirds he can claim three quarters of that from T1, who was three times as much to blame.

THE ACT INAPPLICABLE

Although 'It's your own fault' would seem to be a powerful riposte to any claim, there are certain situations where the defence is not available. Suppose I leave my car on the street unlocked with the keys in the ignition and it is stolen and sold by the thief. The law is that I can claim the full value from the blameless purchaser, even if he no longer has the car. This unfair common law rule is confirmed by the deliberate decision of the legislature to provide that 'Contributory negligence is no defence in proceedings founded on conversion, or on intentional trespass to goods'.[17] It was soon realised that this had to be changed so far as cheques were concerned, for it was manifestly unacceptable to make a bank liable for paying out on a cheque which the drawer had drawn so carelessly as to facilitate fraud.

By its very terms the Contributory Negligence Act applies only in tort cases. Thus it is no answer to a claim for the return of money paid by mistake that it was perfectly idiotic of the claimant to make the mistake.[18] Nor does the Act apply where the claim is based on the defendant's breach of contract,[19] unless the claim could equally well have been based on tort.[20] The strange result of this is that the careless claimant can recover full damages only where his contractor was not negligent at all. The Law Commission has made proposals.

---

[16] *Fitzgerald v Lane* [1988] 2 All ER 961.
[17] Torts (Interference with Goods) Act 1977, s 11(1).
[18] *Kelly v Solari* (1841) 152 ER 24.
[19] *Barclays Bank v Fairclough Building* [1995] 1 All ER 289.
[20] *Forsikringsaktieselskapet Vesta v Butcher* [1988] 2 All ER 43.

FURTHER OBSERVATIONS

Two further observations are in point. The first is that whenever damages are reduced in a personal injury claim, it is the claimant, an uninsured human being, who bears the loss to the extent of the reduction, rather the defendant's insurance company. Secondly, unlike damages, social security payments are not reduced by contributory negligence, and this is of some importance in that any relevant social security payments the claimant has received for the first five years will be deducted in full from his damages for lost earnings, reduced as they are by his contributory negligence, so that he may be left with little or nothing (apart from his (reduced) damages for pain and suffering and loss of amenity).

MITIGATION OF DAMAGE

The 1945 Act is concerned with the effect of the claimant having made a causal contribution to the initial harm, but there is another principle, of judicial origin, whereby the damages which may be claimed for the consequences of the initial harm may be reduced. The principle is that you cannot claim compensation for items of damage you could reasonably have avoided or for expenditure needlessly incurred, and it applies in all claims for damages, whatever their basis, though not to claims for debts. It is always called the 'duty to mitigate the damage', though of course it is not a 'duty' such that you can be sued for breach of it, any more than contributory negligence itself is a breach of duty. The courts have room to play with in determining what is reasonable and what is not. A woman who finds herself pregnant as a result of a botched sterilisation operation clearly cannot be expected to have an abortion in order to reduce the damages payable by the doctor, but in a quite different case the Court of Appeal, reversing the county court judge, held that the owner of a car which he loved could not charge the person who damaged it for the cost of repairs when the repairs cost more than it could be sold for once it was mended.[21] More recently the House of Lords dealt with a case where a builder had installed a swimming pool somewhat shallower than specified but no less valuable for that; although the customer was refused the cost of replacement as being unreasonable, he was allowed a modest sum since its depth was particularly important to him.[22] Surely no less should be

---

[21] *Darbishire v Warran* [1963] 3 All ER 310.
[22] *Ruxley Electronics v Forsyth* [1995] 3 All ER 268.

allowed to a person whose dearest chattel has been negligently wrecked, though insurance companies would deplore such a humane development.

OTHER DEFENCES

Contributory negligence is unquestionably a defence, if only a partial one: it is for the defendant to plead and prove it. There are other defences, some of which have been glanced at, but there are not many. The reason there are not many defences to a claim in negligence is that before any defence is required the claimant must have shown that the defendant behaved unreasonably in breach of duty and that this contributed to harm which was reasonably foreseeable; if all this is established, extenuation is bound to be difficult, especially if considerations of what is 'fair just and reasonable' are taken into account on the preliminary question of the duty of care. However, two defences must be considered. The first is that the claimant consented to the harmful conduct or accepted the risk of ensuing damage, the second that the claim arose out of illicit conduct on the part of the claimant. Until recently these defences were respectively known by the Latin tags *volenti non fit injuria* and *ex turpi causa non oritur actio*.

CONSENT

If the claimant has, as against the defendant, freely and lucidly accepted the risk of injury, it does not seem right for the law to shift its cost back to the defendant. The risk of not being paid for any injury is often covered by a contract between the parties. Here the Unfair Contract Terms Act 1977 comes into play and invalidates any clause in a contract or notice which purports to exempt a business, a professional, or a public authority from liability for personal injury or death negligently caused. This is doubtless because such consent is deemed to have been extracted rather than voluntarily given, as in the case of a lion-tamer in the defendant's employ.[23] As regards other types of harm, however, such a clause or notice may, if reasonable, be effective. Thus a disclaimer in a car park is likely to be upheld, though the House of Lords has held that a disclaimer attached to a valuation of a modest house does not protect the negligent valuer from a claim for economic loss.[24] As between individuals, the defence is

---

[23] Animals Act 1971, s 6(5).   [24] *Smith v Eric S Bush* [1989] 2 All ER 514.

excluded where the claimant is a passenger in the defendant's motor vehicle.[25] Can the risk be taken implicitly? It would be surprising if it could not, but the courts are evidently reluctant to apply this defence. If the court can hold that it was unreasonable of the claimant to run the risk in question, it can take refuge in the flexible, because partial, defence of contributory negligence and split the difference. Yet the defence was applied in a case where, after heavy drinking, the claimant agreed to go up in a plane piloted by his drinking partner: drunk as he was, he must have known that the defendant was incapable and was held to have taken the risk.[26] By contrast the defence was not applied where a person on remand committed suicide by seizing the opportunity provided by the negligence of the police in leaving a flap in his cell door open.[27] A clearer case of harm voluntarily espoused would be hard to imagine—this was not even a case of accepting a risk yet to eventuate, but of embracing the very situation presented by past negligence—but the House accepted the unwise concession of the police that they were under a duty to take care to prevent his committing suicide, and held the defence inapplicable where the harm was the very thing the defendants were under a duty to take care to prevent. The fact is that the courts are uneasy about landing—or leaving—people with the consequences of their deliberate choices. Whether this is consistent with personal autonomy is a question: the Court of Appeal thought not when a soldier alleged that it was a breach of the Army's duty to him to allow him to drink himself into a stupor.[28]

ILLEGALITY

Although, as we have seen, a defendant is not liable merely because his conduct was illegal, the illegal nature of the claimant's conduct may in certain circumstances bar his claim in tort, and not just in negligence. Thus when a youth riding pillion on a motorcycle on the way back from a club urged the driver, whom he knew to be unlicensed, to drive recklessly on the highway and was injured in consequence, his claim (which could not be defeated by *volenti non fit injuria* by reason of the Road Traffic Act) was dismissed on the ground that his injury arose out of his distinctly illegal behaviour.[29] As against that, a burglar who was shot, though not aimed at, by a householder whose shed he was trying, yet again, to burgle

[25] Road Traffic Act 1988, s 149(3).   [26] *Morris v Murray* [1990] 3 All ER 801.
[27] *Reeves v Commissioner of Police* [1999] 3 All ER 897.
[28] *Barrett v Ministry of Defence* [1995] 3 All ER 87.
[29] *Pitts v Hunt* [1990] 3 All ER 344.

was awarded damages, subject to contributory negligence (!). This decision caused public outrage, but no matter: the House of Lords had seen fit to hold, in a case concerned with property rights, that it is of no concern to the law whether or not a decision causes public outrage,[30] the public presumably having no sense of what is fair, just, and reasonable. Even so, the Court of Appeal has subsequently held that a hunt saboteur who violently assaulted a farmer had no claim when struck a blow which proved unexpectedly serious in its effects, on the alternative grounds that the blow was subjectively not unreasonable or that the claimant's claim was barred by his illegal conduct in provoking it;[31] a claimant who killed a total stranger in a Tube station failed in his suit against the hospital which allowed him to be at large;[32] and a person lawfully arrested who broke away from the police and threw himself out of a window had his claim against the police rejected. In this last case, however, Sedley LJ wished to split the difference, and said 'It is clear since the passing of the Law Reform (Contributory Negligence) Act 1945 that the power to apportion liability . . . has afforded a far more appropriate tool for doing justice than the blunt instrument of turpitude'.[33] One can see, therefore, that just as tortious negligence is taking over from the other torts, so contributory negligence is trying to eclipse the complete defences.

---

[30] *Tinsley v Milligan* [1993] 3 All ER 65.
[31] *Cross v Kirkby* [2000] TLR 268.
[32] *Clunis v Camden and Islington Health Authority* [1998] 3 All ER 180.
[33] *Vellino v Chief Constable* [2001] EWCA Civ 1249, para 55.

9

Trespass

TRESPASS AND NEGLIGENCE

The tort of negligence tells us when a person has to pay compensation for harm he has caused without meaning to. The role of the tort of trespass is quite different. Its very important function is to protect and vindicate the basic rights of the citizen against deliberate, even well-meaning, invasion, whether or not any damage is caused: every positive act which directly invades one of those basic rights is trespassory, and leads to liability unless it is justified in law. It is to the tort of trespass one must look if one wants to learn whether a doctor may sterilise an adult patient of very feeble intellect,[1] whether the police may stop or arrest a person in the street or enter a private house or garden,[2] whether people may peacefully gather on the highway without obstructing it[3] and so on. The questions raised and answered in this chapter are a good deal more interesting than the question whether one insurance company has to pay another for accidental damage to property: we are here concerned with rights and liberties. When are you entitled to strike another? When may you seize something in his possession? If negligence law says (after the event) what you should not have done, trespass law lets you know (in advance) what you may do by way of—to use a phrase—direct action.

THE DIFFERENCE IN FUNCTIONS

The functions of the two torts being so different, it is not surprising that their rules are fundamentally divergent. In negligence it must be shown that the defendant owed the claimant a legal duty to take care, whereas trespass is not, according to the House of Lords, a breach of duty at all.[4] In negligence the defendant must have behaved unreasonably whereas this is not a requirement in trespass. In negligence, but not in trespass, the

---

[1] *Re F, F v West Berkshire Health Authority* [1989] 2 All ER 545.
[2] Police and Criminal Evidence Act 1984.
[3] *DPP v Jones* [1999] 2 All ER 257.   [4] *Stubbings v Webb* [1993] 1 All ER 322.

defendant may be liable for an omission. In negligence the defendant is liable for the foreseeable consequences of his conduct, even if indirect, but not for direct consequences which were not foreseeable; in trespass the defendant is liable only for the direct consequences of his act, whether foreseeable or not. In negligence actual damage must always be shown, and there may be liability where the damage is merely financial, whereas in trespass there is no need to show any damage, only the invasion of a protected right, all those rights being physical in nature. This seems like legal schizophrenia, but the difference in rules is explicable by the difference in roles. To try to effect a synthesis is just a waste of time, but awareness of the difference is vital if negligence is not to take over completely, with unfortunate effects on the rights of the citizen.

This great difference between the requirements of claims in negligence and in trespass makes it desirable to try to delimit their respective areas of operation. One attempt emerges from a decision of 1959 in which the plaintiff asserted simply that the defendant had shot him, without indicating whether the shooting was deliberate or careless. As an allegation of a positive act directly invading the plaintiff's person, this looked like a good claim in trespass, but the judge held that the pleadings were insufficient: the plaintiff must allege and prove either that the defendant meant to hit him or was negligent, that is, should have realised that he might well hit him.[5] This dichotomy of intention/negligence is not really satisfactory, however, since in trespass the intention need relate only to the invasion, whereas negligence relates to the damage.

More illuminating, though less explicit, is a later case in the Court of Appeal. Peter Wilson and Ian Pringle, both 13 years old, were walking away from a mathematics class when Ian decided to pounce on Peter. He pulled on the bag slung over Peter's shoulder, and in falling to the ground Peter broke his leg. When Peter sued him (!) Ian pleaded that this was just normal horseplay, but the judge accepted Peter's objection that this was no answer to his claim, which explicitly alleged a trespass, and ordered an inquiry into damages. On Ian's appeal, the Court of Appeal sent the case back for a finding whether the pouncing was 'hostile', on the view that no unconsented touching could constitute the trespass of battery unless it were 'hostile'.[6] Now since it is certainly not the law that an unconsented touching is trespassory only if it is 'hostile' (think of the unwelcome kiss!), one must ask why the Court of Appeal said it was. Surely it was because this was a 'broken leg' case, a claim for compensation for actual

[5] *Fowler v Lanning* [1959] 1 All ER 290.   [6] *Wilson v Pringle* [1986] 2 All ER 440.

harm, not a claim for vindication of his rights by a schoolboy with a grievance. The courts know about broken leg cases, for they hear such claims every day, at least in the county courts, and know what law applies to them: no liability unless the defendant behaved unreasonably and the harm was foreseeable. Here, by contrast, the defendant alleged that his conduct was perfectly normal, and there had been no finding that the harm was a foreseeable consequence of what he did. One can conclude that the distinction between negligence as a tort and trespass should be in functional, not formal terms: are we compensating for harm or vindicating rights? This is important, for when rights are to be vindicated, neither damage to the claimant nor fault in the defendant is relevant to the claim, though the first may affect the remedy and the second the defence.

THE PROTECTED RIGHTS

The rights protected by the tort of trespass are few in number: freedom of movement, bodily integrity, and property in one's possession. The names given to the invasions of these rights are respectively 'false imprisonment', 'assault' and 'battery', and trespass to land and goods. Note that it is the physical aspect which dominates: freedom of *movement*, not belief or expression; *corporeal* integrity, not mental tranquillity; *possession*, that is, the physical relation between person and thing, not *ownership*, which is an economic relationship. Much more numerous are the rights conferred by the European Convention and protected by the Human Rights Act 1998. They include, for example, the right to respect for private and family life, freedom of expression, marriage and, very importantly, procedural rights to a fair trial as well as to an inquiry into every violent death, especially in Ulster or custody—an invention of the Strasbourg court not reflected in the common law.[7] The structure of the Convention is very like that of trespass law—the rights are specified first, followed by a list of the possible justifications for invading them. As in trespass it is easier for the claimant to establish the invasion of his rights than it is for the defendant—in Strasbourg always the State, in Britain a public authority—to justify it; and just as a justification for a trespass will fail if it is exercised in an unreasonable manner, so in Strasbourg the justification will fail if its exercise is disproportionate or discriminatory. But there are important differences, too. Whereas the victim of an unjustified trespass has an automatic right to damages, damages are by no

---

[7] *Re McKerr* [2004] UKHL 12.

means always available under the Act—a fact which led Lord Bingham to state with less than his usual caution that 'the 1998 Act is not a tort statute'[8]; whereas trespass law binds private citizens as well as officials and public bodies, only the latter are directly required by the Act to act compatibly with the rights conferred; and whereas trespass requires a positive act which directly invades the protected right, Strasbourg is increasingly imposing duties on public authorities (which includes the courts) to prevent such invasions by private third parties.

FALSE IMPRISONMENT

Liberty is very strongly protected by the common law, as the remedy of *habeas corpus* indicates. Whenever a person is confined, whether by physical means or the threat of them, so that he cannot move outside an area prescribed by the defendant, this is in law an 'imprisonment', presumptively trespassory. It seems therefore that the victim of rape could complain of imprisonment as well as battery, as could the victim of a knock-out blow, since the claimant need not even be aware of his confinement. It is true that both these victims could sue for battery, but a claim for imprisonment is better, since it entitles one to trial by jury.[9]

BATTERY AND ASSAULT

Corporeal integrity is protected against direct physical invasion by the tort of battery. Physical impact is traditionally required, and this requirement should not be weakened, as was done when it was suggested that it might be a battery to take a flashlight photograph of a person.[10] It is quite unnecessary to extend the scope of trespass because if any actual harm is done, a claim in negligence will surely lie, and if the act is repeated, a claim for harassment, including an injunction. The requisite physical impact need not be by a fist: it is a battery if I throw something at you (and hit you) or get my dog to bite you. Rather eccentrically, however, it is said to be a trespass to the person, called 'assault', to cause a person to fear an immediate attack, and in criminal cases this has been extended very far so as to include heavy breathing on the telephone.[11] Again, negligence or harassment is available here, and there is no need to extend the tort of trespass. Indeed, assault is really just a justification for battery. In a famous seventeenth-century case, just after the Restoration, one bravo

---

[8] *R (Greenfield) v Secretary of State* [2005] UKHL 14.
[9] Supreme Court Act 1981, s 69.   [10] *Kaye v Robertson* [1991] FSR 62.
[11] *R v Ireland* [1997] 4 All ER 225.

poked another in the eye with his sword after the latter had said, in response to some disobliging words, 'If it were not assize-time I would not take such language' and the answer to the question whether the defendant was liable for what was manifestly a battery depended on whether the plaintiff was guilty of an assault.[12] It was held that although the plaintiff had put his hand on the hilt of his sword, he was not an assailant, since what he said neutralised the aggressive nature of what he did. Note the roles of the parties: it was not, as is often suggested, the *plaintiff* who was complaining of assault—it would have been very unmanly of a Restoration stud to complain of *not* being hit; the plaintiff was complaining of an actual battery—he had been blinded—and the assault point was raised by the defendant, for if the plaintiff were an assailant, the defendant could justify his battery as being in self-defence.

TRESPASS TO PROPERTY

A distinct problem is raised by the protection of *property*, whether goods or land, land being what laymen think of whenever they hear the word 'trespass' ('Trespassers will. . .'). Whereas it is clear that only the person confined or battered can claim for false imprisonment or battery, several different parties, such as the owner, the possessor, and others, may have an interest in a piece of property. There is therefore a problem about 'title to sue'. The aspect of property which is protected by the law of trespass is its possession, the physical aspect. Here again the courts have tended to extend the scope of the tort by allowing a suit in trespass by those not actually in possession at the time of the alleged act, but having only a right to obtain or resume possession. The incantation is muttered: 'As against a wrongdoer, title is as good as possession'. This is absurd because one cannot tell whether the defendant was a wrongdoer until one has ascertained that the claimant, as the person wronged, is an appropriate person to sue. This development, unfortunate as it is, was doubtless necessitated by procedural difficulties regarding the repossession of land, but it was extended much further when the Court of Appeal very dubiously held that demonstrators who were determined to stop the construction of a new runway at Manchester Airport could be evicted as trespassers by a construction firm which had never been on the property and had only a contractual right to enter it.[13]

With regard to moveable property there is no reason to let anyone sue

---

[12] *Tuberville v Savage* (1669) 86 ER 284.
[13] *Dutton v Manchester Airport* [1999] 2 All ER 675.

in trespass except the person in actual physical possession at the time of the act impugned: the tort of conversion is available to those who are entitled to possession, whether or not they actually have it. Like battery to the person, trespass to property requires physical contact: it is a trespass to affix a clamp to a car, but not to lock one's gate so as to prevent its exit (needless to say, there is no false imprisonment of chattels). Again one need not actually go on another's land in order to be a trespasser: it is a trespass to dig under the land of another or to construct anything on one's land which protrudes into the airspace over that of one's neighbour.[14] The fact that it is a trespass to put, throw, or build anything on another's land makes trespass a suitable forum for the resolution of boundary disputes between neighbours.[15] But surely it was an improper extension of the law when a judge held that the master of staghounds was liable in trespass whenever 'by his failure to exercise proper control over them he caused them to enter' the tiny 'sanctuaries' sporadically established on Exmoor by the League Against Cruel Sports?[16]

DEFENCES

All the claimant has to do to make a claim in trespass is to allege 'You touched me', 'You came on my land', or 'You clamped my car'. But such conduct is very often justifiable: the defendant may be entitled, authorised, empowered, or whatever to do what he did. If he can prove it, he will escape liability. Such entitlements (we can call them 'rights' if we like, and irritate the jurisprudes) may arise either at common law or under statute, and they are of great interest, since they tell us when we may invade the basic rights of others. Rights, after all, are not inviolable; it is rather that violations must be justified. As one would expect, the range of situations in which one is entitled to invade the rights of others depends on the strength of the right being invaded. A transitory trespass to land can be paid off by the tender of a tiny sum, but that could hardly apply where the trespass was an infringement of liberty. The primacy of liberty of movement is indicated by the existence of *habeas corpus* proceedings (if we may still use the term), by the provision in the European Convention (art 5(5)) that damages *must* be awarded when a person has been unlawfully arrested or detained, and by the fact that the claimant for false

---

[14] *Anchor Brewhouse Developments v Berkley House* (1987) 38 BLR 82.
[15] *Burns v Morton* [1999] 3 All ER 646.
[16] *League Against Cruel Sports v Scott* [1985] 2 All ER 489.

imprisonment (including arrest) is entitled to trial by jury, whereas the claimant for assault and battery is not. This must not be taken too far, however. Parents must not beat their children, but need not let them roam the streets, and convicts may be imprisoned, but not bastinadoed.

FALSE IMPRISONMENT

Apart from children, those most commonly confined are suspects, convicts, and the mentally ill. Arrest of a suspect by warrant is justified by the order of a judicial officer, as is the detention on remand of a person charged or the imprisonment of a person convicted. A warrant is not, however, always required for an arrest. The powers of the police are carefully laid down in the Police and Criminal Evidence Act 1984, as extended by the Serious Organised Crime and Police Act 2005, ss 110 ff, and it is for them to show that the conditions have been satisfied. At common law arrest is simply an instance of imprisonment, specific only that it is a constraint imposed in connection with a criminal investigation, and though the Convention on Human Rights treats arrest and detention alike, our courts have recently drawn a distinction between them.

In one case a person sentenced to two years' imprisonment was due, according to a statute as then interpreted, to be released on 18 November. On 15 November a court held that the previous interpretation of the statute was erroneous, with the result that she should have been released on 17 September. The claimant now claimed damages for her detention from 17 September until 15 November, when she was actually set free. The Court of Appeal's award of £5,000 by way of damages was upheld by a unanimous House of Lords: given that her detention was now recognized not to have been lawful, it was irrelevant that the prison governor could not be blamed at all.[17] Nor could the police be blamed when they arrested Ms Percy for the umpteenth time for breach of a bye-law whose validity they had no reason to doubt. The bye-law was later held invalid, yet her claim for false arrest (= imprisonment) was dismissed by the Court of Appeal.[18] Worse still, the House of Lords has recently held that the police may justify arresting the wrong person provided he is the person named in the warrant.[19] These decisions illustrate how the salutary rules of trespass are being invaded by negligence-type thinking: the police were excused because what they did was perfectly reasonable, they

---

[17] *R v Governor of Brickhill Prison, ex p Evans (No 2)* [2000] 4 All ER 15.
[18] *Percy v Hall* [1996] 4 All ER 523.
[19] *McGrath v Chief Constable* [2001] 4 All ER 334.

were not at fault. But rights must be protected even against reasonable conduct which infringes them, the citizen should not have his liberty restrained for doing what was not an offence or under a warrant intended for someone else, and in any case the constables were not going to pay out of their own pocket, for the money comes out of public funds, as it should when a public body has invaded the citizen's rights.

BATTERY

When may you lay hands on a person without his consent? In self-defence, obviously, and obviously not in retaliation: the distinction is drawn, as we have seen, in terms of whether the party battered was an assailant, so you cannot thump someone just for being unforgivably rude. In order to regain your liberty you may use quite serious force, but you have to be actually (and improperly) confined, not just obstructed: you must, if possible, go round a person who is in your way, and not push past, unless there is no reasonable alternative.

This emerges from a very instructive Victorian case.[20] An entrepreneur had set up seats within an enclosure on one side of Hammersmith Bridge, with a view to charging spectators to sit there and watch the regatta impending on the Thames below. This was clearly a public nuisance, since the entrepreneur had no authority to block the highway, and it irritated Bird, whose fixed habit it was always to use the pavement on that side of the bridge, so he climbed over the fence into the enclosure with a view to climbing out the other end. Jones, an employee of the entrepreneur, blocked his way, and invited him to use the other sidewalk. After a period of stasis Bird tried to push past Jones, who promptly gave him in charge to a policeman for breach of the peace. Bird was locked up in a police cage for the night. On the (correct) assumption that Bird had been arrested by Jones, the question was whether the arrest was justified, as it would be if Bird was guilty of a breach of the peace in unjustifiably battering him in trying to push past. Bird argued that his battery was justified, on the basis that Jones was imprisoning him by blocking his passage and he was entitled to use force to regain his liberty. He would indeed have been so entitled had he been imprisoned, but the court held that he had not been imprisoned at all, only prevented from going in the direction he wanted. In other words, you can use force to get out but not to get past. Note that Bird would not be liable for trespassing to the fence he climbed over: it was a nuisance, and you are entitled to abate nuisances,

---

[20] *Bird v Jones* (1845) 115 ER 668.

if they are things; not if they are people. Very sensible, too. However, there was a furious dissent by a judge who clearly thought that the citizen was entitled to enforce his right of passage: his fury would know no bounds if he knew of the appallingly negative attitude of our present courts towards self-help, for, as the reader will appreciate, self-help is exactly what the defences to trespass are about, and the courts, which fancy that they are there to help people, are very unhappy when people try to help themselves.

That we are concerned with rights and not faults emerges from another illuminating case. Sir John Townley had been behaving so oddly that it looked as if he should be locked up. At that time a person could be lawfully locked up only if two doctors had signed the relevant form, and so two doctors, one of whom had signed and the other had not, went with a constable to Sir John's house. When he withdrew upstairs to his bedroom, the policeman gently approached him to calm him down and was struck a severe blow for his pains.[21] Leaving aside the question of the reasonableness of the blow (struck in defence of his liberty by a person at home with his back to the wall), the question whether the suspected madman was guilty of battery or not depended *exclusively* on whether the second signature was on the form or not, a matter of which neither party knew anything. If the second signature was there, the policeman was entitled to lay hands on the suspected lunatic and the latter was not entitled to defend himself; if it was not, the positions were reversed.

Force may be used to prevent or stop a breach of the peace.[22] This is quite distinct from arrest: breach of the peace is not a serious offence, merely something that should be put an end to. In a public place such force may, and perhaps should, be used by any citizen, not just a constable.[23] It used to be the law that a constable might enter private premises if he reasonably believed that a breach of the peace was imminent there, but now, in deference to Strasbourg, if the premises are a home the constable's action must in addition be 'proportionate' to the risk of disorder.[24]

Force may also be used to protect property. Trespassers may be evicted. This, indeed, is surely why trespass to land is independent of fault: if you have no right to be on another's land, whatever you may think, you are liable to be evicted, and since you can only be evicted if you are a trespasser, a trespasser is defined as anyone who cannot justify his

---

[21] *Townley v Rushworth* (1963) 62 LGR 95.
[22] Police and Criminal Evidence Act 1984, s 25(6).
[23] *Albert v Lavin* [1981] 3 All ER 878.
[24] *McLeod v United Kingdom* (1999) 27 EHRR 493.

presence on the land. It is perhaps a pity that the burglar, the mischievous child, and the bemused wayfarer are all classed as trespassers, for they should surely be treated differently, at any rate as regards their safety. All of them are liable to be shown off the land, however. Eviction must be carried out with the minimum necessary force and damage: you must ask the trespasser to leave before pushing him out, and you must push him out the door not the window. You cannot, of course, detain him, because it is only in order to disencumber your land of the unentitled intruder that you are entitled to use force at all, and justifications for trespasses must be in line with their purpose.

If one may extrude a trespasser, may one scare him away? That is what the aged occupier tried to do in *Revill v Newbery* when thugs were approaching the hut in which he was crouching.[25] He fired a shotgun through a hole in the door, not aiming at anyone, and hit one of the burglars. He was held liable, to popular indignation and the approval of the Law Commission. These are cases where force is used by a person in actual occupation of premises on which the trespasser intrudes. In the interests of avoiding public disorder there are restrictions on the use of force to evict an established trespasser or squatter. Force may be used to enter premises in order to evict a trespasser only by a person who previously resided or is entitled to reside there. The police may act if called by such a person, but all others, and legal persons in particular, must seek a court order.[26] Note that here the legislature draws distinctions according to the nature of the premises being occupied—home or office?—something that the common law is incapable of doing, just as it seems incapable of overtly distinguishing between the different classes of persons trespassing there.

One cannot be evicted as a trespasser if one has a right to be on the premises, though of course when one is lawfully on another's premises one must respect 'No Entry' or 'Private' notices on particular parts of them, and equivalent implicit restrictions. Many persons are entitled to walk or drive over the land of another even without his consent. Such a 'right of way' may be either private, an easement, or public. There are frequent disputes over what is permitted under a private right of way. Then there are public rights of way. The public's right to enter private land has been greatly extended by the Countryside and Rights of Way Act 2000: 'Any person is entitled . . . to enter and remain on any access land

---

[25] [1996] 1 All ER 291.
[26] Criminal Justice and Public Order Act 1994, ss 72, 74.

for the purposes of open-air recreation, if and so long as (a) he does so without breaking any wall, fence, hedge, stile or gate, and (b) he observes the general restrictions in Schedule 2 . . .'. Note that the right is limited by the purpose for which it is granted—recreation in this case. A like limitation used to attach to the exercise of those public rights of way which we know as highways: they could be used only for the purpose for which they were (taken to have been) granted, namely passage, moving along it to one's destination, or crossing it to get to the other side. In a recent decision, however, the House of Lords held by a bare majority that people were entitled to use the highway for any reasonable purpose, such as meeting and gathering there, provided no obstruction was caused to the passage of others.[27]

PROPERTY

We have seen that the occupier of premises may evict an unlawful intruder, by force, if need be. He can also evict a thing, for he is entitled to have his land free of intrusions. But may he clamp a trespassing car? The question is difficult because far from removing a car, clamping it keeps it there. But there were automotive chattels long before the motor car was invented, and at common law if cattle trespassed the occupier could not only shoo them away, but might, if he preferred, detain them. This common law remedy of *distress damage feasant* was judicially extended to inanimate objects (such as a railway engine) and though it was abolished by statute in 1971, it was abolished only as to animals. In principle, therefore, *distress damage feasant* was available as a defence by the occupier who clamped a car. Indeed, one member of the Court of Appeal so held in *Arthur v Anker* in 1996, but the majority decided that detention was licit under this remedy only where the vehicle was causing damage other than merely occupying space.[28] They held instead that the trespasser would be deemed to consent to the risk of clamping (thereby providing a defence) if a prohibitory sign were visible, the charge reasonable, and release swift (conditions which could not be applied to *distress damage feasant*). This was a clever fiction. A later Court of Appeal, however, failed to understand that the consent in such cases is *deemed* to have been given—no one *in fact* agrees to being clamped—and held in *Vine v Waltham Forest LBC* that if the trespasser did not see the sign he could not really have consented to being clamped[29]—as if the reality of his consent were of any

[27] *DPP v Jones* [1999] 2 All ER 830.   [28] *Arthur v Anker* [1996] 3 All ER 783.
[29] *Vine v Waltham Forest LBC* [2000] 4 All ER 169.

interest whatever, as if any enraged driver will admit to having seen a sign, and as if the courts were as competent lie-detectors as they claim. The courts having thus gutted the clever remedy they themselves had invented, Parliament intervened, providing originally that it was unlawful for anyone to clamp or permit the clamping of a trespassing car unless the clamper had a licence to do so.[30] Now, thankfully, such conduct is unlawful only if a charge is to be made for the release[31], so it is to be hoped that the common law as laid down by *Arthur v Anker* will be applied: clamping being a trespass to the car with a defence of deemed consent if release is facilitated. *Vine* is ripe for overruling.

Power is often abused, alas, and that is true also of the occupier's power to exclude others and their property from his premises. The dog in the manger is a familiar and unadmired figure. Suppose your neighbour needs to come on to your land to do necessary repairs to his adjoining house? Can you prevent him, and evict him if he insists? The common law said you could.[32] Now we have a statute which permits your neighbour to enter your land for that purpose provided that he has gone through rather a cumbrous procedure.[33] Likewise an occupier might make unnecessary difficulties about party walls; again there is a recent statutory provision.[34] Suppose a kid's cricket ball gets knocked into the neighbour's garden yet again; may he go in and fetch it? Certainly not. Nor need the neighbour be at the trouble of coming to the front gate and handing over the cricket ball, though he must not use it as if it were his own (that would be a 'conversion'). Here, as in the clamping situation, we see a standoff between the rights of possessors of chattels and occupiers of land.

CONSENT

An act to which one has consented cannot be treated as invading one's rights (unless those rights are inalienable). This seems self-evident: to use a language now forbidden, *volenti non fit injuria*. If the person affected is incapable of giving valid consent, there may be a question whose consent is relevant. And there may be a question whether apparent consent is actual or whether consent given by a person apparently, but not actually, authorised to give it on behalf of another is sufficient. There may be problems about the withdrawal of consent.

---

[30] Private Security Industry Act 2001, Sch 2 para 3.
[31] SI 2005/224.   [32] *Collins v Renison* (1754) 96 ER 830.
[33] Access to Neighbouring Land Act 1992.   [34] Party Wall, etc Act 1996.

It is clear that the use of a scalpel by a surgeon or a hypodermic needle by an anaesthetist constitutes a direct positive invasion of the patient's bodily integrity. The patient has usually consented to the invasive treatment, but if it goes wrong without any negligence in the operation itself, the patient may want to argue that his consent was invalid because he didn't know what he was consenting to. Some jurisdictions hold that respect for the autonomy of the patient requires that the doctor fully explain the implications of the proposed line of treatment, or face the prospect that the court may hold the operation trespassory for want of 'informed consent'. The English courts have not followed this line, and have been criticised for doing what common lawyers usually do, treating it as a question of the defendant's duty rather than the plaintiff's right, as a matter of negligence rather than trespass.[35] Accordingly, while the doctor must answer any questions put to him, he need not volunteer information unless that is required by approved medical practice, subject to marginal control by the courts. Furthermore, it must appear that the patient would not, if properly informed, have proceeded with the operation—to which we must add 'there and then', in order to accommodate the correct decision in *Chester v Afshar* (above p 89), where the tension between the claimant's right and the defendant's duty was particularly prominent.

Not everyone has land to occupy, but those who do should be encouraged by the law to permit others to cross it, and not act like the dog in the manger. To an extent the law actually discourages such sociable generosity, since the occupier of business premises who permits people to enter them lays himself open to suit if they are injured, and he cannot exclude personal or vicarious liability unless they are permitted to be there simply for recreational or educational purposes independent of the business and the injury results from the dangerous state of the premises.[36] It would be an even greater discouragement if the occupier were not allowed to withdraw his consent. This he may do, on reasonable notice, if the permission was just a favour, but if it was part of a deal the matter is more complex. In 1915 the Court of Appeal held, by a majority, that the patron of a cinema who, having paid for his ticket, refused to leave during the show and was physically evicted could claim substantial damages for trespass to his person: the cinema operator could not turn the patron into a trespasser by withdrawing his consent in breach

---

[35] *Sidaway v Bethlem Royal Hospital* [1985] 1 All ER 643.
[36] Unfair Contract Terms Act 1977, s 1(3)(b).

of contract.[37] In this respect one's home would, one hopes, be treated differently from a cinema.

NECESSITY

Sometimes people are unable to consent to an invasion which would be in their interests, perhaps because they are unconscious or unaware of a pressing danger or too feeble-minded to be able to consent or dissent. Trespassory invasions under such circumstances may well be justified under the heading of necessity. This was the case where the doctors wanted to sterilise a mental patient who would have been quite incapable of dealing with pregnancy, parturition, or maternity; even in such a case the intervention is lawful, one member of the House of Lords saying that it would be intolerable if the doctors could be sued in trespass if they acted and in negligence if they failed to do so.[38] The defence of necessity was used again by the House of Lords in a case where a mental patient had been informally admitted to a hospital and arguably detained there,[39] but the Strasbourg Court, noting that the concept of 'deprivation of liberty' in the Convention was wider than that of 'false imprisonment' at common law, held that the common law defence of necessity did not contain adequate safeguards and that the decision of the House of Lords therefore put the United Kingdom in breach of its treaty obligations.[40] Necessity certainly does not justify force-feeding a sane person, for a sane person is entitled to refuse medical treatment even if it is necessary to keep him alive. This is required by respect for the autonomy of the individual, though the courts do not always resist the temptation to treat as insane those who in their view have acted very unreasonably.

THE RIGHT TO TRESPASS

If there is a threat that a trespass will be repeated or continued, the claimant may well seek an injunction to stop it. The court need not grant it, since the remedy is discretionary. If the court could grant an injunction and declines to do so, it may award a sum of damages instead. This effectually legitimates future trespasses of the sort. It amounts to judicial expropriation of the victim. The courts deny this, and proceed to imprison

[37] *Hurst v Picture Theatres* [1915] 1 KB 1.
[38] *Re F, F v West Berks HA* [1989] 2 All ER 545.
[39] *R v Bournewood Community and Mental Health NHS Trust, ex p L* [1999] AC 458.
[40] *HL v UK* (App No 45508/99) (2005) 40 EHRR 32.

for contempt the property-owner who continues to take a sledge-hammer to a building which admittedly encroaches on his property.[41]

THE RIGHTS OF TRESPASSERS

Trespassers do not lose their rights to personal safety. As we have seen, the occupier may not deliberately harm the trespasser; as to unintended harm the occupier was not liable at common law unless his negligence was so extreme as to show an inhumane disregard for the trespasser's safety. This was modified by the House of Lords when an infant trespassed on to an electrified railway line,[42] and a statute intended to clarify the law was passed in 1984.[43] The trespasser can now sue if he suffers personal injury from a danger against which the occupier failed to offer the appropriate protection, supposing that the occupier knew or had reason to know of the danger and the fact that the trespasser would probably be exposed to it.

Determined squatters even got to own the premises on which they trespassed long enough,[44] until the Strasbourg Court held, by a bare majority, that the Act of Parliament which permitted this was incompatible with the protection afforded to possessions (sic) by the First Protocol to the European Convention.[45] It is still, however, the law that by continued crossing of another's land one can acquire a right to do so (easement), provided that the occupier is aware of what one is doing and neither consents nor objects.[46] These provisos may seem odd, but they are quite rational, for their effect is to encourage people to be generous with their permission (which can always be withdrawn) and prejudices only those who know their rights are being infringed and do nothing about it.

---

[41] *Burton v Winters* [1993] 3 All ER 847.
[42] *Herrington v British Railways Board* [1972] 1 All ER 749.
[43] Occupier's Liability Act 1984.
[44] *J.A. Pye (Oxford) v Graham* [2003] AC 419.
[45] *J.A. Pye (Oxford) v United Kingdom* (App No 44302/02) [2005] 3 EGLR 1.
[46] *Mills v Silver* [1991] 1 All ER 449.

10

Nuisance

The tort of trespass vindicates rights, as we have seen, and the tort of negligence offers damages as compensation for harm. The tort of nuisance does both: it can be invoked whether you are complaining that a fire from next door destroyed your house or that the noise infringes your right to sleep. This dual role does not make nuisance any easier to understand, given that rights must be protected even if no damage has been suffered and no fault committed, whereas harm is generally compensable only if due to fault of some kind. Accordingly, the question whether liability 'in nuisance' is strict or not is one which can be endlessly and pointlessly debated.

Trespass and negligence have this in common, however, that they both cover interests in all physical property, land and chattels alike. Nuisance, on the other hand, is concerned exclusively with land, just as the tort of conversion deals only with moveables. But even this does not make nuisance any easier to understand, for whereas negligence protects only the physical integrity of land and buildings, and trespass only the right to undisturbed possession, nuisance embraces all the multifarious rights and interests appertaining to land, that extremely distinctive form of property whose characteristics include uniqueness, durability, fixity, contiguity, visibility, and short supply. Some such rights are natural, others must be acquired; some are absolute, others qualified; some depend on physical possession, others, such as easements, do not. One of these rights is the right to enjoy one's land; indeed, it is commonly said to be of the essence of nuisance. Analysis in terms of such a compendious right is certainly apt enough if your neighbour is making nasty smells or noises, or perhaps when a busy brothel sets up next door, but if your house is burnt down or your garden washed away in a flood it hardly seems apt to say that you are complaining of mere disamenity. However, since actual damage to the fabric of property is of interest to the law of negligence, whereas noises and smells are not, unless they are deafening or poisonous, it may be said that noises and smells are *characteristic* of nuisance law.

REMEDIES

Persons afflicted by recurrent noises and smells generally want them stopped. They seek an injunction rather than damages, welcome though an award of damages always is. Injunctions do not figure much in books on negligence, and arise in the case of trespasses only if they are repeated or continuing. Since you cannot stop an activity or situation unless it is still going on, there is a tendency, assisted by the fact that isolated smells and transient noises are unlikely to be actionable at all, to say that a nuisance (a word which confusingly denotes both the cause and its effect) must be of some duration. This has led the courts to say, absurdly enough but doubtless in response to a foolish argument from counsel, that though the damaging event, such as the escape of fire, happened only once, it nevertheless arose from a continuing state of affairs, that is, an ongoing situation on the defendant's land that was about to result in ignition. A further factor of note is that while even a continuing trespass affects only the particular occupier whose property is invaded, some nuisances may affect the whole environment: we have a category of public nuisances, but not of public trespasses. This helps to explain the very heavy involvement of local authorities in the detection and prevention of nuisances, which will be discussed shortly.

PARTIES

The claimant 'in nuisance' must have a legal right in or over the affected land.[1] The defendant usually has one, too, but this is not a legal require-ment; it results from the operation of the inverse square rule, which tells us how rapidly light and sound (and smells, too, one supposes) diminish in intensity as distance increases: put less pompously, it is generally the people next door who are the real nuisance. We may therefore take it that we are principally concerned with the relationship of neighbours, not in the figurative sense popularized by Lord Atkin in *Donoghue v Stevenson*, but real neighbours, so familiar in our daily life. As every solicitor knows, disputes between neighbours are almost as fractious, irrational, and uncompromising as disputes within the family. The law-and-economics people who say that it is immaterial how the law apportions rights and liabilities in this area since neighbours can always contract around them have obviously never tried to get human neighbours to agree, though

---

[1] *Hunter v Canary Wharf* [1997] 2 All ER 426.

what they say may be true of limited liability companies, concerned only with money, which economists take as the model to which, in a world they suppose ideal, human beings should conform.

In order to indicate the scope of nuisance law and the distinctions which are made within it, let us leave aside for the moment the right to enjoy one's property free from intolerable irritation, and consider other matters which may affect a landowner or occupier. We start with the four elements, earth, air, fire, and water.

EARTH

If a pit is dug close to your boundary, your land may fall into it. If so, you have an automatic action against your neighbour, even if he had the digging done by an expert and it is all a great surprise: your right not to have your land collapse as a result of your neighbour's excavations is absolute.[2] Further distinctions are made: the land itself has a natural right to support, whereas buildings on it have to acquire such a right. If your house, having acquired such a right, collapses because of the defendant's activity, it matters whether he was digging or draining, for if he is draining he is apparently not liable at all, even if it is quite foreseeable that your house will fall down when the wet earth on which it stood dries up and shrinks.[3] It is quite another question if your land collapses without any action on your neighbour's part, but solely as a result of natural forces. Until recently you would have had no claim. A few years ago, however, a hotel in Yorkshire fell into the sea. This would not have happened if the defendant, who had control of the seaward strip of land, had executed its coastal protection plans. Although it did no more than King Canute to keep the sea at bay, the defendant would have been held liable were it not that this novel duty to take positive steps to secure one's neighbour's land from collapse is not absolute but qualified ('measured'), not only in relation to what is objectively reasonable but also what is subjectively appropriate, given the cost of the necessary works and the defendant's resources.[4]

AIR

Domestic premises no longer depend so much on open fires, so the absence of any right to receive an undisturbed flow of *air* is not so important. One

---

[2] *Dalton v Angus* (1881) 6 App Cas 740.
[3] *Stephens v Anglia Water Authority* [1987] 3 All ER 379.
[4] *Holbeck Hall v Scarborough Borough Council* [2000] 2 All ER 705.

is, however, entitled to relatively (but only relatively) pure air, and the neighbour will be liable if he pollutes it to an unreasonable extent by smoke, fumes, and so on. Light is different. A right to *light* has to be acquired by long enjoyment; indeed, your neighbour is entitled to block the light to your building simply in order to prevent your acquiring a right to continue having it and to maintain his right to build so as to block it.[5] Even when the right has been acquired for one's building (there is no right at all to light in one's garden),[6] it is not a right to all the light one used to have, but only to a reasonable amount:[7] there has to be an adjustment between your right to see what is going on in your house and the neighbour's right to build on his land. On the other hand, he is perfectly entitled to block your *view*, however attractive, and, probably, however ugly his building or fence.[8] Thus a distinction is drawn between seeing inside the building and seeing out of it. Even within your house your ability to watch television may be affected by your neighbour's building, as residents of the Isle of Dogs discovered to their dismay when Canary Wharf was built. The House of Lords held that this was not actionable, but indicated that there might be a different outcome if the reception was affected by an activity rather than a building.[9] Television signals, like light, have to come in, cabled or not. We have seen a distinction between seeing inside the house and seeing out of it: might there not be an analogous distinction between what comes into the house and what is kept out of it? Perhaps there is. When householders complained that their supply of gas had been interrupted by negligent excavations it was held that this was not actionable in nuisance (it was clearly not actionable in negligence), since to decide otherwise would significantly increase the scope of the tort.[10]

As to buildings, planning permission is by statute required for any alteration to a building which would raise it to a height of more than four metres if it is within two metres of the boundary and for any boundary wall or fence more than two metres high.[11] (Where planning permission is required, the neighbours may object to its being granted; if it is granted, they cannot sue the authority, unless it has actually caused a danger,[12] but

---

[5] *Allen v Flood* [1898] AC 1 at 46.
[6] *Allen v Greenwood* [1979] 1 All ER 819.
[7] *Carr-Saunders v Dick McNeil Associates* [1986] 2 All ER 888.
[8] *Aldred's Case* (1610) 77 ER 816.
[9] *Hunter v Canary Wharf* [1997] 2 All ER 426.
[10] *Anglian Water v Crawshaw Robbins* [2001] BLR 173.
[11] Town and Country Planning (General Development) Order (SI 1995/418), Sch 2.
[12] *Kane v New Forest DC* [2001] 3 All ER 914.

retain their common law rights, if any, against the occupier.)[13] But a hedge is not a wall or a fence and if your neighbour's untrimmed *cypressus Leylandii* hedge reached its 30-metre height and deprived your roses of light and you of your view there was nothing you could do, save cut off protruding limbs and sever intrusive roots, until the Anti-Social Behaviour Act 2003 (Part 8) gave the local authority power to intervene where a hedge (two or more evergreen or semi-evergreen trees or shrubs close together) is over two metres high.

FIRE

Fire spreads easily. The fabric of a building is easily insured against fire, though special cover is required for contents and consequential 'business interruption', which tort damages will meet. Liability for the escape of fire is not strict, since the occupier 'on whose estate any fire shall . . . accidentally begin' is immune to liability under an Act of 1774, when fire insurance companies were starting up. Even where the fire is wholly accidental, however, such as one started by lightning, the occupier who is aware of it must take all reasonable steps to bring it under control. Furthermore, he is answerable for a fire started or allowed to spread by the fault of anyone he allows on his premises: thus a hostel-keeper has been held liable to a neighbour for personal injury (?) suffered from a fire started by one of the lodgers smoking in a communal room.[14] Less contestably, a householder was held liable when her plumber caused a fire by mismanaging his blowtorch when trying to thaw out a frozen pipe.[15] The latter decision may, indeed, be an instance of an unacknowledged general principle that a neighbour is always liable for property damage done to his neighbour by the fault of his independent contractors, but this is far from certain: there may be a distinction, in law as in fact, between fire and flood, for in an older case a householder was held not liable for a flood due to his plumber's botched attempt to repair a leaky cistern.[16]

WATER

There is certainly a distinction between flood and drought, between too much water and too little. As to flooding, a person who interferes with the

---

[13] *Wheeler v Saunders* [1995] 2 All ER 697.
[14] *Ribee v Norrie* [2000] TLR 825.
[15] *Balfour v Barty-King* [1957] 1 All ER 156.
[16] *Blake v Woolf* [1898] 2 QB 426.

flow of water in a stream, as by damming it so as to produce a pond for his pleasure or business, may well be strictly liable if it overflows.[17] By contrast, if a flood is due not to deliberate interference but to some natural or trespassory obstruction on his land, the neighbour will be liable only if he should have removed it or done something to make the flooding less likely. If water percolates downhill on to your land, you cannot complain, but you may prevent its entering your land, even if this means sending it back to your uphill neighbour. This very proper act of self-help or self-defence may now perhaps be subject to the condition that it be reasonable to do so in order to protect your own land.[18] By contrast, your neighbour is not allowed to let rainwater drip directly from his roof on to your land, much less channel water or sewage underneath it, unless he has an easement to that effect, an easement being a right to have an otherwise impermissible effect on a neighbour's land; it may arise in several ways, by express or implied grant, presumption of grant, or prescription.

As to flooding of dwellings, one may well have no claim the first time one is flooded by water or even by sewage coming from the apartment above, unless one can prove negligence in maintenance or control.[19] If water escapes from the mains, however, the water authority is strictly liable by statute. The position is quite different where water or sewage escapes from the public drains: while the authority may be liable if it fails to keep the existing drains in order, it is not liable at common law for failing to renew a system which is suffering from overload. So held a unanimous House of Lords, reversing the Court of Appeal.[20]

As to deprivation of water, distinctions are drawn depending on whether it is in a stream or not. If the water is merely percolating through the soil, you have no right to receive it at all: it may be intercepted and abstracted with impunity, as Bradford Corporation found when, with a view to forcing a purchase, Mr Pickles prevented the water under his land from reaching their reservoir.[21] But where water in a defined channel is flowing through, alongside, or under one's land one is entitled to receive a reasonable amount from it: to put it another way, upstream occupiers may take only a reasonable amount. A distinction is drawn between abstraction and pollution, for there is liability for polluting

---

[17] *Rylands v Fletcher* (1868) LR 3 HL 330.
[18] *Palmer v Bowman* [2000] 1 All ER 22.
[19] *W H Smith v Daw* (CA, 31 March 1987).
[20] *Marcic v Thames Water Utilities* [2003] UKHL 66.
[21] *Bradford Corp v Pickles* [1895] AC 587.

even percolating water which a lower occupier would otherwise receive pure.[22]

DISTINCTIONS

These examples show that some seemingly quite narrow distinctions are drawn in cases to be found in the nuisance chapter. Are such distinctions justified? The answer depends on whether one is trying to explain the law or to solve disputes, the latter being the more important. After all, there can be little doubt whether one's house has been flooded or burnt down, whether the water was in a stream or not, and whether one is trying to see out of one's building or see within it. Very occasionally, it is true, there may be a borderline case, as where the defendant forced hot water into his land in order to pump up the salt thus liquefied into brine. Was he draining or digging?[23] The fact that the Court of Appeal in that case found the distinction absurd indicates our current preference for generalization over distinctions, even distinctions which are obvious, simple, and useful. Consider damage done by trees. The law used to be clear: if the roots of my tree knocked down your house (by sucking up the water and drying out your subsoil) then I was liable, no questions asked, but if the branch of my tree fell on your greenhouse, I was liable only if I should have realised that this might well occur and should have prevented it. Now, however, the rules have been 'harmonised', and I am liable for the damage done by my tree roots only if I am in some way at fault.[24] A single opinion in the House of Lords has confirmed this development, with two glosses: first, that suit may be brought by an owner who repairs damage done before he bought the property, and secondly, that the victim must notify the owner of the tree which was doing the damage.[25]

It is not clear that this development is advantageous; the distinction between root and branch caused no practical problems, the distinction between what is visible above ground and what is invisible underground is not a trivial one, and it hardly conduces to neighbourly relations if you have to show that your neighbour was at fault, the more so since the exposure to harm from these causes is perfectly mutual. The change may be seen as linked to a general trend from a position where the occupier was strictly liable for the damage done by any activity of his, but not liable

[22] *Cambridge Water Co v Eastern Counties Leather* [1994] 1 All ER 53.
[23] *Lotus v British Soda Co* [1971] 1 All ER 265.
[24] *Solloway v Hampshire CC* [1981] 79 LGR 449.
[25] *Delaware Mansions v Westminster CC* [2001] 4 All ER 737.

for inactivity, to a position where he may be liable for failing to protect his neighbour when he reasonably could have done so (Lord Atkin and Lord Wilberforce, the proponents of negligence law, leading the campaign on this point) and may not be liable for damage due to his activity unless he or his people were somehow at fault.

FAILURE TO ACT

Where the defendant is charged with failing to protect his neighbour, fault is clearly necessary, and seems increasingly to be treated as sufficient. The line of development leading to the case of the hotel which fell into the sea is clear. First it was held that the occupier was liable for a flood due to the misplacing, by persons who had no right to be on the land at all, of a grid in a culvert; the defendants were said to have 'adopted' the nuisance, with the suggestion that they had done something positive, whereas, being monks, they had done nothing whatever, and doubtless had not even noticed the risk, though they could have done so.[26] Next was a fire case: when a tree in the outback was struck by lightning and set aflame, the aged though muscular occupier, having taken professional advice, very sensibly felled it, but then decided to let it burn itself out. He was held liable when a wind arose and fanned the embers into a disastrous fire.[27] Next, and worst, was a decision of the Court of Appeal. In the dry summer of 1976 a hill owned by the National Trust started to crumble and bits of it fell on the plaintiff's vintage house nestling underneath it. Although the Trust had done nothing whatever to cause the fall of earth, it had to meet the bill for sticking its hill together again, as it was required by court order to do. One of the judges rightly doubted whether it is reasonable to make an occupier pay to protect a neighbour from the effect of gravity on the natural condition of land, even if his resources are to be taken into account.[28] Indeed it was only because this anomalous duty of care is said to be a 'measured' one that the Court of Appeal was able to avoid awarding damages to the Holbeck Hall Hotel which fell into the sea off Scarborough after the local authority had failed to proceed with very expensive coastal protection works. In a subsequent case with considerable implications for public expenditure, these twentieth-century decisions were relied on by the Court of Appeal as justifying their view

[26] *Sedleigh–Denfield v O'Callagan* [1940] 3 All ER 349.
[27] *Goldman v Hargrave* [1966] 2 All ER 989.
[28] *Leakey v National Trust* [1966] 2 All ER 989.

that Victorian precedents to the effect that a sewerage authority was under no common law duty to replace overloaded drains were now obsolete. The House of Lords, however, was of a different view: Lord Hoffmann made it clear that the old authorities are 'not about general principles of the law of nuisance. They are cases about sewers' and still good law.[29] It is refreshing to find sensible distinctions being maintained against the relentless determination to treat unlike cases alike under the umbrella of an abstract rule.

Another case where the defendant was held liable for the effects of gravity was where pigeons resting or roosting on its bridge over Balham High Street fouled the highway beneath it.[30] As a claim in private nuisance it was problematical, since the claimant highway authority neither owned nor possessed the highway, but it was argued and accepted that this was a public nuisance for which the local authority had statutory power to sue, on the basis that the situation on the defendant's property was prejudicial to the public at large in their use of the highway. As to the damages, it can be noted that the claimant was required to mitigate its loss—the cost of cleaning the highway every day—by accepting the defendant's offer to let it abate the nuisance at its own, lesser expense. It may be said in passing that public nuisance is quite different from private nuisance, for in the former the claimant need not have any interest in property adjacent to the trouble and provided that the defendant has done something improper which adversely affects a large number of people, such as obstructing a highway, may claim even for merely economic loss provided that it is specific to him over and above what is suffered by the generality.[31]

If the occupier must take steps to deal with actual hazards on his premises, even if he has done nothing to create them, lest they cause damage next door, must he take steps to prevent such hazards arising? The issue was ventilated, but not really resolved, in a case where young hooligans entered a closed-down cinema and deliberately used some film scrap there to start a fire which burnt down the pursuer's church. Lord Goff was of the opinion that there was no general duty on an occupier to take steps to protect his neighbour from the misdoings of trespassers, though there were particular instances where such a duty did arise. The better view may well be to accept that there is a duty to take reasonable

---

[29] *Marcic v Thames Water Utilities* [2003] UKHL 66.
[30] *Wandsworth LBC v Railtrack* [2002] Env LR 9.
[31] *Tate & Lyle Industries v GLC* [1983] 1 All ER 1159.

steps when they are called for by the likelihood of trespassers entering and doing damage, and to decide the matter in relation to breach, as Lord Griffiths did in that case.[32]

NATURE OF THE OCCUPIER'S DUTY

Is the duty of the occupier 'non-delegable', such that he will be liable if his independent contractor causes harm by negligence? The tendency is certainly towards making the occupier liable to his neighbour. It is true that one of the leading authorities against making an occupier liable for the torts of his independent contractor was one in which paid tree-fellers cut down a tree in the occupier's garden so incompetently that it fell against wires over the highway and caused personal injuries to a person, actually the neighbour's son, who was trying to remove the hazard,[33] but it is far from clear that liability would have been denied had the tree fallen on the neighbour's greenhouse. The Court of Appeal has imposed liability on a householder whose contractors, in replacing his roof, failed to make a proper seal with the existing roof of his neighbour, but only by holding, contrary to the evident fact, that the operation was fraught with danger.[34] It would be easier to say that the mutual duties of neighbours not to cause each other harm are non-delegable; after all, the person who employs the contractor knows whom he has employed, and will be able to claim from him either for breach of contract or for a contribution to any damages payable to his neighbour, who may well have no means of identifying the contractor.

DISAMENITY

The tort of nuisance would be simpler if it dealt only with disamenity between neighbours, but even then it could not be very simple, because almost anything a neighbour does—cooking exotic foods, playing the trombone, running a school, adding an extension—affects the person next door or above or below him. Yet since he, just like the claimant, is entitled to enjoy his property, there must be some accommodation between a person's right to hold a party and his neighbour's right to sleep undisturbed: both are asserting the same right to enjoy their property.

---

[32] *Smith v Littlewoods Organisation* [1987] 1 All ER 710.

[33] *Salsbury v Woodland* [1969] 3 All ER 863.

[34] *Alcock v Wraith* [1991] TLR 600.

We have suggested that disamenity, rather than actual damage, is the characteristic of nuisance law, since the latter is compensable in negligence and the former is not. On this point a problem is caused by the decision of the House of Lords in *Hunter v Canary Wharf* which laid down categorically that the (sole) function of the tort of nuisance was to protect land rather than its occupants,[35] and peremptorily overruled a decision of the Court of Appeal that Miss Khorasandjian could sue 'in nuisance' a person who made her life at home intolerable by constant phone calls, the ground for the reversal being that she was not herself the householder but only his daughter.[36] Since one consequence of the Court of Appeal's decision had been that infants in the affected property started to sue their neighbours in order to benefit from better legal aid than their parents could obtain, it was quite sensible for the House of Lords to restrict the number of possible plaintiffs to those with a legal interest in the property. It is, however, odd to say that noises and smells affect the land itself, which has neither ears nor nose.

THE HUMAN RIGHTS ACT 1998

Miss Khorasandjian had no claim in nuisance, according to the House of Lords, because although she was at home it was not her house. The European Convention, by contrast, provides in Article 8 that everyone has 'the right to respect for his ... home ...'. Accordingly, when the plaintiffs in the *Hunter* case, disappointed in the House of Lords, went off to Strasbourg, the Commission held that their right under this Article had been infringed, though the national interest in constructing Canary Wharf and its substructures provided a justification. The national interest has also been held (but only on appeal to the Grand Chamber) to justify the government's statutory approval of the large number of flights in and out of Heathrow Airport which gravely disturbed the home life of the groundlings underneath the flight paths,[37] a decision which was relied on by the House of Lords in reversing the decision of the Court of Appeal that Mr Marcic, whose home was regularly flooded by water and sewage from the public drains, could base a claim on Article 8 of the European Convention.[38]

---

[35] *Hunter v Canary Wharf* [1997] 2 All ER 426.
[36] *Khorasandjian v Bush* [1993] 3 All ER 369.
[37] *Hatton v UK* (App. No. 36022/97) (2003) 37 EHRR 28.
[38] *Marcic v Thames Water Utilities* [2003] UKHL 66.

COMMON LAW: DISAMENITY

If we revert to the common law on disamenity, we must agree that on the one hand, one cannot complain of everything which one finds annoying or 'a nuisance', for it is simply impossible to live close to another without suffering some inconvenience. On the other hand, one has no right to make one's neighbour's life a misery, even if one thinks that what one is doing, and doing quite deliberately, is perfectly reasonable, such as playing heavy metal or Wagner *fortissimo*. Reasonableness is a relevant consideration here, but the question is neither what is reasonable in the eyes of the defendant or even the claimant (for one cannot, by being unduly sensitive, constrain one's neighbour's freedoms), but what object-ively a normal person would find it reasonable to have to put up with. If the claimant is suffering to an objectively intolerable extent, the defend-ant has to stop or limit what he was doing. Characteristic is a case where the plaintiff was a musical family whose members played instruments a very great deal, to which the defendant reacted by banging on the walls. The musicians had admittedly gone beyond what it was reasonable for the defendant to have to put up with, but the defendant, unlike them, was guilty of what Italian road signs call '*rumori inutili*', so the court subjected the defendant to a permanent injunction but only imposed music hours, so to speak, on the plaintiff.[39]

The defendant here was retaliating, and could be described as acting maliciously. So, too, in another case. The sound of shooting is a feature of country living (and urban living, too, in some areas, alas) but when it was shown that the farmer shooting close to his boundary with the plaintiff's land was doing so purely to cause the plaintiff's silver foxes to abort and eat their cubs, the court had no hesitation in enjoining him.[40] Of course there was actual damage to property in that case, and intended damage at that (though not trespassory, because the defendant had not shot the foxes, though he had killed them by shooting).

Gratuitous noise is much more irritating than noise intrinsic to an estimable occupation, such as running a school. As in a claim for neg-ligence, it is relevant whether the defendant's activity is worthwhile or not. Thus one cannot complain of the noise of church bells unless the bell-ringing practice occurs too frequently or goes on too long, but whether the nuisance is gratuitous or not is only one of the factors to be

[39] *Christie v Davey* [1893] 1 Ch 316.
[40] *Hollywood Silver Fox Farm v Emmett* [1936] 2 KB 468.

taken into account in deciding whether what the claimant had to put up with was excessive and unreasonable. All the factors in the context are to be taken into account—the severity of the inconvenience, its duration, and the nature of the surroundings. Building works are inevitably noisy, but permissible if they are not unduly prolonged or nocturnal, and noise and dust are reduced to the practicable minimum. Occupants are entitled to only a reasonable amount of peace and quiet, and the test is objective, much affected by the nature of the neighbourhood. It is very much a matter of judgment, like deciding in a negligence suit whether the defendant was or was not in breach of his duty to take reasonable care, with the difference that the focus here is on the reasonableness of the effect rather than that of the conduct.

It is often said that 'Live and let live' is the order of the day (and night), but living and letting live may be incompatible in fact or unprocurable in law. In *Baxter* the parties lived in adjacent apartments in a Victorian house which had been subdivided by the local authority conformably with standards at the time but whose insulation was so poor that the noise made by the occupants of apartment A, which was no more than the normal noise of daily living (television, dishwashing, toilet flushing, lovemaking), made life intolerable for the occupant of apartment B who could hear, and could not avoid hearing, everything that went on next door. In the lawsuit brought by the occupant of apartment B against their common landlord the House of Lords held that the conduct of those in apartment A did not amount to a nuisance, since they were behaving absolutely normally.[41]

Of course the occupants of apartment B were not at fault in doing what comes naturally, but that is not the critical point. What if it is impossible to blame the neighbour though his distressing conduct is not normal at all? Although at common law the person whose abnormal conduct is making your life a misery is automatically liable to an injunction or an eviction order, any such remedy may be barred by the Disability Discrimination Act of 1995 if all the intolerable and antisocial shouting, banging, swearing, gobbling and raving is due to a condition defined by the Act as a disability—and much (most?) antisocial conduct is due to a disability as defined. The situation is both a social and a legal nightmare, and though the Court has gone some way to relieve the situation and afford some protection to the distressed victim by giving a very extensive meaning to 'health' in the provision which legitimates eviction

[41] *Baxter v Camden LBC* [1999] 4 All ER 449.

of a disabled occupier if that is objectively necessary to avoid endangering the 'health or safety of any person' (s 21D(4)), one understands its pained cry for help from Parliament, whose failure to join up its legislation is at the root of the mess.[42]

LANDLORD AND TENANT

In *Baxter* there was nothing for the landlord to be liable for, though it had let the premises for the purposes of living in, but in any case the landlord could not be liable because the condition complained of was already in existence when the claimant's tenancy started. So it raised two issues: when is a landlord liable for a nuisance committed by a tenant, and when is it a defence that the claimant accepted the situation now said to constitute a nuisance? The first question, whether a landlord can be sued for what the tenant does, is not easy to answer. After all, the tenant has exclusive possession of the premises, and in the common law it is possession, physical control, to which entitlements and liability principally attach. It appears that, even if the landlord knows that his tenant will make, or is actually making, life a total misery for those in the area, even other tenants of his own, he will not be liable if in the lease he has forbidden the tenant to create a nuisance (unlike the employer, who cannot escape vicarious liability simply by forbidding his employee to commit torts). Thus in one case a local authority which installed a problem family under a lease which forbade the creation of a nuisance was held not liable when the family made the neighbours' lives an unbearable misery.[43] This decision may be incompatible with claimants' rights under Article 8, and if the troublesome tenants resist eviction on the basis of their own rights under that Article, they may be met by Article 17 which prevents a person invoking his Convention rights as a justification for invading those of others. It is true that the landlord may have power to evict the tenant who, in breach of that term of the lease, does indeed commit a nuisance, but he is not bound to do so at the instance of third parties affected or even those tenants to whom he has promised quiet enjoyment. Over licensees, however, occupiers of land have much greater powers of control, and may well be liable to neighbours for their activities.[44]

---

[42] *Manchester CC v Romano* [2004] EWCA Civ 834.
[43] *Smith v Scott* [1972] 3 All ER 645.
[44] *Lippiatt v South Gloucestershire Council* [1999] 4 All ER 149.

'COMING TO THE NUISANCE'

The second issue, that a tenant cannot complain of a situation existing at the start of the tenancy, is out of step with a questionable rule of nuisance law which is commonly put in the form 'It is no defence that the plaintiff came to the nuisance'. In other words the fact that you chose to move next door to a chip shop does not prevent your complaining of the attendant noise and smell, if excessive in the area. Although this is inconsistent with the principle underlying the defence of *volenti non fit injuria*, it is quite understandable in terms of history. Until fairly recently, the tort of nuisance was the only way environmental pollution could be controlled: the system depended on private citizens bringing a civil action to stop it. To allow the polluter to carry on polluting just because he started polluting before the plaintiff arrived on the scene would have frustrated this function and stymied *embourgeoisement* and gentrification. Now that we have very powerful administrative methods of reducing such pollution, we could well abandon this rule of private law, as Lord Denning was prepared to do in a case where a person who bought a Wimpey house overlooking a village cricket ground sought to stop cricket being played there on the basis that the cannonade of balls made her feel (and be) unsafe in her garden.[45]

ADMINISTRATIVE AND LEGISLATIVE AUTHORISATION

Doubtless planning permission had been obtained to build houses next to the village cricket pitch, for such permission is required for any change of use of land, but the fact that it has been obtained does not insulate one from liability in nuisance. This is quite right: administrators cannot authorise torts. Parliament, however, may do so, and if the defendant has statutory authority for its activity, as may well be the case where the activity is a really major one like running an oil terminal, it will not be liable even for the very serious effects of its activity provided that it causes no more harm and disruption than is entailed in the exercise of the authority granted to it. Thus although the Manchester electricity company had statutory authority to run a power plant, it was subjected to an injunction precisely because it was operating it without proper concern

[45] *Miller v Jackson* [1977] 3 All ER 338.

for the people in the neighbourhood.[46] Where the authorised public works are properly executed, so that a claim in nuisance at common law is barred, the person affected may well be able to claim compensation from public funds, much as one can claim compensation for expropriation.[47] Alternatively one can sail up the Rhine to Strasbourg (a city, as A. E. Housman noted, 'still famous for its geese') and complain, with a fair chance of success, that the legislature in authorising the works or activity paid too much attention to the national interest and too little to the affected individuals.

Many common law nuisances, such as disturbance by noise, fumes, and so on, are also classified as 'statutory nuisances'.[48] This gives the local authority extensive powers, indeed imposes on it a duty, to require or effect their 'abatement'. Likewise, while you yourself may not enter your neighbour's dwelling and impound the hi-fi gear which is generating an illicit number of nocturnal decibels, the local authority may do so, though it is no longer under a duty, but has only a discretionary power, to respond to a householder's complaint.[49] Statutory nuisances go further, however. For example, premises which are 'in such a state as to be prejudicial to health' constitute a statutory nuisance of which the occupants themselves can complain, as they could not at common law, and have the local authority, which may itself be the landlord, remedy the situation. In this respect the regime has an effect on the quality of housing as well as on that of the environment.

---

[46] *Manchester Corp v Farnworth* [1930] AC 17.
[47] *Wildtree Hotels v Harrow LBC* [2000] 3 All ER 289.
[48] Environmental Protection Act 1990, s 79ff.
[49] Anti-Social Behaviour Act 2003, s 42.

11

Conversion

Property is either tangible or intangible, fixed or moveable, depending on the answer to the lawyer's almost childlike questions (1) can you touch it? (2) can you move it? Tort, as one would expect, is mainly concerned with the physical, the tangible, that is, land and goods, not debts and shares. Trespass and negligence protect both land and goods, nuisance only the former, and the tort of conversion only the latter. Trespass and conversion are alike in that both are in the business of protecting rights, with the result that neither requires the defendant to have acted unreasonably, but the rights they protect differ: to put it bluntly—the qualifications come shortly—trespass protects possession and conversion protects ownership. It is true that trespass to goods, conversion, and negligence have all been grouped together in a statute as 'wrongful interference with goods',[1] but this is for purely procedural purposes: in substance they are quite distinct torts with different requirements and effects, and 'wrongful interference with goods' is just a name and not a tort at all. Conversion is certainly a tort in England (though not in Scotland) and, subject to the important qualifications which follow, is best regarded as the tort which protects the owner of goods not against their being damaged (negligence covers that) but against their being dealt with or detained against his will. It is concerned with loss of goods rather than damage to them.

Every legal system which recognises ownership (as even the communist systems did) must provide a remedy whereby the owner can sue the person who has his property and has no right to keep it. This remedy the Romans called the *vindicatio* since it vindicates the right of ownership, and it is a vital feature in all modern civilian systems. But ownership is not a central concept in the English law relating to moveables and our law has no *vindicatio*, though which of these facts is the cause of the other may be a question. At any rate we have no property remedy whereby the owner of a chattel can sue the possessor simply by claiming 'That's my thing you've got!'. Instead we use the tort remedy of conversion to

---

[1] Torts (Interference with Goods) Act 1977, s 1.

perform the property function of the *vindicatio*. This makes conversion sit rather uneasily in the tort books, since property is concerned with what people have and tort with what people do. What the defendant in a typical conversion case has done is to sell or buy a thing belonging to the claimant. These are the commonest and most characteristic examples of 'denying the plaintiff's title', as it is unhelpfully called.

People who sell goods normally own them—indeed they warrant that they have a right to sell them—so it follows that all those who sell goods are acting as if they owned them, or at least had the owner's authority to sell them, as auctioneers do. If the owner has not authorised the sale, the seller is said to have 'converted' the goods by disposing of them: by implicitly asserting his own title the seller is 'denying the title' of the true owner, as we shall call him for the moment. What of the person who buys such goods? He, too, is implicitly asserting that he (now) owns them, so he too can be taken to be denying the true owner's title, unless, exceptionally, the true owner's title has been lost by the sale, purchase and delivery. In many systems the buyer who bona fide believed the seller to be authorised to sell does acquire title and the true owner thereupon loses his, but this is not the position of the common law: in our law, subject to several statutory exceptions, the buyer is in no better position than the seller himself, and is therefore is liable in conversion if, whatever he may have thought, the sale was in fact unauthorised.

Now it may seem unfair to make the buyer liable when he was in perfect good faith and did nothing more unreasonable than answer an advert in *Exchange and Mart*, but consider the situation as one of property law: if you have my thing and no right to hold on to it, it is hardly an answer to my claim for you to say 'It's not my fault I've got it.' This strict liability, which is really inevitable in property law, is carried over into our tort remedy of conversion. This is odd but not entirely irrational. After all, if you sell my goods, however innocently, you surely owe me the price you got for them; and if you bought my goods and still have them, you must hand them over. The oddity is that in conversion the seller is liable even if he no longer has the price, and the buyer is liable though he no longer has the goods. That is, however, the consequence of using a tort remedy to perform a property function, of looking to what people have done rather than what they still have. It is small comfort for the buyer that he can always sue his seller for failing to make him owner, for the original unauthorised seller, con-man or thief, is probably in Pentonville picking oakum.

In one case, however, it seems peculiarly unfair to make the bona fide purchaser liable to the claimant, and that is where it is due to the claimant's own negligence that the goods got into circulation and the defendant was enabled to buy them. To enable a careless claimant to obtain full damages from a careful defendant flies in the face of proper tort thinking. But of course conversion is not a tort quite like others, and if, as we have seen, it is no answer for the defendant to say 'It's not my fault I've got your thing', Parliament has laid down that it is not an answer either to say 'And, what's more, it's *your* fault that I've got it'.[2] If you leave your keys in the car, you may not be able to claim on your insurance policy but the law allows you to claim from the bona fide purchaser to whom the entirely predictable thief sells it. Odd? Acceptable?

Although selling and buying are unquestionably the paradigm instances of conversion, there is room outside these instances for the application of the untransparent notion which the common lawyers elicited from them, namely 'denying the plaintiff's title'; it certainly applies where the possessor unwarrantably refuses to hand over the goods when proper demand is made on him by the person currently entitled to have them—the very situation where the *vindicatio* is most at home. Suppose you park your car in my yard and I lock the gate. This is wrongful if I make a charge for release,[3] but I have not at common law converted your car, since I make no claim to it. It is, however, likely that I shall have to let you have it back one way or another, though which way is not so clear since the legislator decided to abolish the tort of detinue.[4]

WHAT CAN BE CONVERTED?

We have said that conversion applies only to goods, that is, tangible moveables. Does this need to be qualified? Certainly the law regards cheques, share certificates and other such documents as subject to the tort of conversion[5] but they do have physical form although their significance is purely financial. A licence to use goods may also be worth a lot and liability in conversion was once imposed on a person who, having bought lorries from a hire-purchaser without taking possession of them, was able to deprive the finance company of the valuable licence attaching (in a non-physical sense) to the vehicles; the defendant in that case was in bad faith, however, and could have been held liable on another

---

[2] Torts (Interference with Goods) Act 1977, s 2(1).
[3] Private Security Industry Act 2001, Sch 2, para 3.
[4] Torts (Interference with Goods Act) 1977, s 2(1).
[5] *Marfani & Co v Midland Bank* [1968] 2 All ER 573.

basis.[6] The question came up in much clearer form in 2005 though on very unusual facts. Administrative receivers took over the business of the apparently insolvent claimant company, whose assets included land, goods and contracts. The appointment of the receivers was invalid: they had no right to do what they did. As to the land they were liable in trespass, as to the goods in conversion. But what of the contracts which they terminated or settled at an undervalue? The Court of Appeal divided on the question whether the tort of interference with contractual relations, which requires intentional wrongdoing, was made out, but all agreed that 'there can be no conversion of a chose in action'.[7]

TITLE TO SUE

What entitlement must the claimant in conversion show? In contrast with the *vindicatio* it is neither necessary nor sufficient for the claimant to be owner. This may seem surprising, since the owner is the person with the ultimate economic interest in the property—the person who can turn it into money by selling it—but the common law has always been more interested in the physical than the economic relationship between person and thing, and instead of asking who is eventually to have the benefit of the thing, it asks who is currently entitled to get his hands on it. Accordingly, in order to claim in conversion you must show that at the time of the alleged conversion you were entitled to the possession of the thing, on simple demand, if necessary.

Not all such entitlements qualify. First, it must be an entitlement recognised at common law rather than in equity. The reason for this is that an equitable title yields to a bona fide purchaser, whereas a common law right does not, and since the bona fide purchaser is liable in conversion it would be contradictory to allow the merely beneficial owner to use the tort. This was made quite clear in 1998.[8] Secondly, not all common law entitlements qualify. The same case seems to suggest that a *contractual* right to obtain possession is sufficient, but this is surely wrong, for an analogous reason: interference with a merely contractual right is actionable in tort only if the defendant was aware of the contract, and since there is certainly no such requirement in the tort of conversion, it would stultify the proper rule to allow a person with a merely contractual

[6] *Douglas Valley Finance Co. v Hughes* [1969] 1 QB 738.
[7] *OBG Ltd v Allan* [2005] EWCA Civ 106.
[8] *MCC Proceeds v Lehman Bros* [1998] 4 All ER 675.

right to possession to bring a claim in conversion. Furthermore, since equitable entitlements commonly arise from contractual rights of particular strength, it would be eccentric to welcome the contractual claimant and dismiss the equitable one.

In this light we may consider a case to be found in the contract books.[9] The plaintiff had been negotiating with his nephew for the purchase of a horse and wrote to him offering a compromise price and saying that if he heard nothing further he would consider the horse his. He heard nothing further although the nephew appears to have been willing to sell it to him, for the nephew told the defendant auctioneer who was to sell the rest of his stock that this particular horse was not to be sold. The defendant by mistake did sell the horse, and the uncle sued him. The uncle's claim was dismissed, on the ground that since he had received no acceptance of his offer to buy the horse he had not actually bought it, and had therefore not become its owner. Some commentators think the decision wrong. But consider. If the uncle's claim had been allowed, he would be receiving the value of a horse for which he had not paid and could not be made to pay, and the auctioneer would be paying him the value of the horse or whatever he received from the buyer, although he had already handed the proceeds over to the nephew and could not claim it back. Hardly a fair result? Yet it would be even worse when one considers the position of the person who bought the horse at the auction. If the horse still belonged to the nephew, the buyer at auction would become owner despite the nephew's having told the auctioneer not to sell it, because the auctioneer would be a mercantile agent in possession with the consent of the owner.[10] But that would not be true if the horse was already owned by the uncle, for he had not consented to the auctioneer's possession of the horse and the buyer too would be liable to him in conversion. It would seem clear, then, that one should not allow a person with a merely contractual claim to sue in conversion, for although the buyer of specific goods in a deliverable state is said to become owner, in reality he obtains, until delivery, nothing more than a personal right to obtain possession. In fact, however, even if he becomes owner, the buyer who has not paid for the goods has no right to sue in conversion, for if the seller has a lien on the goods till payment, as is often the case, the buyer has no *immediate* right, but only a conditional right to possession.[11] If A, the buyer of specific goods, has paid B for them, and B resells and delivers them to C, who does not know

---

[9] *Felthouse v Bindley* (1862) 142 ER 1037.   [10] Factors Act 1889, s 2(1).
[11] *Lord v Price* (1873) LR 9 Exch 54.

of the prior sale, B is of course liable to A in conversion, but C is not: that is because C, unlike most bona fide purchasers, is given special statutory protection[12]—or, to put it another way, obtains a good title though his seller was no longer owner.

A commoner case where the owner has no title to sue in conversion is where he has bailed the chattel to another and is prevented by contract or estoppel from demanding it back for the time being. This is the case where the owner lets the thing on hire for a period not yet elapsed at the time of the alleged conversion. In such a case it is the person in justified possession, the bailee, who can sue in conversion and not the owner. When a finance company lets a thing on hire-purchase it becomes the equivalent, as regards chattels, of the absentee landlord, who not only cannot sue a third party in trespass but can actually be sued in trespass by the tenant. But not all those who have granted possession to another are deprived of a claim: the bailor may sue if the bailment is gratuitous or if the terms of the bailment, though for a period not yet expired, have been seriously flouted by the bailee.

Bailment is one of the situations where different parties may have concurrent interests in the property and have claims against the same person in negligence or conversion. In the 1977 Act Parliament sought to allay this 'double liability' by requiring the claimant to identify anyone else with an interest in the property and entitling the defendant to require them to be brought into the lawsuit or abide by its consequences.[13]

PERSONS NOT LIABLE

The strictness of liability in conversion makes life difficult for those who handle large numbers of things belonging to others. Consider bankers, for instance. We have seen (p. 167) that the law regards cheques, share certificates, and other documents representing intangible property as capable of being converted.[14] In the normal case where a cheque in favour of A is drawn by B on his bank X, it is presented by A to A's bank Y, and the Y bank then tenders it to bank X for payment. Bank X then, pursuant to B's instructions (the cheque says 'Pay. . . .'), pays bank Y which credits A's account. On analysis one will see that bank X has effectively sold the cheque to bank Y which has bought it. Now if for some reason A is not

---

[12] Sale of Goods Act 1979, s 24.
[13] Torts (Interference with Goods) Act 1977, s 8.
[14] *Marfani & Co v Midland Bank* [1968] 2 All ER 573.

entitled to the cheque, both banks would, in principle, be liable to B or the 'true owner', but given the literally millions of cheques handled by banks every day it would be intolerable if they were held strictly liable, so they have statutory protection, provided they act with proper care.[15] Carriers also handle goods belonging to many others (consider the Post Office, which admittedly has a statutory immunity),[16] but they are not treated as converters at all if they simply obey the instructions of the consignor, even if he is not the owner or authorised to deal with the goods, for in carrying the goods as instructed the carrier is not 'acting like an owner' or denying anyone's title. Auctioneers, who also handle lots of goods, do not seem to 'act like an owner' either, since they do not suggest that the goods put up for sale are their own. Nevertheless the law is that if an auctioneer delivers the goods to the successful bidder he is liable in conversion to the true owner, though not if the goods remain unsold and he redelivers them to the person from whom he received them.[17] Somewhat similarly, the carrier who delivers the goods contrary to instructions or without the authorisation of the person entitled to their possession will be liable in conversion, as where he delivers to an insolvent buyer despite a proper instruction from the seller not to do so, or where the carrier by sea delivers the cargo to a person not possessed of the requisite document, such as the bill of lading.

REMEDIES

The 1977 Act provides that the court may order the return of the goods or damages or both. As regards return of the thing, there is no real difficulty, but the mismatch between the function and the form of a conversion claim gives rise to serious problems as to the measure of damages. In tort the measure of recovery is usually the claimant's loss, to the extent that it is not too remote, whereas in a *vindicatio* the recovery would be of the thing itself or its value. The tendency therefore was for the measure of recovery in conversion to be the value of the thing itself rather than the loss suffered by the claimant. Since value is objective (what would other people pay for it?) and loss personal, the claimant's loss may be greater or less than the value of the thing. If greater, he will not be fully compensated by the award of the value; if less, he gets a windfall. The former case arises where the thing was being put to

---

[15] Bills of Exchange Act 1882, ss 60, 80.   [16] Postal Services Act 2000, s 90.
[17] *Marcq v Christie Manson & Woods* [2003] EWCA Civ 731.

unusually profitable use, perhaps in conjunction with other property. The latter often arises in hire-purchase transactions where the defendant has bought a thing from a hire-purchaser who had no right to sell it. The finance house which owns the thing is now, by reason of the hire-purchaser's repudiation, entitled to possession and so to claim in conversion, but since it has already been paid part, perhaps much, of the sum due to it under its contract with the hire-purchaser, its loss is only the outstanding amount.[18]

Difficulties as regards causation are caused by the fact that conversion is primarily about vindicating the claimant's right to have the thing rather than damages for actual loss. Consider the Contribution Act 1978. It provides a remedy between those 'liable in respect of the same damage'. Are subsequent converters of a chattel 'liable for the same damage'? Are they liable for *damage* at all? But even supposing that the claimant's damage consists of not having the thing, how can it be said that it would not have arisen 'but for' the second or subsequent conversion when it has already arisen as a result of the first? In a case arising out of the Iraqi snaffling of planes belonging to Kuwait, there was a discussion regarding the requisite link between the conversion and 'consequential loss', that is, 'loss beyond that represented by the value of the goods'. Lord Nicholls was of the opinion that if the defendant was in good faith, the loss had to be merely foreseeable, a test which he described as 'more restrictive', whereas the bad faith converter had to pay for all loss 'directly and naturally' resulting, as in the tort of deceit. Lord Hoffmann, in apparent agreement, would apply 'conventional principles', helpfully stated to be 'the rules which lay down the causal requirements for that form of liability.'[19]

Where the converted goods are not returned, a question arises as to the time at which they should be valued—the time of the conversion (tort) or the time of trial (*vindicatio*)? The question is important, since the passage of time may cause chattels to depreciate physically or appreciate financially, but a single answer is not required for all cases, and the courts feel free to choose the time which gives the fairest result.[20]

LENGTH OF PROTECTION

The concern of the common law of England to protect the legal owner of goods is shown by the fact that he can sue even the good faith purchaser.

---

[18] *Wickham Holdings v Brooke House Motors* [1967] 1 All ER 117.
[19] *Kuwait Airways v Iraqi Airways* [2002] UKHL 19.
[20] *IBL Ltd v Coussens* [1991] 2 All ER 133.

But for how long is he protected? His rights may be cut off in two ways. First, if he sues for conversion and the judgment in his favour is paid, his ownership vests in the defendant or anyone who bought it from him. Secondly, he may lose his ownership by lapse of time: once six years have elapsed after the first conversion in respect of which suit could have been brought, no suit may be brought in respect of any subsequent conversion and the owner's title is extinguished, subject to this, that the six years do not start to run against the victim of theft until the moment when the goods are first purchased in good faith.[21]

---

[21] Limitation Act 1980, s 3.

12

Defamation

It is sometimes useful to consider tort cases in the light of the relative values involved. When the law imposes liability on a person, it normally does so because it places a lesser value upon his activity, or his method of conducting it, than on the interest of the victim affected by it: the liberty of the arrested suspect or peace-breaker yields to the proper enforcement of law and order, whereas the security of the vulnerable pedestrian on a marked crossing is regarded as more important than the motorist's interest in belting down the road in his metal carapace.

When one comes to the law of defamation (libel and slander), however, which constitutes a quite distinct chapter of tort law—for it is often said that one cannot obtain damages for injury to reputation except under the law of defamation,[1] and the Court of Appeal once had to be corrected for holding that you couldn't sue in negligence if you couldn't sue in defamation[2]—it is far from clear that the law's priorities are correct. The claimant's interest is in what people think of him, the defendant's interest is in saying what he thinks, or thinks he knows. Reputation against expression, therefore. A balance has to be struck. The common law of England has struck it in quite the wrong way. That is why it has been held substantively unconstitutional in the United States[3] (which quite exceptionally refuses to enforce the judgments of English courts in this matter[4]) and why the Strasbourg court has disapproved of certain aspects of it.[5] Freedom of expression is of course a protected right under the Convention, and our courts are enjoined by the Human Rights Act 1998 to have 'particular regard to the importance of the Convention right to freedom of expression' (not that they do!). Reputation itself, though mentioned as justifying a proportionate restriction of the right of freedom of

---

[1] *Lonrho v Fayed (No 5)* [1994] 1 All ER 188.
[2] *Spring v Guardian Assurance* [1994] 3 All ER 129.
[3] *New York Times v Sullivan* (1964) 376 US 254.
[4] *Telnikoff v Matusevich* 702 A2d 230 (Md 1997).
[5] *Tolstoy Miloslavsy v United Kingdom* (1995) 20 EHRR 442 (damages), *Steel v United Kingdom* (2005) 41 EHRR 22 (legal aid).

expression, and now treated as implicitly enshrined in Article 8 about private life(!),[6] is not a specially protected right under the Convention, but it is certainly one of the few protected rights in English law, as one can tell from the absence of any need to prove either fault or damage.

It may be worth asking why freedom of expression is so valued. There seem to be two reasons; first, that the expression of views is useful, secondly that it is fun. But speech is useful only if it is critical (especially of powerful public figures), and it is not much fun to be flattering, so it may be argued that our rules of defamation strike at precisely those instances of self-expression which are most desirable. Robert Maxwell was enabled to continue plundering pension funds because he threatened to sue anyone who was about to tell the world what he was doing, and indeed obtained hefty damages from *Private Eye*; another bullying tycoon sought to stop *Private Eye* from mocking him by threatening to sue the distributors of that admirably disrespectful periodical, and was allowed by the courts to do so.[7]

The basic rules of the common law of defamation can be stated quite simply. A is liable for saying anything to C about B which would be apt to make an average citizen think worse of the latter. Certain qualifications will have to be made later, and it will be seen that one or two defences are available, but in principle B can sue A without having to show that what A said was false, that it caused him any harm, or that A was at any way at fault in saying it. Just consider how remarkable this is in a tort book! Normally in cases where a tortious misrepresentation is alleged, the claimant has to prove falsehood, fault, and loss, as in *Hedley Byrne v Heller*. None of these have to be established where what is said might affect what people think of the claimant. The protection thus afforded to a person's reputation is as strong as that afforded by the law of trespass to his liberty, his person, and the property in his possession—surely more important values—and it is afforded not against positive invasive action but against mere speech, which is a recognised right in itself. The protection may be thought to be all the odder in that the only kinds of harm apt to result from being badmouthed are emotional upset and financial loss, neither of which is very readily redressible in the law even where the defendant's negligence has been demonstrated.

---

[6] *Cumpana v Romania* (2005) 41 EHRR 200 at 91.
[7] *Goldsmith v Pressdram* [1977] 2 All ER 566.

WHAT IS DEFAMATORY?

Since these special rules apply only when A's communication to C is defamatory of B, it is essential at the very outset to discover what is 'defamatory' and what is not. It is not defamatory, for example, to say that B has gone out of business (though he may well lose custom if he has not), for no one thinks worse of a person for changing jobs or taking early retirement. In such a case, where the words are not 'defamatory', the normal tort rules apply: unless A was under a special duty to look after his interests, B must show that the statement was false, that A knew it, and that B suffered harm in consequence. But courts have been very generous in treating statements as potentially defamatory and leaving it to the jury to say whether they were really so or not, though even the jury is not asked whether people actually did think worse of the claimant, only whether they might well do so. In one recent case it was held that it was potentially defamatory to call someone ugly,[8] and an actress has sued a journalist for saying she had a big bum.[9] It has been held that it is defamatory to say that a business is insolvent. This seems to be wrong, for though it is certainly defamatory to say of the managing director that he continued to trade knowing of the company's insolvency, since that is an offence, whereas insolvency by itself is just a misfortune,[10] as to the company it appears to be merely a damaging statement, so that the company should have to prove falsehood and knowledge. It should also have to prove that it was damaged, but need not do so, since in 1952 Parliament unwisely dispensed with that requirement in such circumstances,[11] and our courts are perfectly happy to make the Press pay damages to foreign corporations which do not even offer to prove that they have suffered any harm at all.[12] In one nineteenth-century case the House of Lords held that it was not defamatory for a firm to state 'We shall not accept cheques drawn on [the plaintiff]'.[13] It has been roundly criticised for so holding, on the ground that the words were clearly harmful, since people panicked and made a run on the bank in question. But the House was clearly right: the fact that a statement causes harm does not make it defamatory any more than a statement ceases to be defamatory just because it does not

---

[8] *Berkoff v Burchill* [1996] 4 All ER 1008.
[9] *Cornwell v Myskow* [1987] 2 All ER 504.
[10] *Aspro Travel v Owners Abroad* [1996] 1 WLR 132.
[11] Defamation Act 1952, s 3.
[12] *Jameel v Wall Street Journal* [2005] EWCA Civ 74.
[13] *Capital and Counties Bank v Henty* (1882) 7 App Cas 741.

seem to have caused any harm. After all, is it to be actionable if a store puts up a notice stating that it does not accept VISA cards?

THE MEANING OF STATEMENTS

Contrary to what is often believed, the truth or falsity of a statement is irrelevant to the question whether it is defamatory or not: truth is a matter of defence only. But it does have to be decided what the statement means, and though a statement can have several different meanings, some worse than others, the law has decided that it can only have one; it is for the parties to propose what meaning should be attributed to it, for the judge to decide which of them are possible, and for the jury to decide which is actual, that is, what the average addressee would understand by it. Libel practitioners have managed, in their own interests, to complicate the law on the question of the meaning of words to a remarkable extent; the degree to which they have done so can be inferred from a provision in the Defamation Act 1996: 'In defamation proceedings the court shall not be asked to rule whether a statement is arguably capable, as opposed to capable, of bearing a particular meaning or meanings attributed to it'. (s 7)

In other torts the matter or manner of pleading is not very important, but in defamation cases it seems actually predominant. Indeed its complexity, leading to what has been described as an 'archaic sarabande',[14] is both the result and the cause of the high specialization of the libel bar, whose members have no incentive to diminish it (even when promoted to the Bench, since some defamation experts have to be there in order to deal with its complexities). Thus with regard to meaning, the rule seems to be that while the claimant must specify the defamatory meaning he attributes to the matter impugned (and within limits he can select the matter he complains of, though not just the meat of an indiscerptible sandwich), the defendant need not plead an alternative lesser meaning but must, if he seeks to justify any particular meaning, give sufficient detail in his pleadings that the claimant knows what case he has to meet. Here there is a 'somewhat subtle distinction . . . between (a) the meaning of the words complained of for which the defendant contends (as the practice stands at present, the defendant is not obliged to plead that meaning) and (b) the meaning of the words which, if it is the true meaning of those words, the defendant will seek to justify (that is a meaning which the

---

[14] *Morell v International Thomson* [1989] 3 All ER 733 at 734.

defendant must now spell out sufficiently to enable the plaintiff to know what case he has to meet)'.[15] It is now possible for either party to ask the judge to rule on the acceptability or otherwise of any meaning or meanings of the words complained of. Such rulings gave rise to an unsuccessful appeal by Jessye Norman, complaining that a music magazine had falsely attributed to her the remark 'Honey, I ain't got no sideways'.[16]

In one important case reputable newspapers stated that the Fraud Squad was investigating the plaintiff firm. This was true. The plaintiff argued that this would be understood to mean that the firm was guilty of fraud, while the defendant argued that it meant simply what it said. The House of Lords held that it could not mean that the firm was guilty, but did mean more than it said: the average reader would infer that the firm had behaved suspiciously, so the defendant would be liable unless it could prove that there were adequate grounds for the Fraud Squad's investigation.[17] How, one might ask, is the press to inform the nation of an investigation which is under way? Do the courts not care whether such information may be published, and is the commercial reputation of London Rubber Improvements, actually under investigation, more important than public awareness of the fact? To be noted is that if the imputation is that the plaintiff has behaved suspiciously and the defendant seeks to justify this, he must prove it by reference to actual conduct by the plaintiff and not by reference to the suspicions entertained even by third parties, however trustworthy, including, one supposes, the Fraud Squad itself.[18]

The addressee is taken to be only averagely credulous, but it is accepted that he will understand statements in the light of facts known to him (and perhaps not known to the defendant) which may render an apparently innocuous statement quite damaging ('innuendo'). If so, it must be shown that there were persons who had that special knowledge. In one case *The Sun* reported that in a particular week a young woman had been kidnapped by a dog-doping gang and kept in a flat in Finchley. There was no reference whatever to the plaintiff, but several witnesses knew that he had had that young woman staying in his flat in Willesden the week previous to that stated, and testified that they supposed that despite the discrepancies of time and place the article was referring to the plaintiff. They also said that they didn't believe the supposed imputation.

[15] *Prager v Times Newspapers* [1988] 1 All ER 300 at 311.
[16] *Norman v Future Publishing* [1999] EMLR 325.
[17] *Lewis v Daily Telegraph* [1963] 2 All ER 151.
[18] *Shah v Standard Chartered Bank* [1998] 4 All ER 155.

The House of Lords by a majority upheld the jury's decision for the plaintiff on liability, thereby reversing the Court of Appeal, and laid it down as self-evident that it was quite irrelevant to liability whether any-one believed what was said.[19] The reader may be excused for inferring that as soon as the door of defamation is opened, common sense flies out the window. It is true, however, that there may be no liability if no one in his right mind could believe in the truth of what was said,[20] or if a false impression conveyed by a headline, for example, is immediately corrected by the text.[21]

'PUBLICATION'

The fact that no action lies unless the communication has been made to a third party (a single third party will suffice!) shows that the tort is con-cerned with reputation rather than self-esteem: you can be as rude as you like *to* a person (provided you don't cause a damaging physical reaction),[22] or keep doing it (harassment), but you cannot be rude *about* him, unless he is dead (the proposal that speaking ill of the dead should be actionable has fortunately not been accepted, or writing history would be impos-sible). The act of communication is called 'publication' and at common law it was a publication every time anyone communicated anything to anyone else. In the old days when people had secretaries who took dicta-tion and handed the letter back for signature this caused stupid problems, but nowadays, thanks to the Act of 1996, strict liability attaches only to the author, editor, and commercial publisher of the material; others are not liable provided they 'published' with reasonable care, having no reason to believe that the material was defamatory. 'Publication' does suggest some positive act on the part of the publisher. Do internet service providers qualify as publishers when some subscriber transmits defama-tory material? As usual, the common law looks for some analogue in the pre-technical age, and found it in a golf-club where a member posted a defamatory message on the club notice board.[23] The question whether a defendant is liable for failure to act being whether he should have acted, the result in the case of internet defamation appears to be that the service provider is liable only if it had notice of the defamatory nature of the

[19] *Morgan v Odham's Press* [1971] 2 All ER 1156.
[20] *Blennerhassett v Novelty Sales* (1933) 175 LTJ 393.
[21] *Charleston v News Group Newspapers* [1995] 2 All ER 313.
[22] *Wilkinson v Downton* [1897] 2 QB 57.
[23] *Byrne v Deane* [1937] 1 KB 818.

material and failed to remove it.[24] What one spouse says to another is not published at all, a good rule doubtless attributable to the absurd fiction that husband and wife were one person, and therefore one which some rational reformer will soon propose should be abolished simply because the reason for it is poor. It has yet to be decided whether this good rule applies, as it should, between cohabitants in a recognised civil partnership, whose intimacies may well be enriched by defamatory chit-chat.

LIBEL AND SLANDER

One distinction which rational reformers (perhaps those who cannot distinguish between 'verbal' and 'oral') have girded against for years is that between writing and speech, for at common law the former is called libel, as opposed to slander, and treated as more serious, since in most cases of slander the claimant must prove damage, whereas in libel he need not do so. Some speech is, however, now treated as libel (broadcasts, plays in commercial theatres) and some spoken defamations are actionable without proof of damage, as when one imputes criminal conduct, repellent disease, incompetence in a job or position, or lewdness in a female (lustfulness in a male being presumably a praiseworthy attribute). The distinction between libel and slander is frequently criticised, but it is sound enough, for unless the claimant can be shown to have suffered some quantifiable harm apart from silly mortification, the courts have better things to do than hear complaints about what was said over the garden wall or at lunch-time in the canteen.

DEFENCES

One would expect the range of defences to be inversely proportional to the ease with which the claimant can state a case. Thus there are many defences to a claim in trespass. In defamation, however, there are only a few, and they turn on a distinction between allegations of fact and statements of opinion. As to apparent allegations of fact, the only defences are truth (called 'justification') and privilege; for statements of opinion, which cannot be false but at the most simulated, the defence is 'fair comment on a matter of public interest'.

It might be thought that in a tort concerned with the protection of reputation it would be open to the defendant to show that the claimant's

---

[24] *Godfrey v Demon Internet* [1999] 4 All ER 342.

presumed reputation was totally undeserved, that though he smiled and smiled, yet was he a villain: otherwise one would be rewarding the con-man and the whited sepulchre. It was therefore right that the Defamation Bill 1996 proposed that the defendant might give evidence of the claimant's misconduct in the relevant area of life (for example, that an allegation of fraud in transaction X might attract evidence of fraud in transaction Y, though not evidence of sexual perversion), but this excellent proposal was dropped by our representatives in Parliament (on the basis of a specious argument by a Law Lord) and replaced by a clause which extended *their own right* to sue in respect of allegations about their misconduct in Parliament![25] By an appropriate irony the first beneficiary of this improper substitution, Jonathan Aitken, ended up in jail for causing his daughter to give perjured evidence in his libel action against *The Guardian*. It is more to be regretted that the original clause was displaced, for when a claimant does not deserve the reputation he is presumed to have (and there are many such claimants), all the defendant can try (dangerous though it is) is to plead that what he said was true and thereby bring in relevant material which can be used in mitigation of damages even if the plea fails; and that if he doesn't plead justification he may seek to mitigate the damages by showing that the claimant had a bad reputation, but not, by proving specific acts of wickedness, that he did not deserve the reputation he had, 'case management' being used for this purpose.[26]

TRUTH

Apart from the statutory rule that one must not dig up and ventilate a convict's peccadilloes,[27] truth is a defence to a claim for defamation. But why should it be for the defendant to prove that what he wrote was true, at least in essence, rather than for the claimant to disprove it, as is normal in claims for misrepresentation? Can the law be so stupid as to suppose that if an imputation is disagreeable, it is more likely to be false than true, that virtue is commoner than vice, competence than fecklessness? The effect of the rule, ironically enough, is that no claimant ever leaves the defamation court 'without a stain on his character', for even if he can run all the way to the bank with his winnings, he has not proved that what the defendant said was false—it is simply that the defendant has failed to

---

[25] Defamation Act 1996, s 13.   [26] *Burstein v Times Newspapers* [2001] 1 WLR 579.
[27] Rehabilitation of Offenders Act 1974, s 8.

prove that it was true, though if he doesn't even try to do so, the judge, disposing of the case summarily, may issue a 'declaration of falsity' and thereby run the risk of rewriting history.[28] This absurd reversal of the normal burden of proof encourages claimants to sue even if they know that what the defendant said was perfectly correct; this is a dangerous ploy, as has been discovered by Oscar Wilde, Jonathan Aitken, Neil Hamilton and Lord Archer among others. Likewise the footballer Grobbellaar must regret suing the newspaper which reported that he had taken bribes and fixed games, for though the jury awarded him £85,000, presumably on the basis that though he had taken the bribes he hadn't been proved to have earned them by actually fixing any games, the House of Lords, in reinstating the jury's finding of liability which had been reversed by the Court of Appeal, reduced the damages to £1.[29] Of course claimants for personal injuries often lie about the circumstances or extent of their injury, but they cannot, except in the case of psychiatric harm, pretend to an injury when there was none at all.

One might have thought that Grobbellaar would run foul of the provision in the 1952 Act that where words contain two or more charges, a defence of justification is not to fail just because the truth of every charge is not proved, provided that the unproved charge is relatively innocuous in the light of the proven truth of the other charge. How does this square with the observation of Brooke LJ that 'It is no defence to a charge that "You called me A" to say "Yes, but I also called you B on the same occasion, and that was true"'.[30] The answer depends on the charge of which the claimant is complaining. He is entitled to object to a whole article but to complain of only one of the stings within it, and the defendant cannot justify any other if it is clearly separate; but if the charges are intertwined and indissociable it is not open to the claimant to pick and choose. However, the whole article will be before the jury and it will be open to them to find that in the light of the article as a whole, the charge complained of is not defamatory at all; thus the court held that the remark about Jessye Norman's girth, embedded in an article which was generally very laudatory, was not defamatory, but that observations about the effectiveness and genuineness of the marriage between Tom Cruise and Nicole Kidman (shortly to end in divorce) were separate charges not neutralised by an associated article which was very favourable to the latter.

---

[28] Defamation Act 1996, s 9(1)(a).
[29] *Grobbellaar v News Group Newspapers* [2002] UKHL 40.
[30] *Cruise (and Kidman) v Express Newspapers* [1999] QB 931.

PRIVACY

We have seen that while liability in defamation depends on the offensive material having been published (which does not mean 'made public') there is no liability if it is proved to have been true. But there may well be liability for making public matters which though perfectly true, were obviously supposed to be kept private, even if no one would think any the worse of the person as a result of the publication. Indeed, while the right to one's reputation is now said to be implicitly enshrined in Article 8 of the Convention of Human Rights, that Article is perfectly explicit about 'the right to respect for . . . private life', and public authorities, including the courts, are under a duty to safeguard it against invasion by third parties, such as the Press.

In recent years England, stimulated in part by the Convention, has developed a liability for publishing private information. It developed from, and was long called, 'breach of confidence', but as soon as it was decided that the information need not have been confided at all, the name became inappropriate, and indeed it was said, in one of the two decisions which must suffice here, that 'the effect of shoehorning this type of claim into the cause of action of breach of confidence means that it does not fall to be treated as a tort under English law.' The claim in question was by Michael Douglas and Catherine Zeta-Jones who were determined that no one, not even their 350 guests, should take photographs of their wedding—apart from *OK!* Magazine which had paid them £500K each for the exclusive right to publish them. Alas, *OK!* was scooped by *Hello!*, which rapidly published six illicit photographs for which £125K was paid. In the ensuing trial, the celebrities were awarded £3,750 each for their distress (Ms Zeta-Jones, a talented actress, having professed anguish at having been shown eating her own bridal cake), plus £7,300 each for interference with the commercial exploitation of their event; *Hello!* was awarded £1 million as assignee of the Douglases' commercial rights. On appeal the awards to the personal claimants were upheld, but the decision in favour of *Hello!* was reversed, on the ground that the Douglases' interest in the confidentiality of the information was not transferable and had not been transferred, so that *Hello!*, as a mere licensee, could not complain of interference with property rights, but only (unsuccessfully) with their business.[31]

---

[31] *Douglas v Hello!* [2005] EWCA Civ 595.

The other English decision to mention is the claim by Miss Naomi Campbell who was said by the defendant newspaper to be having treatment for drug addiction and was shown, in a photograph taken covertly, leaving premises identifiable as those of Narcotics Anonymous. Since Miss Campbell had previously said that she was not on drugs, she did not complain of the statement that she was an addict (to stay as thin as a rake, it is best to be one) but only of the revelation that she was undergoing treatment, which she said was a private matter. The Court of Appeal held that the text was unobjectionable and that the photograph added nothing to it, but a bare majority of the House of Lords held that the photograph made all the difference (as it had in the *Douglas* case) and reinstated the trial judge's award of £2,500 compensatory and £1,000 aggravated damages,[32] thereby entitling the claimant (and her legal advisers) to a huge sum in costs (the bill submitted, yet to be taxed, was over £1 million), huge because the lawyers had stipulated for twice their normal fee in the event of success, even as marginal as it was in this case.[33]

A decision in Strasbourg must be mentioned, for our courts are required to have heed to what falls from the judges there. Princess Caroline of Monaco—who does not sell, but only sues—had been snapped dining with her family in the back room of a restaurant, and while the German courts had awarded damages in respect of the photograph of the children, they denied the claim of the mother since she was a 'public figure par excellence', every one of whose doings were of public interest (though Goodness knows why!). This was held to put Germany in breach of its treaty obligations under the Convention: even photographs of public figures par excellence may be published only when they are engaged on public activities (launching yachts and opening hospitals?). So there we are, or probably will be.

PRIVILEGE

There is a distinction between what the public is interested in (of which the Press must be fairly good judges) and what the judges think is of public interest (of which . . .). This distinction lies at the heart of the defence of privilege which is all the Press can rely on if, when sued for defamation, they cannot prove the truth of what they have reported.

Privilege is sometimes *absolute*, in the sense that (like a finding of 'no

---

[32] *Campbell v MGN* [2004] UKHL 22.
[33] *Campbell v MGN (No. 2)* [2005] UKHL 61.

duty' in negligence) no inquiry into the communicator's attitude or conduct is permitted. Sometimes absolute privilege is accorded by statute, as to the Director of the Competition Commission, but the judges have been very reluctant to find absolute privilege, though they and the other lawmakers enjoy it in court and Parliament respectively.

Normally the privilege is *qualified* in the sense that even if the facts alleged are admittedly false the claimant will fail unless he can establish that the defendant was actuated by malice, that is, did not really believe in the truth of what he said or was motivated by some oblique purpose. When does such privilege attach? It attaches when the situation is such that a decent person who believed in the truth of what he had to say would think it right to say it, hurtful though it was. He has to say it to the right person, however. The traditional formula was that the defendant must have been under a kind of a duty to speak (though it is surely odd to say that you have a right to speak only when you are under a duty to!), and the recipient must have a proper interest in the matter. For centuries this made it virtually impossible for the press to invoke privilege, for they had no *duty* to disseminate information—they did it for gain—and they were addressing the whole world, whether or not it was at all interested. This meant that the papers were liable if they got their facts wrong, however hard they had tried to get them right. Some freedom of expression!

In 1999, however, the House of Lords, faced with a claim by the Prime Minister of Ireland in respect of a suggestion that he had misled his Parliament, held that qualified privilege can indeed be invoked by the media. The House did not, however, abandon, but only weakened, the twin requirements of duty in the defendant and interest in the addressee (the public). The decision, ungenerous as it is, has been applied rather ungenerously by the lower courts, one judge, indeed, going so far as to hold that the Press had no privilege unless they could be blamed for not publishing what they did! The courts still insist on the primacy of matter published being 'in the public interest': only of such matter has the public a right to be informed and the Press a duty to inform them. Once this requirement has been met, the conduct of the journalist is scrutinised in order to see whether he has met the courts' exacting standards of responsible journalism. It is normally essential, among other factors listed in a quasi-legislative manner by Lord Nicholls, for the matter to be put to the person affected, even if the question would be futile, like asking George Galloway whether he really was a traitor.[34] But at least, and at last,

---

[34] *Galloway v Telegraph Group* [2006] EWCA Civ 17.

exculpation is now possible, for it has certainly taken long enough for the courts to go any way towards respecting the freedom of the Press to inform the receptive electorate of the shenanigans of the temporarily great, the apparently good and the certainly rich.

In one case where a newspaper was held liable because it had made no investigations of its own, the Court of Appeal reversed on the ground that the newspaper was simply reporting, without adopting, what had been said ('reportage')—a majority decision subsequently cold-shouldered.[35] Statute does, however, permit reportage, if fair and accurate, of what is said to or by a large number of specified bodies with public functions.[36] Two points should be noted. First, the statutory provision was necessary in order to avoid the effect of the common law rule that merely to repeat defamatory matter uttered by someone else renders you liable. Secondly, in certain listed cases the privilege is lost if the publisher declines to publish a reasonable letter or statement by way of explanation of contradiction, the only instance in Britain of the useful continental device of 'right of reply'.

COMMENT

Fortunately one's freedom to express one's *opinions* does not depend on one's duty to do so. Even so, there are limits, and they are too restrictive. First, the matter on which comment is made must be 'of public interest'; gossip, the most interesting part of any conversation, is forbidden, but public performances may be criticised, even quite sternly. Secondly, the facts on which the comment is based must be indicated clearly enough to show that the statement is indeed the maker's opinion on those facts, and furthermore the facts must be accurate. This is a regrettable restriction: surely one should be free to comment on the basis of what one believes to be true. A judge once said to a doubtless impressionable jury that comment could hardly be fair if it were based on inaccurate facts! At least the judges do not have to agree with the comment impugned: the comment need not be 'fair', only honest—the ventilation of opinions you do not hold is not protected. But suppose the commentator, though honest, is spiteful. It has often been said that the defence fails if the commentator was actuated by 'malice', which is rather worrying, since in the academic world at any rate, negative comment is as often the result of personal

---

[35] *Al-Fagih v HH Saudi Research and Marketing* [2001] EWCA Civ 1634.
[36] Defamation Act 1996, s 15.

animosity as of genuine difference of opinion. Lord Nicholls, sitting in Hong Kong, has caught this hare: 'Honesty of belief is the touchstone. Actuation by spite, animosity, intent to injure, intent to arouse controversy or other motivation, whatever it may be, even if it is the dominant or sole motive, does not of itself defeat the defence.'[37] His Lordship distinguished the defence of privilege, which is granted for a particular purpose and fails if the occasion is used for any other, from the defence of fair comment, whose purpose is to simply to permit the citizen to state his honest opinions regardless of his motive.

LEGISLATION

Although legislation has sometimes made the situation worse (for example, by dispensing with the need to prove damage in certain cases of slander) it has gone some way towards moderating the common law's ingrained antipathy to freedom of expression. Under the Defamation Act 1996 summary judgment is now possible, and the courts can now control the ludicrous, antisocial, and profitable excesses of the specialist bar. They can also now exercise some control over the awards of damages made by the jury, for if the courts put an absurdly high value on a person's reputation when formulating the rules of liability, the jury still does so when it comes to awarding damages. The Strasbourg Court frowned when a jury awarded the sum of £1.5 million,[38] and the Court of Appeal has laid down restrictive rules.[39]

CONCLUDING REMARKS

In 2005 the Strasbourg court had another occasion to consider the English law of defamation. It arose out of the famous *McLibel* case in which McDonald's sued two unwaged pamphleteers who had accused it of shabby and shady practices. The damages of £60K awarded after a trial which lasted 313 days were reduced by the Court of Appeal, after 23 days of argument, to £40K, and the House of Lords refused leave to appeal. The doughty defendants went back to Strasbourg and complained that they had not been given a fair trial (Art 6) since they had not been granted any assistance with their defence, and that their freedom of expression

---

[37] *Cheng v Tse Wai Chun Paul* [2000] HKCFA 88.
[38] *Tolstoy Miloslavsky v United Kingdom* (1995) 20 EHRR 442.
[39] *John v MGN* [1996] 2 All ER 35.

(Art 10) had been infringed. The court there upheld their complaints, and awarded them €35K non-pecuniary damages between them: 'the Court does not consider that the correct balance was struck between the need to protect the applicants' rights to freedom of expression and the need to protect McDonald's rights and reputation.'[40] This will not, of course, put an end to the flow of smug pronouncements 'of the highest authority' (in England) to the effect that the English law of defamation is fully consistent with Article 10 of the Convention.

The Strasbourg court was much affected by the absence of legal aid for the individuals here, who were not suing but were being sued and were trying to defend their right of freedom of expression. Claimants seeking damages for alleged injury to their reputation also get no legal aid, but the substitute provided by Parliament is even worse: lawyers can take up a case on the terms that they will get double if the case is won, thereby increasing the bill for costs payable by the defendant should he lose, costs which the solicitors already have an incentive to inflate. The chilling effect on the Press is admitted by the House of Lords, as is their inability to do anything about it. Those in doubt should read the case about the costs claimed by Naomi Campbell (see p. 185), who could well have afforded to meet the costs herself.[41]

Even before this deplorable situation, it was surprising how many claims were brought by persons such as police constables who were not obviously rich enough to face the expense. The explanation is that their claims were funded by their trade union. (Advice to the reader: do not say that you were thumped in the police cell unless you can prove it to the hilt.) Somewhat similarly, local councillors, in order to assuage their umbrage, used to use the name (and funds) of the local authority to bring suit, until the House of Lords had the good sense to stop that.[42] So, too, individuals with corporate associations have the company join them in the suit (the company need not prove any loss) and then get the costs from the shareholders. The message is: if you want to muzzle someone, just use the tort of defamation! You will find the legal profession eager to help you (and themselves). There is a lot of money here. Defamation is quite big business. The 'honey-pot', as one judge has called it, attracts a lot of bees and bears. In 2004 no fewer than 267 proceedings for defamation were started in the Queen's Bench (as against 749 for personal injury,

---

[40] *Steel v United Kingdom* (2005) 41 EHRR 22.
[41] *Campbell v MGN (Costs)* [2005] UKHL 61.
[42] *Derbyshire CC v Times Newspapers* [1993] 1 All ER 1011.

119 for other negligence (including professional negligence) and 30(!) for other torts—trespass, nuisance, assault, wrongful arrest). Hardly marginal, then.

One cannot conclude these observations about this tort, which is a blot on the lawscape, without adverting to the oddity, perfectly manifest in the law reports, that a tort designed to protect reputation should attract and reward the most disreputable and shabby elements of civil society, and not only our fellow-citizens: disreputable foreigners come here to sue for libel much as adulterers used to flock to Nevada for a quick divorce.[43] Anyone tempted to join the list should remember two things: (1) to claim within a year of the publication, an unusually short period;[44] (2) to stay alive, for the claim collapses on the death of the party allegedly defamed, as well as that of any human defendant.[45]

---

[43] See *Berezovsky v Forbes Inc* [2000] 2 All ER 986, especially per Lord Hoffmann, dissenting.

[44] Limitation Act 1980, s 4A.

[45] Law Reform (Misc Prov) Act 1934, s 1(1).

13

Economic Torts

We have seen that if purely economic harm is *unintentionally* caused, the victim who has no transactional connection with the defendant has considerable difficulty in obtaining damages 'in negligence', at any rate as compared with the claimant complaining of injury to person or property: while one is certainly under a duty to respect the integrity of one's neighbour's body and property, there is in general no liability for merely unreasonable conduct which causes harm to his pocket only. But what is the law to do when the economic harm is *intended* by the defendant, or virtually certain to occur as a result of his deliberate conduct? The question of policy is not easy to answer. On the one hand, it seems morally objectionable to wish to visit harm of any kind on a fellow citizen, yet on the other, the economic field is one where liberty of action may well conduce to the public good, and practical considerations suggest moderation in constraining it by too ready an imposition of liability. It is therefore perhaps unsurprising that in English law the answer is far from simple.

One reason it would be impractical to hold that intended harm must always be compensated (and the defendant consequently enjoined) is that it would put an end to competition between tradesmen and to strikes by the workforce. These two types of economic warfare have something in common, but they also differ: competition hurts the competitor but benefits the customer, while strikes inconvenience the customer in order to force out of the employer a benefit which will eventually be paid for by the customer. The fact that competition must be encouraged and strikes permitted shows that there are at least some situations in which it must be lawful to cause deliberate harm. Commercial competition and labour disputes are not the only areas to consider, however. There are examples in daily life: the person who bids the most at an auction intends to deprive the underbidder of the item coveted by both, and the prize-fighter does his best to wrest the prize from his opponent. A moment's thought will therefore show that it would be impossible to impose liability on all those who can be said to be the knowing and deliberate cause of economic harm to others.

The choice for the legal system is therefore between saying that to cause such harm is *prima facie* actionable, but can be justified if the defendant had a good reason for doing what he did, and saying that the claimant must show more than the mere fact that the defendant intended to cause him harm. Against the first is that, given that there are so many justifications for committing trespasses to person or property, there must be so many more for invading less important rights or interests that the defences might eat up the cause of action. If the second is adopted, as really it must be in a free capitalist system, the question is what more must be shown. Some systems have adopted a general rule that the defendant must have acted deplorably (Germany), improperly (United States), or unreasonably (France). England's *residual* position is more restrictive of liability, more libertarian, than any of these, for it must be shown that the methods adopted by the defendant were actually unlawful, and not just deplorable, improper, or unreasonable. But this tort of deliberately causing harm by wrongful means is only the fallback position, not recognized until quite recently, though it may yet take over the other specific torts, as negligence tends to do as regards unintentional harm. Meanwhile, there are several different fact-patterns from which liability can arise. Hitherto our chapters have been devoted to a single tort, but now we must deal with a plethora of different torts, whose differing components make it difficult to present a simple picture. It is small comfort that if the position is difficult to understand, it is perhaps because it has not been understood.

The different torts include deceit, malicious falsehood, passing-off, inducing breach of contract, intimidation, and conspiracy (in two forms). The first three involve *deception*: deceit is telling lies to the claimant; telling lies to a third party is malicious falsehood; misleading a competitor's customers, even bona fide, is passing-off. The other three torts all involve *collaboration*, whether reluctant, as a result of threats, complaisant as a result of positive incentives, or spontaneous.

NATURE OF THE HARM

It might seem that the nature of the harm would be a unifying feature in this area, since the claimant is complaining that he would be better off had the defendant not acted as he did. But this is a unifying factor only at the factual level. At the legal level there are important differences. Part of the trouble is that the torts cover both harm caused and rights invaded, which, as we have seen in comparing the torts of negligence and trespass, involves differences in treatment. As to harm, though it is generally true that the claimant seeking damages must prove that he suffered loss, except where Parliament has said otherwise,[1] in many cases he seeks not damages but an injunction, and an injunction may be granted against the possibility that actionable harm might result. As to rights, in some cases the defendant has infringed a specific right of the claimant, for example a copyright, a patent right, or a registered trademark; at the other extreme it is merely the claimant's expectations that have been frustrated. In between, rather tiresomely, comes a contractual right, which is a stronger entitlement than a mere expectation of gain, but weaker than a registered trade-mark, for example, in that in principle it is good only against the other party to the contract; furthermore, despite what some contract lawyers seem to think, not all contracts are the same, for a distinction can surely be drawn between the individual who loses his job and the company that loses a deal. The interest in issue in the tort of passing-off is different again: it is said to be the claimant's 'goodwill', which is certainly more tradable than a mere expectation, yet the firm has no right to the loyalty of its clientele, for unlike the contractor, potential customers are free to choose whom to patronize, though preferably to choose lucidly, without being deceived by a competitor.

THE DEFENDANT'S CONDUCT

The defendant's harmful conduct may take different forms. He may indulge in lies, threats, or bribes. Lies, characteristic of the torts of deceit and malicious falsehood, are always wrong; honesty is not only the best policy but an inflexible requirement in law, since lies disable freedom of choice. So, too, do threats. They are intrinsic to the tort of intimidation, but since the objective criterion of truth/falsehood is inapplicable and has to be replaced by the more subjective test of licit/illicit, threats are generally wrongful only if what is threatened is itself wrong (though a threat to tell the truth may make you guilty of blackmail). Bribes are distinguishable from other payments only as being offered for the commission of a wrong, notably to induce an act of disloyalty to his principal by an agent for purchase or supply.

---

[1] Defamation Act 1952, s 3.

THE DEFENDANT'S PURPOSE

Usually in this area the defendant is out to acquire something for himself which the claimant would otherwise get, but he may want to inflict harm simply for kicks: he may be a robber or a wrecker. In one situation the distinction certainly makes a difference, for while people who cooperate in order to advance their own interests at the expense of another are not liable to the latter unless the methods they use are independently wrongful, it is tortious in itself to gang up simply to do someone down: 'It is unlawful to combine with others with the sole or predominant object of causing injury to another person, even if the means used are not themselves unlawful'.[2] In cases other than conspiracy, however, where the defendant has behaved objectionably one might think there is no great difference between causing gratuitous harm and causing harm for one's own benefit: even Robin Hood could hardly deny that he caused harm and did so intentionally (his justification being another matter).

THE BASIC RULE

The basic proposition is that it is not of itself enough to render one liable that one deliberately caused even serious economic harm to another. This was affirmed by the House of Lords in 1897 in *Allen v Flood*,[3] which a distinguished writer has termed 'the most important decision in the law of tort'. The events happened in a shipyard. While work on the wooden and metal parts of a vessel was being done by woodworkers and ironworkers respectively, all of whom were employed by the day, the ironworkers discovered that two of the woodworkers had previously done ironwork on another vessel in a different port. The defendant, the ironworkers' union official, went to the harbourmaster and said that unless the two woodworkers were shown the door, his men would not turn up for work the next day. The submissive harbourmaster told the woodworkers not to return. A majority in the House of Lords, reversing the courts below, held that the woodworkers had no claim against the union official, despite the fact that he had encompassed the harm to them, the loss of their job, quite deliberately and perhaps even 'maliciously', since it was done not in order to obtain their present jobs but to punish or make an example of them for what they had previously done.

---

[2] *Lonrho v Fayed (No 5)* [1994] 1 All ER 188 at 208.   [3] [1898] AC 1.

In order to understand the scope of this important decision, it is essential to appreciate that all the workers involved were employed by the day: they were neither entitled nor bound to work the next day. Otherwise liability could be imposed under one or other of the specific torts; had the woodworkers had a contractual right to continued employment, the defendant would have been liable under the already established tort of 'inducing breach of contract', and if the metal workers had been bound to return to work the following day and threatened not to do so unless the woodworkers (even if merely day labourers) were fired, that would have been actionable under the subsequent decision of the House of Lords in 1964, extending the tort of 'intimidation'.[4]

Favourable though it was to the union official, *Allen v Flood* had little effect in the industrial area, for when workers obtained the greater security of longer-term contracts, the existing tort of inducing breach of contract made it unlawful for anyone to persuade them to go on strike during the currency of their employment. Parliament, therefore, not only conferred on trade unions an immunity in tort equalled only by (and prolonged beyond) that of the Crown itself, but also granted immunity to individuals who, in furtherance of a trade dispute, committed the tort of inducing breach of a contract of employment. This statutory immunity was progressively extended to cover the new heads of liability, such as 'intimidation', which the courts invented purely in order to sidestep it.

COMPETITION

The commercial field differs from the industrial scene in that the customers one seeks to wean away from one's competitor are not usually bound to him by a long-term contract. Accordingly, fierce competition does not necessarily involve inducing breaches of contract, though of course it does so if one bribes one's rival's agents or otherwise suborns his staff. Here there was no tension between the courts and the legislature. The courts decided that they would not police competition simply on the ground that it was unfair, saying 'To draw a line between what is fair and unfair competition . . . passes the power of the Courts' and asking 'What is unfair that is neither forcible nor fraudulent?'.[5] Nevertheless the courts did have at their disposal a special tort by means of which they were able to

---

[4] *Rookes v Barnard* [1964] 1 All ER 1129.
[5] *Mogul Steamship Co v McGregor, Gow & Co* (1889) 23 QBD 598 at 626, [1892] AC 25 at 47.

stop tradesmen using practices which were apt to mislead the plaintiff's clientele as regards his goods, even if that were not his intention.

PASSING-OFF

Since competition does not work properly if customers are misled and consequently unable to make an informed choice, it is wrong to make your goods look so like those of a competitor that the customer who thinks he is buying your competitor's wares is actually buying yours: you thereby get the profit that your competitor would otherwise have obtained, and the customer gets something other than what he thought he was buying. This tort is called 'passing-off'. As a form of competition it is obviously unfair, and though a generalized tort of unfair competition has never developed in Britain, in contrast with other systems of law, passing-off has been much expanded from the classic case where the defendant pretended that the goods he himself made were made by the plaintiff. Thus a manufacturer of egg-flip who sold it under the misnomer 'English Advocaat' and thereby damaged the market for those like the plaintiffs who made genuine advocaat was held liable, though there was no suggestion that the defendant's drink was made by the plaintiffs: customers thought they were getting advocaat when they were actually getting egg-flip, and this hurt the plaintiffs.[6] In one puzzling case, producers of Scotch whisky were permitted to try to enjoin the defendant from selling as 'Welsh Whisky' what was actually Scotch whisky, purchased quite lawfully from a Scottish producer, with some herbs added. Here, though the defendant was doubtless telling lies, it is difficult to see either that customers were misled at all, since there is no such thing as Welsh whisky, or that the producers themselves, who had been paid for what was being sold, had suffered any harm.[7] Then there were the relentless efforts of the producers of Parma ham to enjoin British supermarkets from selling authentic Parma ham packaged in England, on the ground that under Italian law it must be packaged in Parma (a city notorious for its commercial integrity), efforts which were eventually successful because of a silly EU law.[8] This flexible tort has also been used to enjoin persons who registered as internet domain names which they then offered for sale the trade names of well-known firms such as Marks & Spencer.[9] The peculiarity of the tort is

---

[6] *Erven Warnink BV v Townend* [1979] 2 All ER 927.
[7] *Matthew Gloag v Welsh Distillers* [1998] FSR 718.
[8] *Consorzio del Prosciutto di Parma v Asda Stores* (Case C-108/01) [2003] 2 CMLR 21.
[9] *BT plc v One in a Million* [1998] 4 All ER 476.

that whereas competition is really for the benefit of the customer, it is the competitor, not the customer, who sues, just as the Office of Fair Trading is much more concerned with firms than individuals.

The utility of the common law was reduced somewhat when Parliament permitted the registration of trade marks, and reduced still further when the range of registrable marks was recently extended. Originally any unpermitted use of the registered trade mark was actionable. This meant that comparative advertising was virtually impossible, since one can hardly compare without identifying the comparator. Nowadays comparative advertising is permitted provided that the use of the competitor's trademark is neither unfair nor deceptive.[10] The courts themselves had been indifferent to comparative advertising, and declined to decide, under the head of malicious falsehood, whether comparisons were accurate or not, unless spurious data were adduced in purportedly factual support of the defendant's claim to superiority.[11] The courts' desire to liberalize competition was praiseworthy, but unrestrained competition can destroy itself, so Parliament has rendered unlawful two kinds of competitive (or anti-competitive) conduct which the common law tolerated, namely agreements in restraint of trade and abuse of a dominant position.

ANTI-COMPETITIVE CONDUCT

If an agreement unreasonably restrained a person's right to work or a firm's ability to trade, the common law simply refused to enforce it: one was free to leave a union or cartel, but those who stayed in were free to implement the agreement, even to the extreme disadvantage of the party who had jumped ship. That indeed was the famous decision in the *Mogul Steamship Co* case in 1892.[12] Nowadays even to make such agreements is prohibited.[13] Nor did the courts repress the singlehanded abuse of economic power, as the case of the woodworkers showed in 1897. However, given that 'it is excellent to have a giant's strength, but tyrannous to use it like a giant', it has been made unlawful to distort competition by abuse of one's dominant position in the relevant market (not an easy concept!).[14] The provisions follow European law, the right to damages of those adversely affected by infringements having been reinforced by the Enterprise Act 2002.[15] Even so, there is no reason to doubt that those

[10] See Unfair Commercial Practices Directive (2005/29/EC), Art 14.
[11] *De Beers Abrasive Products v International General Electric Co* [1975] 2 All ER 599.
[12] [1892] AC 25. [13] Competition Act 1998, s 2. [14] *Ibid.* s 18.
[15] Enterprise Act 2002, s 18 ff.

targeted by such prohibited conduct, as opposed to mere incidental victims, may claim damages under the residual common law tort of causing harm by unlawful means.

INDUCING BREACH OF CONTRACT

It was in the field of competition that the common law tort of inducing breach of contract originated. In 1853 it was held that an impresario would be liable for persuading a prima donna to sing for him when he knew that she had promised to sing exclusively for the manager of the rival opera house.[16] The decision is susceptible of two analyses. This is due to the simple fact that a contract has two sides—a right in the creditor and a duty in the debtor. Was the defendant liable for deliberately interfering with the plaintiff's contractual *right* to have the singer perform for him, or was he liable for knowingly persuading the singer to breach her *duty* by doing something they both knew she was bound not to? The analyses lead in different directions. The former leads towards holding a person liable even if he made no direct approach to the intermediary, even if he provoked no breach, even if he did nothing independently unlawful, and even if the effect of what he did was not to deprive the plaintiff of what had been promised to him but to make it harder for him to render the performance he himself had promised, so that an action would be granted not only to the disappointed creditor but also to the discomfited debtor. This is surely to give too great a third-party effect to a private contractual arrangement. The courts were led into extending the proper tort of 'inducing breach of contract' into the false tort of 'interference with contract' as a means of sidestepping the immunities which Parliament had conferred on trade unionists. This attempt was immediately thwarted by Parliament which forthwith extended the immunity to cover 'interference with contract', an act which the courts took as legislative confirmation of the existence of the tort! But this extended tort ought not to exist and if it does it should be abolished: it is quite enough if, in addition to being prevented from seducing the claimant's contractor by lawful means, the defendant is barred, as he is under the residual tort, from using unlawful means in order to hurt the claimant, whether or not that involves interference with any existing contract to which the claimant is a party.

Even if properly limited, this tort remains perplexing. Is it for his own

---

[16] *Lumley v Gye* (1853) 118 ER 749.

misconduct in bribing or otherwise inducing the intermediary to be false to his promise that the defendant is held liable, or should his liability be seen as secondary to the breach of contract, the wrong committed by the intermediary in acceding to his blandishments or bludgeonings? The second analysis has the advantage of doing away with 'interference with contract', for then there would be liability only if there was a breach and only the creditor would be able to sue, but has the disadvantage of making it more difficult to associate this tort with the residual tort of causing harm by wrongful means, of which it looks rather like a variant. Once again, as with the question whether a defendant is vicariously liable for his employee or personally liable for a breach by his delegate of a non-delegable duty, we see that even if there is no way to square a circle, there are two ways of going round a triangle.

THE VARIOUS TORTS

INTENTION

Let us now consider the various 'economic torts' in terms of their various components. In the residual tort it is fairly clear that the defendant must be shown to have intended to cause harm to the particular claimant, and the same seems to be true of the tort of intimidation: the victim must have been 'targeted'. This is the strongest intention requirement. In other torts it seems to be weaker. In the tort of inducing breach of contract, the defendant need not have intended to cause harm but must have intended to cause the claimant's contractor to act in breach of his contract with the claimant. In the tort of deceit the defendant need only intend that the claimant rely on the truth of what is falsely asserted, not that the claimant suffer harm; indeed the liar may well hope that no harm is done. Nor need the defendant sued for malicious falsehood have intended to cause harm: it is enough if his false assertion about the claimant was intrinsically 'calculated' to cause him harm. In the tort of passing-off the defendant need not have intended any harm to the claimant at all.

The question of the requisite intention in the economic torts was thoroughly investigated by the Court of Appeal when considering whether the trial judge, who awarded modest damages to Michael Douglas and Catherine Zeta-Jones for their distress at the publication by *Hello!* magazine of illicit photographs of their 'private' wedding, was correct to award much heavier damages to *OK!* magazine, to which the bridal pair had, for a considerable consideration, granted the exclusive right to publish photographs which met with their approval (see above p 184). The award to *OK!* was on the basis that *Hello!* had by wrongful conduct (breach of confidence) caused deliberate harm to their rival fanzine. The Court of Appeal reversed the award: 'The essence of the tort is that the conduct is done with the object or purpose (but not necessarily the predominant object or purpose) of injuring the claimant or, which seems to us to be the same thing, that the conduct is in some sense aimed or directed at the claimant.' The court held that, on the facts as found by the trial judge, *Hello!* had no subjective intention of causing any harm: *Hello!* was doing itself good but not intending any harm to *OK!*, since the publicity pool would not be emptied by their scoop.[17] The House of Lords gave leave to appeal.

CONDUCT

Given that the defendant has the appropriate intention, what must he have done in order to be liable? In deceit and malicious falsehood the defendant must have communicated the falsehood to someone—in malicious falsehood to a third party, and in deceit to the claimant himself. In passing-off the defendant must have engaged in practices which were apt to mislead the claimant's clientele. In the tort of inducing breach of contract he must, in our view, have persuaded the claimant's contractor to act in a manner known to be inconsistent with his contractual obligations to the claimant. In the tort of conspiracy the defendant must have actively associated with others in causing harm to the claimant, with the additional requirement, if the group was seeking to promote its own interests, that unlawful means were used. In intimidation the defendant must have used threats to commit a wrong against a third party unless he agrees to and does cause harm to the claimant. Likewise in the residual tort it must be shown that the defendant himself did something unlawful or prompted others to do so.

WRONGFULNESS

Wrongfulness being a component in several of the torts, we must ask what, apart from force and fraud, is 'wrongful'? Criminal conduct would seem to be clearly wrongful, yet there is some doubt about it. We have seen, under the unsatisfactory rubric of 'breach of statutory duty', that the *unintended* victim of a statutory offence is very commonly unable to sue, partly because statutory offences may be committed without any

---

[17] *Douglas v Hello!* [2005] EWCA Civ 595.

fault. It certainly does not follow that the victim of a *deliberate* statutory offence committed with the *intention* of harming him should not be able to sue. Yet one can pause before endorsing the decision that demonstrators who deliberately held up the construction of a bypass could be subjected to a civil injunction in tort, whose breach would be punishable by imprisonment, on the basis that they were deliberately harming the Department of Transport by committing the offence of obstruction, for which they could be exposed to a paltry fine.[18]

The wrongfulness point was considered, *obiter*, by the Court of Appeal in *Douglas v Hello!* (see p 184), where it concluded that the conduct of *Hello!* would satisfy the requirement of wrongfulness, notwithstanding that it did not breach any duty of confidence owed to *OK!*, since it did constitute a breach of confidence owed to the Douglases: given the requirement of a strict intention to cause harm to the claimant, the use by the defendant of any means which are wrongful in any way would be sufficient, along with the causing of actual economic harm, to constitute the residual tort. That does not, however, mean that it was appropriate to issue an injunction against the demonstrators.

IN CONCLUSION

It must now be very clear that an introductory book on tort cannot begin to cover the often subtle details of the various economic torts, but we may finally consider a case involving neither competition in trade nor industrial warfare.[19] A number of musicians contracted with Dreampace to do the backing for a recording of songs which Shirley Bassey had agreed to sing under a contract with Dreampace, her own production company. When she decided not to sing after all, she was sued by the musicians, who were unable to earn their fee. A majority of the Court of Appeal held that their case was arguable. Now the singer's refusal to sing as arranged with Dreampace certainly caused Dreampace to repudiate its contract with the musicians, but to cause a person to breach a contract (as opposed to persuading him to do so) is not a tort at all unless wrongful means are used, and even if they are, the defendant must be shown to have 'targeted' the claimant. The singer's deliberate breach of her contract with Dreampace might well count as wrongful means, but it was not suggested that the singer had the musicians in mind at all, much less that

---

[18] *Minister of Transport v Williams* [1993] TLR 627.
[19] *Millar v Bassey* [1994] EMLR 44.

she had targeted them. Had she persuaded Dreampace to fire these musicians and hire others, then certainly she would be liable, possibly with a defence if they were incompetent, but it was surely an error for the majority of the Court of Appeal to hold it even arguable that the claimants might win simply by showing that the defendant had deliberately broken her contract with a third party with the foreseeable effect of causing the third party to break its contract with them to their pecuniary disadvantage. The decision is now recognised to have been aberrant, especially since the Court in *Douglas v Hello!* has emphasised that it is not enough that the defendant foresaw the harm or was even reckless as to its occurrence: he must actually have had a specific intent to harm the claimant (see further p. 184 above).

14

Damages

Most victims of torts want money, indeed, as much money as they can get. In the old days they had to go to the courts of common law, which, rather like post offices, could issue nothing but money orders, requiring the defendant to pay his debt or come up with damages. Those who wanted an order of a different kind, such as an injunction to stop noise or smells, had to go to a court of equity. Nowadays all courts can issue any order: in particular, they can order a defendant to hand over a specific chattel, or grant a temporary injunction pending the final determination of rights and wrongs, provided the claimant undertakes to pay compensation if its issuance later proves to have been unjustified. Nevertheless, damages remain the order of the day in tort cases where claimants are complaining of harm already suffered. That damages are so characteristic a feature of tort explains Lord Bingham's statement that the Human Rights Act 1998 is not a tort statute, for damages are not always payable for the invasion of a Convention right if 'just satisfaction' can be procured otherwise,[1] whereas damages are payable for a quite harmless trespass, though not for the innocuous invasion of a 'constitutional' right.[2] Conversely, a claimant may be awarded damages when what he really wants is an injunction to put an end to a continuing wrong: here the damages are not compensatory at all, but just a sop, and not one which the complainant would regard as 'just satisfaction'.[3]

COMPENSATION

Indeed, while it is relentlessly repeated that damages are compensatory, this needs to be heavily qualified. The very idea of compensation involves redressible damage which can be computed in monetary terms. Yet damages are awarded in cases of trespass and libel though no damage has been

---

[1] *R (Greenfield) v Secretary of State* [2005] UKHL 14.
[2] *Watkins v Home Office* [2006] UKHL 17.
[3] *Jaggard v Sawyer* [1995] 2 All ER 189.

established, and as we shall see, damages may be awarded to punish the defendant by making him pay the victim more than would be enough to compensate him. Again, the notion of compensation is put under strain whenever damages are awarded for pain and other non-economic afflictions, since they can hardly be computed in monetary terms, though an estimate has to be made. Finally, when losses, even of an economic variety, which are expected to arise in the future, are met with a lump sum paid in advance, this is commutation, not actual compensation: as Lord Reid said, 'Such damages can only be an estimate, often a very rough estimate, of the present value of . . . prospective loss'.[4] Because of this, statute has provided that where victims of personal injury are claiming damages for future pecuniary loss the court must consider making an order for periodical payments rather than awarding a lump sum, even if the claimant would rather have the lump sum to which, as regards other heads of harm, he is entitled.[5]

DAMAGE

If damage is the proper object of compensation, it is surprising how little attention courts and lawyers have paid to the concept. Is it 'damage' that one is now going to die sooner than expected? Here Lord Wright said '. . . normal expectancy of life is a thing of temporal value, so that its impairment is something for which damages should be given'.[6] This is clearly wrong: life is not a good thing in itself, but merely the neutral condition of other things, good or bad, a point now taken by the legislature.[7] The Court of Appeal, by contrast, was right to hold that a child born handicapped could not complain that but for the defendant's negligence his mother would have had an abortion: the essence of his complaint was not that he was handicapped but that he was born at all,[8] and being born is no more 'damage' than dying. Likewise the proper answer to the question whether the reluctant parents of a healthy unwanted child can claim the cost of bringing it up is to say that to have a healthy child cannot be counted as 'damage', even though parenthood involves considerable expense.[9] If 'value' is a social construct, so is 'damage'.

In the normal case, damage consists of having fewer good things to

---

[4] *British Transport Commission v Gourley* [1955] 3 All ER 796 at 808.
[5] Courts Act 2003, s 100.   [6] *Rose v Ford* [1937] AC 826 at 846.
[7] Administration of Justice Act 1982, s 1.
[8] *McKay v Essex Area Health Authority* [1982] 2 All ER 771.
[9] *McFarlane v Tayside Health Board* [1999] 4 All ER 961.

enjoy or more bad ones to put up with than one would otherwise have had. This applies in both the economic and the human spheres, which should be distinguished: the French speak of *dommage matériel* as opposed to *dommage moral* and the Scots distinguish patrimonial loss from *solatium*. Damage in the former means less income and more expenditure, in the latter less pleasure and more pain, the former being common to natural and legal persons alike, the latter being the privilege and penalty of the human condition.

ECONOMIC HARM

Let us leave aside for the moment claims by companies and other merely legal persons, noting only that they constantly profess to be unable to prove the trading loss for which they are claiming, though one would suppose that if they couldn't prove it, they couldn't know of it and had probably not suffered it, or at any rate not suffered it by reason of the conduct for which they are trying to make the defendant pay. Their professions in this regard led a ductile Parliament to dispense with their need to prove harm in certain cases, and say, absurdly, that if words were likely to cause loss it is likely that they did so.[10] We shall stay for the moment with human claimants.

LOST INCOME

The human victim who has been disabled from working is entitled to the take-home pay he would have earned, subject to deductions discussed below. He is entitled to the wages lost not only through the injury but also through his accelerated death, that is, wages he will now not live to earn. This rather odd rule is designed to help his dependants who, once his own claim has been met, cannot themselves claim what they would have received out of what he would have earned.[11] Even if the injured claimant has not actually lost any wages, having been kept on by his employer at the same wage, he may still be paid something for the disadvantage he would face in the job market if his employer should downsize or be taken over by a predator.[12] One may also claim for lost earnings even if one never had any: recent decisions enabling young adults to sue for any diminution in their earning ability traceable to abuse or inadequate

---

[10] Defamation Act 1952, s 3(1).
[11] *Pickett v British Rail Engineering* [1979] 1 All ER 774.
[12] *Moeliker v Reyrolle* [1977] 1 All ER 9.

education or care are going to present the courts with formidable problems of estimating how much they would have earned in the absence of such maltreatment or neglect, given that often the prognosis would in any case have been very dismal.[13] Claims by injured infants have the feature that the earnings they would have made lie so far in the future that a relatively small sum, given the interest it would attract over the intervening period, may be adequate.

INCREASED EXPENDITURE

Increase in outgoings is as compensable as diminution of income. In the case of personal injury these include, among much else, the cost of medical treatment, post-operative care, prosthetic devices, and specially adapted accommodation. The expenditure has to be actual, already incurred, or to be incurred in the future; thus nothing can be claimed for medical treatment provided free by the National Health Service. Often the care a person needs after being turfed out of the hospital bed is provided free by a relative, who perhaps gives up a job in order to look after him: the gratuitous carer has no claim of his own against the tort-feasor as his loss is purely financial, and he cannot sue his patient unless remuneration was promised, so a fair result is reached by allowing the victim himself to claim a reasonable sum in respect of such care, which he then holds in trust for the carer, unless of course the carer is himself the tortfeasor.[14]

SET-OFFS

Compensation does not mean overcompensation. That is why the disabled victim gets only his take-home pay net of tax (the damages, unlike the interest they earn when invested, not being taxable in the victim's hands), why in his claim for the wages he will now not live to earn he must give credit for being spared the cost of living, and why he must deduct from his claim for lost wages any sums he obtains in alternative employment. Thus a policeman who had to leave the force because of his injury was required to give credit against his lost wages for the wages he obtained in civil employment, and likewise to give credit against his lost police retirement pension for the civil retirement pension he would eventually receive. Quite right. But the House of Lords went on to hold that he did not have to give credit against his lost wages for the disablement

---

[13] *Barrett v Enfield London Borough Council* [1999] 3 All ER 193.
[14] *Hunt v Severs* [1994] 2 All ER 385.

pension he was actually receiving: pension and wages were said to be different, and like could be set off only against like. It is true that this principle now applies in respect of social security benefits and is reflected in the judicial holding that the joys of parenthood cannot be set off against the expense of rearing a child originally unwanted,[15] though statute inconsistently provides that where a person is maintained at public expense the value of such maintenance is to be deducted from the damages for lost earnings,[16] and the Court of Appeal has held that a statutory payment to a victim of mesothelioma should be deducted from whatever damages were payable by the firm responsible for his affliction.[17] The result in the policeman case, however, was that he was made better off because of the tort than he would have been without it, and though the House of Lords has subsequently stuck to its guns, the view of the two dissentients is preferable.

The victim would be overcompensated if he could claim full damages from everyone responsible for the harm (and one must remember that everyone whose tort contributes to an indivisible harm is liable for the whole of it). The clear rule therefore is that his claim against a second person is reduced by anything already paid by the first: you are not entitled to double damages just because two people are liable to you. Indeed if you settle with one tortfeasor without reserving your rights against the others, you may be held to have been fully satisfied.[18] The victim of a tort may have a contractual claim in debt against another party. Thus in their suit against the bank which negligently certified the creditworthiness of their customer Hedley Byrne would have to give credit for any sums received from that customer, and the bank that makes a loan to a customer on the basis of a negligent valuation of the property made by the defendant must give credit for any sums the customer has repaid or perhaps can repay. What if the contractual claim of the victim is against his insurer? Here, most unsatisfactorily, sums received from the insurer do not reduce the victim's claim against the tortfeasor. If the insurance is indemnity insurance, the insurer can claim its money back from the insured victim who has recovered from the tortfeasor, lest the victim be unjustly enriched by double compensation; if it is accident rather than indemnity insurance, the victim can keep both the proceeds and undiminished damages: this is said to be the reward for the victim's

---

[15] *Macfarlane v Tayside Health Board* [1999] 4 All ER 961.
[16] Administration of Justice Act 1982, s 5.
[17] *Ballantine v Newalls Insulation Co* [2001] ICR 25.
[18] *Jameson v Central Electricity Generating Board* [1999] 1 All ER 193.

thrift. Nor need a victim give credit for sums received from persons charitably disposed: it is said that such persons intended to benefit the victim not the tortfeasor.[19] These last two exceptions, though dubious in policy, are less objectionable than the House of Lords' decision that policemen and firemen can claim full damages for lost wages while retaining the disability pension to which the very risks of the job entitled them.

SOCIAL SECURITY PAYMENTS

Disabled persons very likely receive some social security benefits. If so, some adjustment to the damages must be made, since one can hardly keep unemployment benefit as well as damages for being unemployed. For years many such benefits were split 50–50 between victim and tortfeasor, who were often employee and employer and had both contributed to the victim's entitlement. It was the state which was the loser under this statutory compromise, for it had no tort claim against the tortfeasor since its loss was purely financial, and it was not subrogated to the rights of the recipient, unlike the Criminal Injuries Compensation Authority. Since 1997, however, the tortfeasor is required to remit to the government the total amount of specified social security payments received by the victim for the five years after the injury.[20] The victim may retain the whole amount of any damages for pain and suffering and loss of amenity, but will receive in respect of other heads of loss only what is left after the deduction of the relevant social security benefits, if anything; there may indeed be nothing left, since the damages will have been reduced for any contributory negligence on his part before the social security benefits are deducted in full.

This system of 'recoupment' is fairly simple and horribly effective, but it works only where the benefits take the form of payments. The National Health Service, by contrast, provides services not money, and since the victim could not claim the value of medical services which he had received free of charge and the tortfeasor did not have to pay the National Health Service for its purely financial loss, the odd result for many years was that the person to blame for the injury did not have to pay the cost of curing it. That has now changed, in a big way. If the victim of any tort has been carried in an ambulance to a National Health Service hospital and had treatment there, any person paying him compensation (including the Motor Insurers Bureau) is liable to pay the State the certified charges,

---

[19] *Hodgson v Trapp* [1988] 3 All ER 870.
[20] Social Security (Recovery of Benefits) Act 1997.

reduced, if the victim was contributorily negligent, by the same percentage as the damages.[21] The effect of this legislation is quite different from that of the recoupment system in that it imposes a new liability on the tortfeasor's insurer without diminishing the damages payable to the victim, who never had any claim for the value of the medical services he did not have to pay for.

Services in kind are often rendered by local authorities to the victims of torts, but the central government has not come to their aid in this regard: the authority cannot claim from the tortfeasor the cost of the care they provide to his victim.[22] Uncertainty about whether such care will be provided or prove adequate makes for grave difficulties in determining the appropriate amount of damages in case of serious injury.[23]

DUTY TO MITIGATE DAMAGE

As was seen in the case of PC Parry, a person claiming damages for lost wages must give credit for any wages he actually receives from alternative employment. Indeed, he must go further and do his reasonable best to find such alternative employment. This is an example of the 'duty to mitigate', which applies to all those claiming damages, for whatever reason. Like contributory negligence, this is not a duty in the sense of a duty to take care, breach of which leads to liability: it is simply that one cannot claim compensation for a loss one could reasonably have avoided, any more than one can claim for a loss to the extent that it is due to one's own fault. It is, however, like the duty to take care in that the claimant need only do what is reasonable. Thus the damages (if any) payable to a woman dismayed to find herself pregnant are not to be reduced because she might have proceeded to an abortion.[24] Had she proceeded to an abortion, however, it would not have counted against her that she went to a private clinic, for though one might think it reasonable to take free medical treatment if it is available, the victim is permitted by statute to ignore the National Health Service and claim the cost of private treatment (provided that the cost itself is reasonable).[25] The claimant who reasonably attempts to mitigate his loss may claim for any increase in the loss attributable to the attempt; if it is successful, he must give credit for any benefits over and above the avoidance of the loss.

---

[21] Health and Social Care (Community and Health Standards) Act 2003, s 150 ff.
[22] *Islington LBC v University College Hospital* [2005] EWCA Civ 596.
[23] *Sowden v Lodge* [2004] EWCA Civ 1370.
[24] *Emeh v Kensington and Chelsea Area Health Authority* [1984] 3 All ER 651.
[25] Law Reform (Personal Injuries) Act 1948, s 2(4).

HUMAN HARM

In claims for economic loss yet to be suffered, the courts have to scry the future and guess how much the claimant would have earned, what the cost of medical and rehabilitative treatment will probably be, and so on. The guess once made, however, will be in money terms: there is no problem of translation. Similar imponderables also arise in claims for damages for pain and suffering and loss of amenity, but here there is the additional problem of translation into figures, even as regards the past. What is the cost of pain? How much is a leg worth? In giving an answer, the courts generally follow the *Guidelines* issued by the Judicial Studies Board; the Criminal Injuries Compensation Authority presently has an extremely detailed tariff, with 400 types of injury and 25 levels of award; but the law also allows the claimant to decide for himself what his limbs are worth, in the sense that if he insures them, he may keep both the proceeds of such insurance and undiminished damages in tort.

Damage here, as in the economic sphere, includes a reduction in what is good and an increase in what is bad. What is good is pleasure and what is bad is pain. The loss of pleasure may cause pain, but only if one is conscious of the loss. What if the victim is comatose, in a persistent vegetative state? The decision whether such a person should receive substantial damages (over and above medical costs, of course) has split legal systems other than ours. In ours it split the House of Lords in 1963, of which a bare majority was in favour of awarding very substantial damages, Lord Reid saying that 'It is no more possible to compensate an unconscious man than it is to compensate a dead man', with Lord Morris observing that 'the fact of unconsciousness does not eliminate the actuality of the deprivations of the ordinary experiences and amenities of life'.[26] At that time the common law also awarded damages for loss of time on earth, but Parliament has intervened here; no longer can you claim, even if you are alive, just because you are going to die sooner rather than later, but damages may be payable if you are really unhappy at the prospect.[27] The distinction between the subjective and the objective figured also in *Baker v Willoughby*, discussed above, pp. 78–9, where the subsequent and independent amputation of the leg which the defendant had injured put an end to the plaintiff's pain but not to his loss of amenity.[28]

---

[26] *West v Shephard* [1963] 2 All ER 625.   [27] Administration of Justice Act 1982, s 1.
[28] [1969] 3 All ER 1528.

PAYMENT OF DAMAGES

The old rule that damages must be awarded in a lump sum at the end of the trial has been modified in several respects—we have already seen that the court, when assessing a personal injury victim's future economic loss (loss of earnings, increased medical and care costs) is now bound to consider ordering periodical payments rather than a lump sum. Minor but useful modifications have introduced *interim payments* when it seems wise to wait for a final award (the question of liability can be resolved before any decision on the quantum of damages), and *provisional damages* when it seems that the claimant's condition may worsen. Nevertheless lump sum payments, desired by the claimant and simpler for the defendant, are still quite frequent. The purpose of damages is clear, namely to put the claimant in the position he would have been in if the tort had not occurred, and although it may be far from easy to say what that position would have been, the damages must be adequate.

In the last decade damages were very greatly increased by judicial decision, both as to economic harm and human harm, which overall are about equal in personal injury cases. As to the former, it was done by reducing the 'discount rate' applied to the gross damages, a discount being necessary when damages are paid in a lump sum, since the money paid now in respect of future losses and expenses will be earning interest in the meantime before the losses would have been incurred. When the House of Lords unanimously decided that the rate applied in the past must be reduced (it has now been reduced still further) the effect in just one of the cases before them was to increase the damages by no less than £300,000.[29] As to human harm, the Law Commission produced a Report which proposed a doubling of the awards in serious cases. Incoherent and impertinent as the Report was, the Court of Appeal responded to it and ordained an increase of up to £200,000 in the most serious cases, proportionally less in other cases, and none at all in minor claims.[30]

At the same time as the judges were increasing the sums they themselves were awarding, they were limiting those which could be awarded by juries in actions for false imprisonment, malicious prosecution, and defamation. As regards defamation, Parliament gave the courts some power to modify jury awards, and the Court started to limit them, Elton

[29] *Wells v Wells* [1998] 3 All ER 481.   [30] *Heil v Rankin* [2000] 3 All ER 138.

John providing an early opportunity.[31] As to awards against the police, the Court of Appeal has now laid down, quasi-legislatively, a limit of £50,000.[32] Much larger sums are awarded to a person who has been wrongly convicted and spent years in prison (Andy Evans was awarded £945,500 for 25 years inside), but this is a statutory award,[33] not damages in tort, for there is no tort unless the police concocted the evidence.[34]

It is amusing that in its Report the Law Commission, normally deeply antipathetic to the civil jury, relied on jury awards in Scotland and Northern Ireland as evidence that the awards made by judges in England were too low. A full Court of Appeal under Lord Denning had effectively abolished the jury in negligence cases in England in 1965,[35] on the stated ground that juries awarded different sums in similar cases, and that the law required like to be treated alike (even if all were treated erroneously?). It is true, indeed, that different juries may award different sums not only in different cases but in the same case. For example, in one Scottish case the jury awarded the pursuer £120,000 as damages for pain and suffering, and when the case was sent back for a new trial on the ground that this award was out of all proportion to the harm in question (the pursuer had had a serious arm injury which affected not only his employment but terminated his career as a clay pigeon shot of international repute), the second jury awarded him £95,000. Although the judges thought the appropriate sum was about £30,000, the House of Lords upheld the decision below to let the second jury's award stand.[36] It is likely, however, that the English judges who abolished the jury were at least as much concerned with the practical advantages of predictability as with the moral quality of uniformity; unpredictability makes the system of 'payment in' less useful, and diminishes the chances of settlement.

FATAL ACCIDENT CLAIMS

The death of a relative, like personal injury, can cause both economic and human harm—loss of support and grief—but it differs in that the survivors themselves suffer no physical injury, unless they see it happening and suffer pathological shock. This made it difficult for the *common law* to

---

[31] *John v MGN Ltd* [1996] 2 All ER 35.
[32] *Thompson v Commissioner of Police* [1997] 2 All ER 762.
[33] Criminal Justice Act 1988, s 133(1).
[34] *Darker v Chief Constable* [2000] 4 All ER 193.
[35] *Ward v James* [1965] 1 All ER 563.
[36] *Girvan v Inverness Farmers Dairy* 1998 SC (HL) 1, [1997] TLR 665.

compensate widows and orphans, and it did not and still does not do so: all claims arising out of the unwitnessed death of a person are *statutory*. There are two statutes, the 1934 Act which allows dead victims to sue for pre-death harm and the 1976 Act which grants 'dependants' (the inaccurate statutory phrase) a claim for the financial harm they themselves suffer as a result of the death of a specified relative. The 1934 Act may be left aside here: it simply permits the estate of a decedent, whether he died naturally or as a result of a tort, to claim what the decedent himself could have claimed, not including any losses occurring after the death. It did not even cover the claim of a person crushed to death in the Hillsborough disaster, since death supervened so quickly on the injury.[37]

Under the much more important Fatal Accidents Act 1976, originally from 1846, a claim may be brought only for the persons listed therein. These include most relatives as well as former spouses and current partners of whatever sex, who have lived together in quasi-matrimonial mode for at least two years. The claim is only for economic loss, for what they have personally lost as a result of the death, if tortiously caused.

The loss need not result from deprivation of future support, though the statute unfortunately uses the word 'dependants' as a global description of those entitled to claim: it is inaccurate because the claimant need not be dependent, as was shown when a person who had received a large capital gift from a relative obtained an indemnity for the tax he had to pay because the defendant tortiously killed the donor within the seven-year period which would have exempted him from payment of the tax.[38] Very usually, however, the loss does take the form of deprivation of money or services which the decedent would have provided out of his earnings. This is not a matter of law but of fact, since it is only earnings, and not investments, apart from annuities, which are terminated by death. Though the ultimate aim in each case is to find out how much each particular claimant has lost, in the normal situation the easiest way is to estimate the family's monetary loss by guessing how much the decedent would have earned and deducting the amount he would supposedly have spent on himself.

Even where the survivor's income has diminished as a result of the death, there is one accepted but dubious qualification. Although the statute states clearly that the award is to be for the loss resulting from the death, the courts insist that loss can only be claimed if it is due to

---

[37] *Hicks v Chief Constable* [1992] 2 All ER 65.
[38] *Davies v Whiteways Cyder* [1974] 3 All ER 168.

the claimant's relationship with the decedent. On this false basis a husband was unable to claim the loss he had suffered when his wife's death deprived him of a prize-winning dancing partner,[39] and a husband who lost his care allowance when the wife he was caring for was killed was unable to claim for this loss on the ground that he suffered it in his capacity as carer, not that of husband.[40]

GRIEF AND BEREAVEMENT

Although the original Act of 1846 provided that 'the jury may give such damages as they may think proportioned to the injury resulting from such death to the parties respectively . . .', and although the jury would unquestionably have included a sum for grief resulting from such death, the courts were quick to lay down that only financial harm could be compensated.[41] This was very harsh on parents whose young child was killed: their grief might be immitigable, but they could claim no more than the expense of the funeral, children being a poor investment. Then the 1934 Act was passed. Though principally designed to allow living victims to sue dead tortfeasors (since quite often a motorist managed to kill himself while injuring others), it also entitled dead victims to sue.[42] The courts were then presented for the first time with the claim 'He killed me', though in order that the harm could be said to occur before the actual death, it was dressed up as a claim not for having been killed but for having been about to be killed. As we have seen, the courts said that if life was good, then its abbreviation must be bad and therefore, if due to a tort, damage which must be compensated. Inevitably (and, one would have thought, foreseeably) there were problems of valuation: some juries awarded a lot to a baby killed in its pram because it was deprived of so many years of life, others a lot to an old man expiring in his bath-chair because every moment of his remaining time was especially valuable. This could not go on, so in 1941 the House of Lords said that compensation could be given only for the good things of life, not for the pains one was spared. Offsetting the bad against the good left a credit balance of £200 in the money of the day (now over £6,000), and that was the sum payable by the tortfeasor to the estate of the deceased, as opposed to the £1,200 awarded at first instance.[43] Since the decision involved a small

---

[39] *Burgess v Florence Nightingale Hospital* [1955] 1 All ER 511.
[40] *Cox v Hockenhull* [1999] 3 All ER 577.
[41] *Blake v Midland Railway* (1852) 118 ER 35.
[42] Law Reform (Miscellaneous Provisions) Act 1934.
[43] *Benham v Gambling* [1941] AC 157.

child, the £200 inevitably went to his parents. Now £200 (or £6,000) is not a wholly inappropriate amount to pay parents who lose a child, so in this roundabout manner a fairly acceptable result was achieved. Then in 1982 damages for being killed (or being about to die) were abolished and, lo and behold(!), 'bereavement damages' were introduced, a fixed sum originally £3,500, now £10,000.[44] Whatever anyone says (and the Law Commission describes this as a 'misconceived impression'), it is manifest that this sum is not designed as compensation for grief but is simply, like the earlier award, a replacement in money for the life lost. The lump sum is standard because people are equal, not because they are equally regretted. It is available only to spouses and parents of unmarried minor children, being split between the parents if the child was legitimate, and it is not heritable.

SET-OFFS

In the old days the courts insisted that any benefits accruing to the plaintiffs from the death had to be set off against any losses alleged to result from it. This included even the proceeds of life insurance and the amount inherited from the estate (or, more accurately, the value of its being received earlier). There was nothing wrong with that, but the courts also held that a husband's death was a benefit to the widow in that she was now free to find another husband to support her. She therefore had to give credit for the chance that she might do so. This involved the judges in making a declaration of nubility, all the more fallible in that a decision that the plaintiff would not remarry rendered remarriage that much more likely. Parliament responded to criticism by passing a statute which provided that in a claim by a widow (but only a widow, not also a widower or orphan!) no account was to be taken of remarriage, prospective or actual. At the same time Parliament provided more widely that in assessing damages no account was to be taken of *any* benefits actually or possibly accruing to the plaintiff as a result of the death.[45] This is pure sentimentality, like the rule that there is no recoupment of social security benefits in wrongful death cases. The relationship of loss and benefit is subtle. What of the case where a feckless mother is killed and the hapless child is looked after by a splendid grandmother: has the child lost at all by the death of the sluttish mother, and does the grandmother's care constitute a benefit resulting from the death, so that it must be disregarded? The decisions are in confusion, as always happens when

[44] Fatal Accidents Act 1976, s 1A.   [45] Fatal Accidents Act 1976, ss 3(3), 4.

tort enters the unhappy home, but it seems that there is a loss, as there are services that only a mother can provide (whether she did so or not?), and that substitute services are a benefit which by statute must be disregarded in computing the damages, part of which may be held in informal trust for the surrogate carer, provided he is not himself the tortfeasor.[46]

It must be said that the whole development of the law of tort when death is in the picture reflects poorly on both the judiciary and the legislature, and hardly justifies smug observations about the 'logical development of the law'.

PROPERTY DAMAGE

One might think that in comparison with claims for personal injury and death, claims in respect of property would be simple: after all, a damaged thing, if inanimate, is not going to get better or worse after the trial, though a lost thing may be found. But things go up and down in value through time, and the cost of repair may go up through inflation, so it may be critical what date is chosen for the valuation, date of loss or date of judgment or in between? There may also be a choice between the cost of repair or replacement and diminution in value, but repair may cost more than the item is worth, exact replacement may be impossible, and reinstatement may be much more costly than market value and disallowed as unreasonable. Nor is market value a panacea, for there may not be a market—and even if there is, the number of successful lawsuits against professional valuers testifies to the difficulties of valuation. Furthermore, as was noted in connection with remedies for conversion, the loss resulting to the owner from not having the thing may be much greater than its value. In one case a firm whose dredger was sunk by the defendant's fault while engaged on work under a contract stipulating penalties for delay was unable to buy a replacement through lack of money and hired one at exorbitant rates, amounting to far more than the value of the dredger itself.[47] It was held that only the value of the dredger 'as a going concern' was recoverable, not the full loss. The decision seems to be right in the result: a firm should not embark on a risky (and therefore profitable) project without having adequate liquidity or a sufficient policy of insurance, not only against the loss of its equipment but also against the loss to its business as a result of the loss of such equipment.

---

[46] *MS v ATH* [2002] EWCA Civ 792.   [47] *The Edison* [1933] AC 449.

Unfortunately the sole speech in the House of Lords made the decision turn on causation and remoteness rather than valuation, and the decision came to be treated, and vilified, as laying down a rule that extra expense due to the claimant's 'impecuniosity' could not be recovered. Any such rule has now been disavowed by the House of Lords in a case involving an individual's motor car.

The owner of a car which has been tortiously damaged is entitled to the cost of repair, and to the price of a replacement if it is a write-off. To find the cost of replacement one goes to the market in new or second-hand cars. The owner is also entitled to general damages for the loss of its use during the period required for repair or replacement, and to special damages if he reasonably hires a substitute. Just as the capital value of a car is easily ascertained from Glass's Guide, the value of the use of a car is easily found, since there is a vibrant market in which firms such as Avis and Hertz compete to provide customers with the use of a vehicle. Such firms, however, insist on the production of at least one credit card. Suppose the car-owner has no credit card? Well, there is a market here too. If the owner probably has a claim against a tortfeasor certain firms will provide him with the use of a car for a notional sum, which they do not expect him to pay since they reimburse themselves out of the damages (which will, of course, include the charge they make for the provision of the car on these terms). The sum they charge is about half as much again as the cost of hiring a car from a car hire company, and this the tortfeasor's insurer is reluctant to pay.

In 2002 the House of Lords decided that the difference was not payable by the tortfeasor since it was not in respect of the use of the car as such, and the owner could have gone to one of Hertz's competitors.[48] The next year, however, the claimant had no such option, being impecunious, and by a majority the House held that the extra charge was compensable: 'a claimant's lack of means should not be taken into account when assessing his loss.'[49] *All* claimants? Could our courts not distinguish companies and their commercial property from individuals and their private property, as is done by the Consumer Protection Act 1987?

One very human being who dearly loved his car was distraught when it was totalled by the careless defendant, and had it repaired rather than replaced by a different model, doubtless equally good in anyone else's eyes. The court disallowed the cost of repair, which exceeded the value

---

[48] *Dimond v Lovell* [2001] 1 AC 384.   [49] *Lagden v O'Connor* [2003] UKHL 64.

(to others) of the car once repaired.[50] Here we come close to the notion of 'sentimental value'. Although the courts can be counted upon to be hostile, it is not certain that the last-mentioned decision can stand with recent authority in the House of Lords, shaky though it is, allowing what economists, with their usual uncharming jargon, call 'consumer surplus'.[51] A man who wanted a deep swimming-pool was allowed £2,500 because the swimming-pool as built was slightly shallower at the deep end than specified, though the difference made it no less valuable. More recently a businessman who bought a house in the Gatwick area which was worth what he paid for it was allowed to claim money from the surveyor who had failed to report, though specifically asked to do so, that it was subject to aircraft noise.[52] It is true that in these and comparable cases the parties were in a special, indeed a contractual relationship, so it is possible that in the absence of such a relationship of reliance the courts will adhere to their dislike of sentimental value. Nevertheless, if the defendant shoots your pet under your very eyes he will likely have to pay aggravated damages in your trespass claim.

AGGRAVATED DAMAGES

Aggravated damages, which do not feature in Scots law,[53] have been awarded recently in cases of malicious falsehood[54] and racial discrimination,[55] but they live in an illogical limbo between compensatory damages, which are very common, and punitive damages, one of the most controversial issues in the area. Aggravated damages are more than compensatory damages since they are triggered by the bad conduct of the defendant, but less than punitive damages. But since anything more than compensation must be punitive, one might suppose that either compensatory damages are not fully compensatory or aggravated damages are punitive. However, just as a dog is said to know whether it has been kicked or just tripped over, and feels more aggrieved in the former case, then perhaps—but only perhaps—there is always more to compensate if the defendant had behaved badly. Nevertheless, it looks very much as if aggravated damages are a compromise or cop-out, and the ambiguity of

---

[50] *Darbishire v Warran* [1963] 3 All ER 310.
[51] *Ruxley Electronics v Forsyth* [1995] 3 All ER 268.
[52] *Farley v Skinner* [2001] 4 All ER 801.
[53] *D Watt (Shetland) v Reid* (EAT, 25 September 2001).
[54] *Khodaparast v Shad* [2000] 1 All ER 545.
[55] *Racial Equality Council v Widlinski* [1998] ICR 1124.

the concept contributed to the rather disingenuous judicial demolition of the law relating to damages which are frankly punitive. Matters are not greatly clarified by the decision of the Court of Appeal which was designed to diminish the damages which juries were awarding against the police. It was held that the jury should make separate awards for aggravated damages 'where there are aggravating features about the case which would result in the plaintiff not receiving sufficient compensation for the injury suffered if the award were restricted to a basic award . . .' and that 'It should also be explained that if aggravated damages are awarded such damages, though compensatory and not intended as a punishment, will in fact contain a penal element as far as the defendant is concerned'.[56] But when the Court of Appeal in 1915 upheld the jury award of £150 (now over £6,000) to a patron who had been quite peaceably evicted from a cinema, were these aggravated or punitive damages?[57] Who can tell?

PUNITIVE DAMAGES

If the role and nature of aggravated damages is ambiguous, there is no doubt about the function of punitive or exemplary damages: they are awarded to punish the defendant who has behaved deplorably by making him pay his victim a sum greater than the equivalent of the harm he caused. But there is much doubt about whether punitive damages should ever be awarded in a civil claim. The very idea is anathema to our friends on the continent, as is shown by the provision in an EU Regulation ('Rome II') that in the application of foreign law the award of 'non-compensatory damages, such as exemplary or punitive damages shall be contrary to Community public policy'.

The history of the matter in England is depressing. Before 1964 it was accepted law that punitive damages could be awarded whenever the defendant had behaved outrageously, and they were awarded by a jury in the famous case of *Rookes v Barnard*.[58] In that case members of a trade union sought to make an example of a colleague for leaving the union, and threatened to go on strike in breach of contract unless their employer gave him notice, as it did. This factual setting can hardly have conduced to clear thinking, for the Court of Appeal held that the defendants were not liable at all, so that it was only when the case reached the House of Lords that the question of punitive damages arose, and only one of their Lordships, Lord Devlin, addressed the matter at length. He held that

[56] *Thompson v Commissioner of Police* [1997] 2 All ER 762 at 775.
[57] *Hurst v Picture Theatres* [1915] 1 KB 1.   [58] [1964] 1 All ER 367.

they were anomalous (and therefore objectionable), but since on rare occasions they could serve a useful purpose, he proceeded to limit their availability to two categories of case at common law, not suggested to him by counsel on either side: where a government official had acted unconstitutionally and oppressively, and where the defendant had committed the tort with a view to profiting from it. This led Lord Denning shortly afterwards to state that 'Lord Devlin threw out all that we ever knew about exemplary damages' and 'knocked down the common law as it had existed for centuries'.[59] His Court of Appeal accordingly said that the House of Lords decision was wrong (*per incuriam*!), refused to follow it and instructed lower courts to do likewise. This unprecedented rebellion was put down by an afforced House of Lords which reasserted the Devlin position by a majority, despite serious doubts expressed by Lord Wilberforce and Viscount Dilhorne.[60]

The next stage was in 1993 when the Court of Appeal, by now clearly hostile to punitive damages, decided that even if the case fell within one of Lord Devlin's two categories punitive damages could not be awarded unless such damages had, prior to his decision in 1964, been awarded in the specific tort of which the defendant was alleged to be guilty.[61] The problem with this is that it naturally excludes the most recent torts (such as discrimination on grounds of race or gender, where aggravated damages are available[62]), and is thus at odds with the view of Albert Camus that it is the truths most recently discovered which seem the most fundamental. The Law Commission in its turn was minded to propose the abolition of punitive damages until it discovered that of those it consulted 49% wanted them to be more widely available, while only 28% were in favour of abolition. It therefore produced a compromise proposal extending their availability but removing their award from the jury.

Then in 2001 the matter came before the House of Lords again—not, one supposes, for the last time. The claim was against the Chief Constable of Leicestershire in respect of the scandalous conduct of one of his constables, allegedly constituting the 'resurgent' tort of misfeasance in public office. The courts below struck out the claim for punitive damages because such damages had never before been awarded for that tort. The facts of the case offered the possibility of discussing the propositions (a) that punitive damages should never be awarded, and (b) that they could

---

[59] *Broome v Cassell & Co* [1971] 2 All ER 187 at 198.
[60] *Cassell & Co v Broome* [1972] 1 All ER 801.
[61] *AB v South West Water Services* [1993] 1 All ER 609.
[62] *Armitage v Johnson* [1997] IRLR 162.

not be awarded against a defendant whose liability was purely vicarious, but counsel declined to argue these points or to suggest that either of the previous House of Lords cases was wrong, so the only question was as to the correctness of the decision of the Court of Appeal in 1993. On that narrow point the House decided against the Court of Appeal and reinstated the claim as arguable.[63] Lord Phillips and Lord Hutton seemed favourable to an extension of punitive damages, but Lord Scott, distinctly hostile to punitive damages in general, was determined that they should never be awarded in a case of vicarious liability. His speech starts out with a fine example of question-begging, that is, assuming what you are setting out to prove, otherwise known as *petitio principii*: 'My Lords, the function of an award of damages in our civil justice system is to compensate the claimant for a wrong done to him'. Well, that is *one* of its functions, but it is surely better to agree with Lord Wilberforce that 'It cannot lightly be taken for granted, even as a matter of theory, that the purpose of the law of tort is compensation, still less that it ought to be . . .'.[64]

This little story reflects no credit on the judiciary. Not the least serious objection to Lord Devlin's opinion that it has split the common law world, for *Rookes v Barnard* has been repudiated throughout the Commonwealth, as their Lordships were aware in 1973 when they reaffirmed it. In the United States it would be laughed out of court, and rightly so.

[63] *Kuddus v Chief Constable* [2001] 3 All ER 194.
[64] *Cassell & Co v Broome* [1972] 1 All ER 801 at 860.

15

Other Systems

The law of tort is by no means the only source of alleviation for harm suffered by individuals. We have already glanced at private insurance and social security, and their interaction with the law of tort, and we should briefly note that a criminal court, on convicting the perpetrator of a crime other than a motoring offence or one resulting in death, is required by law to order him to pay a sum by way of compensation to his victim. The crime need not be a tort, though it usually is, and the sum will not be the equivalent of damages in tort, since it takes account of the convict's resources. The civil courts are antipathetic to this jurisdiction, established by statute though it is, and the victim may never get the compensation ordered (though £22 million was collected in a recent year). There are, however, two other schemes which are designed precisely to ensure that a victim of a wrong actually receives compensation. The wrongs in question are, respectively, negligent driving and criminal assault.

MOTOR INSURERS BUREAU

Many persons are injured or killed by motorists who do not have the insurance required by law against their liability. Such a motorist is usually penniless, but if the victim obtains a judgment against him and it is not paid off in seven days, it will be met by the Motor Insurers Bureau, representing the firms doing such insurance business in England. This follows from an agreement made with the Minister for the Environment and Transport as long ago as 1945, long before the EC Directive which required Member States to have some such fall-back system in place. The British scheme is peculiar in that it has no formal legal basis—the Motor Insurers Bureau is a stranger to the statute book, so the terms of the agreement are not easy to find, and it figures in the law reports only because the courts subject its decisions to judicial review. Even so, it is not clear how a mere agreement between the MIB and the Minister can give any rights to third parties such as the victims: 'The MIB has never put to the test whether its liability . . . is enforceable against it by the injured third party'[1], but in a typically British way the scheme works well enough.

Its operation was, however, scrutinised in Luxembourg for compliance with the Second Motor Insurance Directive (of five!) and although the Advocate General lambasted our scheme as inadequately formalistic, the Court itself cavilled only at its failure to provide that interest be payable on awards to victims of unidentified, as opposed to uninsured, vehicles (a point on which the Directive was silent).[2] The Directives themselves do, however, distinguish the victims of unidentified and uninsured vehicles respectively, for the former can recover for property damage, subject to a deduction of €500, only if significant personal injury was also suffered, whereas it is no longer permissible to apply any deduction in the case of the latter.

A decision of the Luxembourg Court in 2005 is, however, rather worrying. While observing that 'as Community law stands at present, the Member States are free to determine the rules of civil liability applicable to road accidents', and notwithstanding the fact that the Directives themselves permit the denial of an award to passengers who were aware that the vehicle was stolen or uninsured, it proceeded to invalidate as inconsistent with the purpose of the Directives a Finnish statute which provided that no award be normally made to a passenger who knew that the driver was drunk or drugged. Some role as regards such contributory negligence is apparently left to national courts, but it is not certain how much.[3]

The most striking effect of the Directives has already been mentioned: in traffic accident claims (only) suit may be brought directly against the tortfeasor's insurer or the Motor Insurers Bureau.

CRIMINAL INJURIES

The Criminal Injuries Compensation Authority is unlike the Motor Insurers Bureau in that it makes awards out of public funds and eventually managed, after 31 years in legal limbo, to achieve a statutory basis. One will, however, scrutinise the Criminal Injuries Compensation Act 1995 in vain for the details, for it merely empowers the Minister to draw up a Scheme subject to Parliamentary approval. Even the 2001 Scheme is not in the form of a statutory instrument, and it is therefore

---

[1] *White v White* [2001] 2 All ER 43, 53 (HL).
[2] *Evans v Secretary of State* (Case C-63/01) [2004] 1 CMLR 47.
[3] *Candolin v Pohjola* (Case C-537/03) [2005] 3 CMLR 17.

no easier to find than the terms of the agreements with the Motor Insurers Bureau.

The Authority is a very important source of reparation. In a recent year it received over 66,000 applications and made about 38,000 awards totalling £170 million: most awards are of between £1,000 and £2,000, and the cap of £500,000 is very rarely reached. Whereas in tort cases the award for pain and suffering and loss of amenity is tailored to the precise situation of the claimant, in the light of Judicial Guidelines and conventional figures, the award made under the Scheme depends strictly on a tariff: each of the 400 types of injury listed attracts one of the 25 levels of award, which range from £1,000 to £250,000.

An award is payable only where personal injury is directly attributable to a crime of violence, but it is not necessary for the criminal to have been convicted (or there would have been problems after the terrorist bombings in London on 7 July 2005). In cases of domestic violence, however, the assailant must in general have been prosecuted and the parties must have ceased to live together.

There are interesting differences between the Scheme and the rules of tort law, most of the deviations from which seem quite justifiable. The Scheme makes a very extensive application of the *ex turpi causa* idea, for an award may be denied or reduced if a full award would be 'inappropriate' in the light of the claimant's conduct in relation to the event, including whether he was affected by drink or drugs, or even his bad character as evidenced by previous convictions unrelated to the event. The 'thin-skull' rule also seems to be modified: if the claimant had a pre-existing condition, the award covers only the exacerbation due to the crime. As to psychiatric harm, while the conditions of an award to those who witness a criminal assault on a loved one are generally in line with the tort rules, a stranger must show not only that he was in the area of physical risk but that he actually feared for his own safety.

As to lost earnings, no award is made for the first 28 weeks or for net lost earnings in excess of 150% of gross average earnings in industry. A disablement pension will be taken into account (contrary to *Parry v Cleaver*).[4] Outgoings may attract an award, but not the cost of private medical treatment unless it was reasonable to incur it (contrary to the statutory rule applicable in tort cases).[5]

If the victim dies, his claim to the basic award dies with him, whereas in tort cases his estate can sue for pain and suffering prior to death. His

---

[4] [1969] 1 All ER 555.   [5] Law Reform (Personal Injury) Act 1948, s 2(4).

lost earnings may be claimed by his dependants. The Scheme was more generous as regards 'bereavement damages' than the Fatal Accidents Act. Unmarried partners, even of the same sex, and children may claim as well as parents and spouses. The lump sum is £11,000 as opposed to £10,000, if only one person is entitled, £5,500 each if more than one. In addition, a child under 18 will receive £2,000 per year in respect of the loss of the parental services of either father or mother. As regards financial loss suffered by dependants, their own resources are taken into account and the limits on lost earnings claims by living claimants apply. In particular, pensions and social security payments are deducted, contrary to the rule in the Fatal Accidents Act, s. 4.

The Home Office is considering amending the Scheme by making higher tariff payments to those with serious injuries (only 11% at present receive more than £5,500) removing the £500,000 cap, and doing away with payments for lost earnings and care costs. Those less seriously injured would find their payments replaced by benefits in kind (and kindness), but no change would be made in cases of sexual violence or fatality. The result would be to speed up the processing of applications and reduce the overall cost—at present Britain pays out more than all other EU countries put together.

OTHER SCHEMES

There are other more specific schemes in the statute book, as well as particular schemes operated *ex gratia* by government departments. For example, under the Vaccine Damage Payments Act 1979 money is available for those damaged as a result of vaccination against specified diseases: it has not worked very well because the disablement must be at least 60%, the maximum lump sum payment is £60,000 and the claimant must prove that the injury was actually attributable to the vaccination, just as in a claim of tort. Then in 2001 a trust was set up with a fund of £67.5 million (reviewable when the deaths reach 250) to provide payments in respect of those afflicted with vCJD, the human variant of mad cow disease. There has been some dissatisfaction with the operation of the trust, though nothing like the scandals attaching to the formation and operation of the Coal Health Compensation Schemes, the largest government-run personal injury compensation scheme in the world. When the courts held that the British Coal Corporation was liable for failing to protect its employees from respiratory ailments and vibration white finger, so many persons became entitled to damages that in 1999 the

Department of Trade and Industry entered Claims Handling Agreements with the two major trade unions (sworn enemies), proceedings under which must be exhausted before resort to the courts is allowed. The cost is expected to reach £6.9 billion, two-thirds of which will go in compensation. According to a Report in late 2005, the scheme has generated 'an astonishing degree of suspicion, animosity and recrimination'—certainly both the Serious Fraud Office and the Law Society are investigating the way claims have been handled—and the Report concluded that the government should not go down this path again, since the scheme is costly, productive of conflict, difficult to plan, insusceptible of formal Parliamentary oversight, and neglectful of value for money.

Not very different from actual litigation, one might think, which is characterised in the Explanatory Notes to the NHS Redress Bill 2005 as complicated, unfair and slow, costly both in fees and the time of health professionals, prejudicial to morale in hospitals, and productive of defensive and secretive attitudes when patients really want an explanation and apology. The Bill accordingly envisages a scheme, the details of which are to be contained in a statutory instrument, whereby compensation, limited in amount as regards pain and suffering, would be provided without recourse to litigation whenever in the view of a specified person an NHS unit would be liable in tort for medical fault. The applicant would lose her right to sue by accepting compensation under the scheme, but not by applying for it.

OMBUDSMEN

These schemes deal with harms which could well figure in tort claims, but as we have seen, there is no 'general right to indemnity by reason of damage suffered through invalid administrative action'.[6] However, those who suffer injustice as a result of poor administration by public bodies may seek the help of an Ombudsman, even if judicial review might be possible. The position of Parliamentary Commissioner for Administration was created in 1967 and an analogue for local government seven years later. These are the principal Ombudsmen. The Parliamentary Ombudsman can accept complaints only if they are referred to him by a Member of Parliament, unless they arise from the National Health Service. In addition to health authorities, the Parliamentary Ombudsman can inquire into the activities of over 200 bodies including government

[6] *Factortame v Secretary of State (No 2)* [1991] 1 All ER 70 at 119.

departments, the Inland Revenue, Customs and Excise and the Criminal Injuries Compensation Authority, and receives over 4,000 new complaints each year, about half of which are on the health side. The Ombudsman's investigations were largely responsible for forcing the government to find £150 million for the 18,000 depositors in Barlow Clowes, whose affairs the Department of Trade and Industry had been slothful in monitoring, and an investigation is current into the failure to tackle the difficulties of the Equitable Life Assurance Society. Those who should be grateful for the intervention of the Ombudsman include the farmers whose poultry was slaughtered during the salmonella scare, those distressed by the deplorable comportment of the Child Support Agency, those misled by information about the State Earnings Related Pension Scheme, and those for whom the health service improperly refused to provide free clinical care.

The Parliamentary Ombudsman cannot inquire into maladministration in local government, which typically takes the form of delay in processing inquiries and claims, inaccurate information or poor advice, failure to adhere to a stated policy or to respect a relevant Code of Conduct, and so on. Local government falls under the jurisdiction of the three Local Government Ombudsmen, who can receive complaints directly once the complainant has complained to the council in question. Over 18,000 such complaints were received in 2004–2005, most concerning planning and housing matters. There has been a progressive diminution in the number of findings of maladministration causing injustice, down to 121 in 2004–2005. Although there is no method of compelling a recalcitrant council to accept the proposal of a Commissioner, they can require the insertion into a local paper of their findings, along with the council's reasons for doing what it did. Very often, however, the councils can be nudged into making a payment: before long social services will have paid about £45 million in restitution to those whom they improperly charged for accommodation on their release from compulsory detention in a mental hospital.

Although these Ombudsmen do not have a very high profile, the institution is clearly a success. Their proceedings have advantages over litigation in tort: there is no cost to the parties, the proceedings are informal and private, inquisitorial rather than adversarial. The government has thoughts, perhaps not wise thoughts, about amalgamating the two principal Ombudsmen. One such amalgamation has resulted in a super-Ombudsman in the financial field. The Financial Ombudsman, created by the Financial Services and Markets Act 2000 (s 225 ff) as a result of combining eight other ombudsmen, has a powerful remit, and received 110,963 complaints in 2004–2005, relating, among other things, to banking, credit cards, insurance, endowment mortgages, investments and pensions. He differs from the governmental ombudsmen in that he deals with disputes between customers and the firms they dealt with, and his monetary awards are capable of enforcement through the courts, which can subject his decisions to judicial review.

Some professions in the private sphere have set up schemes of their own for the resolution of disputes with customers and clients, analogous to arbitration but without the need for a special arbitration agreement. There is thus an Ombudsman for Estate Agents. Not all estate agents are members, and though the Minister has power under the Housing Act 2004 to require certain estate agents to join some such redress scheme, he has not yet exercised it. The Removals Industry Ombudsman and the Funeral Ombudsman, in comparable lines of business, are completely private.

Index